MUSIC BUSINESS

Music Business: The Key Concepts is a comprehensive guide to the terminology commonly used in the music business today. It embraces definitions from a number of relevant fields, including:

- general business
- marketing
- e-commerce
- intellectual property law
- economics
- entrepreneurship.

In an accessible A–Z format and fully cross-referenced throughout, this book is essential reading for music business students as well as those interested in the music industry.

Richard Strasser is Assistant Professor in the Department of Music at Northeastern University. He has written several articles on the music business and is co-author of *The Savvy Studio Owner* (2005).

ALSO AVAILABLE FROM ROUTLEDGE

Popular Music: The Key Concepts (Second Edition)
Roy Shuker
978–0–415–34769–3

**Communication, Cultural and Media Studies:
The Key Concepts** (Third Edition)
John Hartley
978–0–415–26889–9

World Music: The Basics
Richard Nidel
978–0–415–96801–0

Finance: The Basics
Erik Banks
978–0–415–38463–6

Management: The Basics
Morgen Witzel
978–0–415–32018–4

Marketing: The Basics
Karl Moore and Niketh Pareek
978–0–415–38079–9

MUSIC BUSINESS

The Key Concepts

Richard Strasser

Routledge
Taylor & Francis Group

LONDON AND NEW YORK

First published 2010
by Routledge
2 Park Square, Milton Park, Abingdon, Oxon OX14 4RN

Simultaneously published in the USA and Canada
by Routledge
270 Madison Ave, New York, NY 10016

Routledge is an imprint of the Taylor & Francis Group, an informa business

© 2010 Richard Strasser

Typeset in Bembo by
Book Now Ltd, London
Printed and bound in Great Britain by
TJ International, Padstow, Cornwall

British Library Cataloguing in Publication Data
A catalogue record for this book is available from the British Library

Library of Congress Cataloging in Publication Data
Strasser, Richard, 1966–
Music business: the key concepts / Richard Strasser.
p. cm.
Includes bibliographical references and index.
1. Music trade—Dictionaries. I. Title.
ML102.M85S77 2009
338.4′778—dc22
2008055419

ISBN10: 0–415–99534–5 (hbk)
ISBN10: 0–415–99535–3 (pbk)
ISBN10: 0–203–87505–2 (ebk)

ISBN13: 978–0–415–99534–4 (hbk)
ISBN13: 978–0–415–99535–1 (pbk)
ISBN13: 978–0–203–87505–6 (ebk)

CONTENTS

ACKNOWLEDGEMENTS

Life grants nothing to us mortals without hard work.
(Horace, *Satires*)

To my girls: Paola, Ginevra and Tosca who constantly support me.

Special thanks to Constance Ditzel for supporting and encouraging music business research. Also thanks to David Avital at Routledge and Richard Cook at Book Now, for their infinite patience.

LIST OF KEY CONCEPTS

Compulsory License
Consumer
Contingent Scale Payment
Contract
Contributory Infringement
Controlled Composition
Convention for the Protection
   of Producers of Phonograms
   Against Unauthorized
   Duplication of Their
   Phonograms
Copublishing
Copyright
Copyright Arbitration Royalty
   Panel (CARP)
Copyright Royalty and
   Distribution Reform Act of
   2004 (CRDRA)
Copyright Royalty Board
   (CRB)
Copyright Term Extension Act
   of 1998
Creative Commons
Cross-Collateralization
Cue Sheet
Demo
Derivative Work
Development Deal
Digital Audio Recording
   Technology Act (DART)
Digital Media Association
   (DiMA)
Digital Millennium Copyright
   Act (DMCA)
Digital Performance Right in
   Sound Recording Act of
   1995 (DPRA)
Digital Rights Management
   (DRM)

Directive Harmonizing the
   Term of Copyright
   Protection
Disc Jockey (DJ)
Display
Distribution
Dramatic Rights (Grand Rights)
E-Commerce
Entertainment Retailers
   Association (ERA)
European Information,
   Communications and
   Consumer Electronics
   Technology Industry
   Associations (EICTA)
European Union Copyright
   Directive (EUCD)
Exclusive Rights
Fair Use
Fairness in Musical Licensing
   Act of 1998
Federal Communications
   Commission (FCC)
Federal Trade Commission
   (FTC)
Festival
Fiduciary Duty
First-Sale Doctrine
Fixation
Folio
Foreign Royalties
Four Walling
Fund
General Agreement on Tariffs
   and Trade (GATT)
Geneva Phonograms
   Convention
Global Entertainment Retail
   Alliance (GERA)

INTRODUCTION

The Music Industry is a large and complex business sector that covers a multitude of activities, disciplines, and organizations. As with any complex field, the need for effective and knowledgeable leaders is essential, especially in such a rapidly evolving industry. As the music industry embraces technological innovation, and in order to be successful, it is vital that globalization and new legal definitions stay in tune with these events and adapt to future changes seamlessly. Therefore, obtaining an overall knowledge of the structures, techniques, and technologies as conceptual systems may be just as important as skills and experience gained in the field.

The term *music business* generally refers to a full range of economic practices necessary for production and performance of music products and services. As such, the music industry by its very nature an interdisciplinary field both in terms of its structure and the manner in which it is studied. Examining this multidimensional field requires an understanding of several diverse activities and disciplines that often result in a dispute over which activity has greater importance in defining the field. Although specific terms and concepts lend themselves directly to the music industry, there are many concepts that are borrowed from other disciplines such as business, law, economics, sociology, and technology. Music industry scholarship has traditionally concerned itself with understanding the creation, management, and selling of music as a physical/digital product or as a performance or as a bundle of intellectual property rights. Within this context, the music industry has been studied as a homogenous entity. Hirsh in *The Music Industry* (1969) considers recording and radio industries as the primary structural forces behind the music industry. Secondary influences included promotion, managers, and agents. Chapple and Garofalo's *Rock and Roll Is Here to Pay* (1977) examines radio, artists, managers, agents, promoters, and the rock press in addition to the recording industry. Baskerville in his seminal work, *The Music Business Handbook and Career Guide* (8th ed., 2006) offers an in-depth and thorough overview of the music industry. However, Baskerville's work does not accurately represent the complex interaction between disparate industries and their common interests. Geoffrey Hull's *The Recording Industry* (2nd ed.) approaches the study of the music industry from an economic perspective. The text divides the music industry into three parts: recording, songwriting/publishing, and live performance. This approach, unlike Baskerville's, ties the various divergent parts of the music industry through copyright. In 1981, Harvey Rachlin attempted to define the field through his book *The Encyclopedia of the Music Business*. Although this book covers a vast number of terms associated not only with the music industry, but popular music in general, the information is more than 20 years old and many of the organizations and laws presented in the text are no longer valid.

Although a thorough knowledge of these divergent disciplines is essential to the operation of music corporations, to include every concept in this diverse field is impossible and not practical to a text such as this. Therefore, this book attempts to identify some of the key terms and concepts within the field of music business. Terms have been selected from what is considered to be influential and seminal texts in the field of music business. As very few models exist for this kind of comprehensive, scholarly reference work on music business, extensive research was undertaken to develop a systematic, subject-based taxonomy for such a new field of study. Therefore, the main intent of this book is to investigate the enormity and complexity of issues pertaining to this field. While the text format is alphabetical, the 175 terms presented in the book are organized in "sets" of related concepts. These concepts revolve around the three primary income streams of the music industry: recording, publishing, and live performance. This grouping can be further refined when assessing financial actions: record production, music publishing, artist management, concert promotion, recording services, and online music services. Eight different groupings can be found when evaluating the music industry from an artistic perspective. Finally, the conceptual framework adopted for this text includes external influences on the music business as a whole. This grouping includes the legal environment and related concepts, the economic environment the political environment, and the many organizations that have been established to monitor the music business.

Although the primary source of terms for this text are those derived directly from the creation, distribution, and consumption of music products and services, the range of the concepts in this multidisciplinary field require a wider approach. For example, recent developments on the World Wide Web and other digital media have changed the way in which people consume and use music content. These new media have made it possible for people to not only consume entertainment in a traditional sense, but to share preproduced works of music as well as their own creations with others. This has enabled the emergence of a new paradigm of music business concepts such as e-commerce, ringtones, and sampling. Within this text there exists a group of concepts that are associated with primary terms, but function independently of the music business. Also included in this group are organizations that are essential to the functioning and administration of the music industry. For example, federal government administrative organizations, such as the **Federal Communication Commission**, **Copyright Royalty Board** (**CRB**), and the **Federal Trade Commission** (**FTC**), are included to emphasize their regulatory impact on the music industry. Similarly, international trade organizations were included to underline the global nature of the music industry today. The **World Trade Organization** (**WTO**) and the **World Intellectual Property Organization** (**WIPO**) have become increasingly important to a field that has such a global reach. Furthermore, many of the treaties negotiated within these international agencies have a direct impact on the music industry and the ability of music companies to operate in the global business environment. Much attention in this text has been paid to copyright law and international copyright treaties. This is because, copyright, both on a national and international level, provides the foundation on which much of the music industry operates.

Although the music industry by its very nature is a multidimensional field that is reliant on a diverse range of disciplines, there are certain concepts that have been eliminated from this text. Terms that have a specific musicological basis were excluded, including terms that deal with Western art music, popular music, and concepts associated with ethnomusicological subjects. Furthermore, individuals (artists and managers) who have contributed directly to the development of the music industry have been avoided as entries. Concepts that are business specific were not included, and the reader is provided with enough references from specialist dictionaries and texts of accounting, banking and finance, economics, business law and taxation, international business, marketing, operations management, organizational behavior, and strategy, and so on. A detailed listing of these texts is found in an expansive bibliography at the conclusion of the book. Furthermore, because this book is one of the few works of its type that relate to music industry, it is important that its text is limited in size in order that it encompasses critical information yet avoid redundancies; for this purpose, the number of relevant concepts is reduced to what is considered useful for the intended readers' benefit. Nonetheless, there are instances of overlap of terms between diverse areas, when discussed outside of their domain, to elucidate a specific point for the reader's benefit.

Within these structural characteristics, the audience for such a text is of three types: students, practitioners, and general readers. However, in spite of such a diverse mix of audience, the need is perceived as one and the same for all: a concise, authoritative, comprehensive, and clear summary of each topic, with information on specific research if greater detail is required. Unlike encyclopedias, which connote a comprehensive treatment of the aspects of a particular subject, this book follows in the tradition of the "Key Concepts" series, by moving beyond a summation or definition of a particular field and providing a detailed insight and understanding of the complex interaction of the music business. It is hoped that readers will turn to this book as the first point of reference in defining a particular term, topic of issue, or industry sector within the music business. Finally, the extensive bibliography and bibliographical reference found at the end of the text and at the conclusion of each concept is intended to provide guidance for the reader to obtain a more detailed exposition of a particular topic.

In a creative industry, such as the music industry, concepts, descriptions, and sources are constantly being invented and redefined, and new terms come into circulation year after year. The material presented in this text is up-to-date at the time of writing. However, due to the ever-changing nature of the music industry and the speed at which such changes occur, many of the concepts may have altered by the time the book hits the stores. Although there does not exist a universally applicable set of terms that represents the totality of this subject, this book intends to be an important contribution to the debate of what constitutes the music business and will provide an understanding of this complex and fascinating field.

MUSIC BUSINESS

The Key Concepts

ADVANCE

Monies paid by one party to another as an incentive to sign a **contract**.

In a recording or **publishing** contract, this payment is often a prepayment of **royalties** from future earnings. In effect, this income is a loan to an **artist** or songwriter for the production and delivery of one or more recordings or songs. Unless otherwise specified, advance monies are **recoupable**, which entitles the party who provides the funds to be reimbursed before the artist or songwriter receives royalties. This amount is due irrespective of whether an **album** or song is profitable or not. For example, if an album does not make a profit, a record label will **cross-collaterize** the advance against future album sales.

See also: **contracts**; **controlled composition**; **copyright**; **independent record label**; **major record label**

Further reading: Halloran (2007); Holden (1991); Krasilovsky (2007)

ADVERTISING

A paid nonpersonal communication used to promote a product, brand, or service by an identified sponsor to a target audience.

This form of communication is transmitted through mass media vehicles such as television, **radio**, newspapers, and magazines, or by nontraditional forms of advertising such as buzz **marketing**, social networks, blogs, or user-generated content Web sites. Advertising can be divided into several categories. Product advertising endeavors to sell a specific good or service, such as a new **album**, by describing a product's features, benefits, and price. Corporate advertising creates goodwill for a company rather than selling a specific product. By improving its corporate image a company can enhance the consumer perception of their products, which in turn will strengthen their stock value. Covert advertising is placement of products within other entertainment media, primarily film and television. This may involve an actor mentioning, wearing, or using a particular product. Interactive advertising is communication in which a customer controls the type and amount of information received. This form of advertising takes numerous forms, including Web sites, viral marketing, and SMS text messaging. For any advertisement to be successful it must appeal to its target audience. An advertisement appeal falls into one of two categories:

logical and emotional. A logical appeal focuses on a product's or service's features, price, value, and data. Advertisement based on price value tends to have a high recall value to a specific market. Emotional appeals function by manipulating a recipient's emotions and desires. The range of emotions elicited by the advertisement depends often on the product and the outcome of the advertiser. Humor appeals are one of the most commonly used appeals today. Combined in a well-integrated advertisement campaign, humor appeals have been shown to enhance attention, credibility, recall, and purchase intention. Fear appeals draw attention to common fears and risks and then associates a solution using a particular product. Poorly conceived and executed fear campaigns can anger an audience or cause them to block out the message. Celebrity appeals are based on the perception that people will use a product if it is endorsed by a celebrity. Celebrity endorsers often possess characteristics that resemble a product or the image a company wishes to project. These messages are usually part of an overall strategy known as the advertising campaign. Campaigns vary considerably in duration, form, and media. In an integrated marketing system, campaigns comprise of more than one carefully planned and sequenced advertisement in different media vehicles that target specific demographics. A campaign will make use of several desirable qualities in an advertising message to elicit a response from a target audience. This process, known as the AIDA model (awareness, interest, desire, and action), is used as the basis for directing a **consumer** from awareness of a product or brand to the final stage of purchasing. Each stage has a specific role in developing this process, especially in an age when it is difficult to gain consumer attention. The first stage is creating an awareness of an unknown or new product or service in a target market. The second stage requires the advertisement campaign to develop interest in the consumer by offering features, benefits, and advantages of using the product. If the campaign is successful, a consumer will develop a desire for the product that satisfies their needs, thus leading them to purchase the product or service.

Regulation of advertising is conducted at the national level with each country regulating how messages are transmitted to particular audiences, especially in the areas of child, tobacco, and alcohol advertising. In the United States the **Federal Trade Commission (FTC)** regulates advertising primarily in the areas of false advertising and health-related products. In 1997, the FTC began an investigation into record distributors' practice of forcing retailers into setting minimum prices for CDs. Under **minimum advertised price (MAP)** policies retailers seeking any cooperative advertising funds were required to observe the distributors' minimum advertised prices in all media advertisements, even in advertisements funded solely by the retailers. The FTC found that MAP violated Federal Law by restricting competition in the domestic market for recorded music.

In the United Kingdom the Advertising Standards Authority (ASA) is a self-regulated organization that has developed a code of advertising ethics. Because the organization does not have regulatory powers, it does not bring legal action against violators. Rather, the ASA posts the information of acts of transgression on their Web site or to **Ofcom**, the communications industry regulatory body in the United Kingdom. Funding for the organization is generated by voluntary fees levied on advertising costs.

See also: **artist**; **consumer**; **e-commerce**; **independent record label**; **major record label**; **marketing**; **music video**; **public relations (PR)**; **retail**

Further reading: Aaker (1998); Agwin (2006); Andersen (2006); Barrett(2001); Bayler (2006); Dunbar (1990); Jacobson (2007); McCourt (2005); Maslow (1970)

AGENT

A person or organization that acts on behalf of or represents individuals and groups by implied or express permission.

In the music industry, agents are bona fide representatives of an **artist** (principle) hired to procure employment. When a **contract** is signed the principle is held legally liable for acts performed by the authorized agent. Agents act as an intermediary between **managers** and **promoters** or **venue** operators. For the procurement of employment, agents are compensated via **commissions** that range between 10 and 20 percent of an artist's gross payment. Unions such as the **American Federation of Musicians (AFM)** and the **American Federation of Television and Radio Artists (AFTRA)** limit the total compensation amount to 20 percent. Contractual duration last on average three years for musicians and seven years for artists associated with film and television. Several states require agents to be licensed, including New York, California, Illinois, Texas, Minnesota, and Florida. The penalties for unlicensed action include black listing by an artist's representative union or annulment of all contracts by a state labor commissioner. The consequences of contractual annulment include the reimbursement of all commissions with interest to the artist under the stated agreement in the contract. Licensure is further dependent on the union that represents the artist booked by the agent. Due to complexity of the music industry agencies fall into three categories based on their geographic coverage. Local agents provide employment within in a particular city or nearby cities. They book small venues such as clubs, bars, and at personal engagements. A regional agent's geographic coverage is somewhat greater than a local agent. Regional agents operate in larger cities, adjoining states, or a larger geographic region, such as the Southwestern United States. A regional agent will procure employment for an artist at large venues or conduct small tours within their geographic realm. National agencies cover entire countries and often international areas. Most national agencies will only work with substantial artists that have a recording contract with a major label. As these agencies are structured as a corporation, they will have multiple artists on their roster, and the gross earnings of these agencies run to several million dollars per annum.

See also: **AFTRA**; **contract**; **independent record label**; **major record label**

Further reading: Frascogna (2004); Howard-Spink (2000)

AIRPLAY

The act of **broadcasting** a song or series of songs via **radio** or television.

On radio, this term refers to the number of times a song is played on a station. Traditionally, in the recording industry, airplay has a **marketing** function. The premise associated with the use of radio airplay is that **consumers** will only purchase recorded material that they have previously heard. Thus, the goal of record labels has been to get as much airplay of their songs to generate consumer interest in purchasing music. If a song has been played several times during the day, it is considered to have a large amount of airplay time. Radio stations will rotate (spin) a series of songs in a given period of time, usually a week. Several rotations of a song within a period of time is known as a *power rotation* or *heavy rotation*. Airplay is also applicable to the number of times a **music video** appears on a music video station. Quantitative data of radio airplay is provided by several trade publications such as Billboard and Radio and Records in the United States and Music Week in the United Kingdom. These publications receive their data from AC Nielsen's **Broadcast Data System** (**BDS**). BDS is not only important for the purpose of ranking songs on **charts** but is also essential to songwriters and publishers, as airplay results in performance **royalties**. If a song receives airplay that doesn't translate into record sales, it is termed a *turntable hit*.

See also: **charts**; **marketing**; **payola**; **performing rights organization (PRO)**

Further reading: Barnes (1988); Brabec (2006); Burnett (1996); Hull (2004); Krasilovsky (2007); Napoli (2003); McBride (2007)

ALBUM

A phonograph record in the format of a CD, LP, or **MP3** file.

Albums consist of several songs, unified by a theme or individual tracks. Album sales in the United States are measured by several organizations, including **SoundScan** and the **Recording Industry Association of America** (**RIAA**). In the United Kingdom record sales are measured by the British Phonographic Industry (BPI) and the **International Federation of the Phonographic Industry** (**IFPI**).

See also: **ASCAP**; **copyright**; **major record label**; **mechanical rights**; **phonorecord**

Further reading: Andersen (1980); Brabec (2006); Hull (2004); Krasilovsky (2007)

ALL RIGHTS RESERVED

A notice that establishes evidence of a **copyright** owner's intention to release any rights appropriated to the **author** by copyright law.

The notice is not required under current copyright law. Under the **Buenos Aires Convention**, the statement was required to offer protection in signatory countries. Article 3 of the Buenos Aires Convention states as follows:

> The acknowledgement of a copyright obtained in one State, in conformity with its laws, shall produce its effects of full right, in all the other States, without the necessity of complying with any other formality, provided always there shall appear in the work a statement that indicates the reservation of the property right.

Because all the members of the Buenos Aires Convention are signatories to the **Berne Convention,** the term has no legal significance, and the Berne Convention states that all rights are automatically reserved, unless explicitly stated. Furthermore, the Berne Convention does not require copyright registration as protection is granted automatically for fixed works within signatory nations.

See also: **creative commons**; **GATT**; **WIPO**; **WTO**

Further reading: Hull (2004); Schulenberg (2005)

ALLIANCE OF ARTISTS AND RECORDING COMPANIES (AARC)

A nonprofit organization formed to collect and distribute **royalties** from the sale of digital home recording equipment and blank media.

The organization came into existence as a consequence of the **Audio Home Recording Act** of 1992. As a nonprofit organization the AARC is administered by a board of directors consisting of 13 record label representatives and 13 members representing **artists** and **copyright** holders. Royalty payments to the organization establish the structure of the board of directors. The AARC also represents members before the **Copyright Royalty Board** and other government agencies. AARC also offers members legal representation and negotiates home tapping agreements with foreign collecting agencies.

See also: **BIEM**; **EICTA**; **GERA**; **IFPI**; **PRO**

Further reading: Holland (1994, 2004)

AMERICAN FEDERATION OF MUSICIANS (AFM)

A national trade union representing musicians, **arrangers**, and copyists.

The AFM negotiates on behalf of its members' **contract**s with employers in areas such as recording, television, live entertainment, and motion pictures. Membership is open to musicians and others who are citizens of the United States and Canada. Founded in 1896 the organization expanded to include Canadian musicians in 1900. AFM operates on two levels: local unions and the international union.

Local unions are granted a charter to operate within a specified territory. Each local union has jurisdiction over wage **scale** and working conditions of members in **venue**s and broadcasters. All officers and governing board are elected by the membership of the union. The International Union has exclusive jurisdiction over recordings, **broadcasting**, and film throughout the United States and Canada. The organization's officers and executive board are elected at the annual international conference by delegates from local unions. Members are required to pay an initial fee to a local union they join, and also a national fee as well as other periodic fees. A local union may require a member to pay a percentage of a scale wage to a local union if that member does not reside in that jurisdiction. AFM also provides pension, health, and welfare benefits for its members.

Apart from funds earned via membership, AFM receives monies from two sources for special purposes. The Music Performance Trust Fund (MPTF) is a trust established in 1948 under an agreement between the recording industry and the AFM. The purpose of the MPTF is to sponsor free live instrumental performances in connection with a patriotic, educational, and civic occasion in the United States and Canada. Administered by an independent trustee, funds are generated by the recording industry on a semiannual basis from record sales. The second nonmembership funding to AFM is the Phonograph Record Manufacturers' Special Payment Fund. This **fund** requires record companies to contribute a percentage of income earned from record sales, which is disbursed to musicians based on their scale wages.

AFM is affiliated with the American Federation of Labor and Congress of Industrial Organizations (AFL–CIO), a national federation of unions made up of 54 members, including the American Federation of Musicians (AFM), **American Federation of Television and Radio Artists (AFTRA)**, **American Guild of Musical Artists (AGMA)**, American Guild of Variety Artists, and the Screen Actors Guild.

See also: **agent**; **venue**

Further reading: Armbrust (2004); De Veuax (1988); Passman (2006); Seltzer (1989)

AMERICAN FEDERATION OF TELEVISION AND RADIO ARTISTS (AFTRA)

A national trade union representing actors and musicians in **radio**, television, and sound recordings.

AFTRA membership includes actors, singers, narrators, and sound-effects technicians. Membership is contingent upon union fees, which are paid at initiation, regular dues and a member's good standing. The union negotiates wages and working conditions on behalf of its members. AFTRA also negotiates on behalf of its members in regards to the production of phonographic recordings. The AFTRA Code of Fair Practice for

Phonographic Records is an agreement between the recording industry and AFTRA. This national agreement provides regulation on minimum **scale**, distribution of funds, reporting, contractual agreements, and arbitration. The agreement between AFTRA and the recording industry requires record companies to contribute between 11 and 12.65 percent of the performer's gross compensation. Gross compensation includes salaries, **royalties**, **advances**, bonuses, and earnings. The welfare benefits of the **funds** may be used for hospitalization, medical, and temporary disability needs.

AFTRA is affiliated with the American Federation of Labor and Congress of Industrial Organizations (AFL-CIO) and is a member of the **Associated Actors and Artists of America**.

See also: **agent**; **venue**

Further reading: Armbrust (2004); Halloran (2007); Hull (2004)

AMERICAN GUILD OF MUSICAL ARTISTS (AGMA)

A national labor union representing opera singers (soloists and choristers) as well as ballet and modern dance companies.

AGMA was founded in 1936. The organization negotiates **contract**s on behalf of its members with agents, concert **manager**s, and classical organizations. Membership is open to any performer within the jurisdiction of AGMA. Membership dues are scaled in accordance to earned income. Although the organization title denotes a **guild**, AGMA operates as a union for its membership in regard to contracts. Thus, on behalf of its members, AGMA negotiates contracts with employers and managers. Contracts establish minimum compensation, rehearsal hours, overtime payment, and sick leave. Contracts with mangers deal specifically with compensation, terms of contracts between managers and AGMA members, and minimum earnings. Under the basic agreement the maximum **commission** a manager may charge is 20 percent of his or her client's earnings from a concert and 10 percent from opera, ballet, and concerts.

AGMA is affiliated with the AFL-CIO and is a member of the **Associated Actors and Artists of America**.

See also: **agent**; **broadcasting**; **manager; venue**

Further reading: Hull (2004); Passman (2006)

AMERICAN SOCIETY OF COMPOSERS, AUTHORS AND PUBLISHERS (ASCAP)

A U.S. **performing rights organization** that **license**s music on behalf of songwriters, lyricists, and music publishers.

ASCAP was established in 1914. The organization has over 300,000 members. The society licenses nearly every genre of music with the exception of **nondramatic** works, and distributes **royalties** to its members from **radio**, television, the Internet, and live performances. According to the organization's articles of association, ASCAP's objective is to act as a supporter of reforms in U.S. intellectual property law and promote uniformity in international intellectual property law, by entering into agreements with similar associations in foreign countries. Furthermore, the articles state that ASCAP facilitates the administration of **copyright** laws, arbitrates differences between its members and others in regard to public performance, and advocates against music **piracy**.

Royalties are collected via specific per-use or per-program nondramatic licenses or **blanket license**s. Data for per-use licenses is collected via several methods. For live performances ASCAP makes use of logs provided by concert **promoter**s, performing **artist**s, and members. For radio, ASCAP makes use of Mediaguide, a digital tracking technology that lists works performed on sampled stations, station logs, and recordings of actual broadcasts. For television and other media, ASCAP relies on station logs and **cue sheet**s. The cost of a license is determined by several factors including the medium (television, radio, etc.), the type of performance (background music, jingles, theme songs, etc.), and the economic significance of the licensee (national broadcasters pay more than small local **venue**s). Other determining factors include the physical size of a venue, the amount of music performed, and the total audience reach of a medium.

Payment to artists and publishers is through a complex **weighting formula** expressed via a credit system in which each credit is worth a specific dollar value. According to ASCAP, the number of credits given to an artist or publisher is determined by several factors including how the music is used, (feature, theme, background, etc.), where the music is performed (radio, national television, etc.), how much the licensee pays ASCAP, the time of day (for TV or radio), the importance of the broadcast (highly rated TV shows receive TV premium payment credits), the length of a work, and the amount of **airplay** a song receives within a quarter.

Once the amounts for artists and publishers is calculated, ASCAP, along with the other **PRO**s, pays writers and publishers a 50/50 rate. If there is more than one writer or publisher, ASCAP will disperse the payments according to the instructions of the writer or publisher. ASCAP deducts operating expenses from the collected royalties.

ASCAP has its headquarters in New York and has membership offices in Los Angeles and Nashville as well as an international branch in London. As a nonprofit organization the organization operates via bylaws established by a board of directors elected by the membership. The board consists of a president and chairperson of the board, a **publishing** and writer vice chairperson, a treasurer, and a secretary. The board comprises of 12 writers and 12 publishers who not only establish and maintain the rules of the organization but also elect the society's officers. ASCAP also provides its members medical, dental, and musical instrument insurance, honors its members via the ASCAP Awards, and provides grants via the ASCAP Foundation.

See also: **BMI**; **copyright**; **publishing**; **SESAC**

Further reading: Fujitani (1984); Krasilovsky (2007); Muller (1994); Nye (2000); Ryan (1985)

ANONYMOUS WORK

A **copyright** term used to define a work that has no identifying **author**.

In many cases, anonymous works are associated with **artist**s who use a pseudonymous title rather than their birth name. In some situations a **publishing** company will file on behalf an artist who wishes to remain anonymous. The term of copyright for an anonymous work endures for 95 years from the year of its first publication or 120 years from the year of its creation.

See also: **publishing**

Further reading: Frith (1993); Hull (2004); Muller (1994)

ARBITRON

A **radio** rating service of the American Research Bureau.

Arbitron collects data from a random sample of the population via a self-administered diary. The diary describes radio listening habits over a period of a week for 48 weeks. Recently, the organization developed the Portable People Meters (PPM), an electronic measuring system that will replace the handwritten diary. Currently, PPM service is used in Houston and Philadelphia and is slated for expansion, reaching 50 top radio markets by 2010. The results of Arbitron's research are expressed via two outcomes, namely, ratings and shares. A rating is the percentage of all people within a demographic group in a survey area who listen to a specific radio station. A share is the percentage of all listeners in a demographic group who listen to a specific radio for at least 5 minutes during an average quarter hour in a given day. Arbitron also offers Arbitron Information on Demand (AID), a computer-based system that produces customized reports. These include Arbitrends, a monthly estimate of station ratings; Maximizer, an analysis of the radio audience by demographics, geographic location, and time period; and Scarborough Reports, which provide local market information on **retail**, product, and media data.

See also: **advertising**; **marketing**

Further reading: Belville (1988); Buzzard (2002); McBride (2007); Napoli (2003); Patchen (1999)

ARRANGER

A person who orchestrates or adapts a musical composition by scoring a new version for voice or instruments that is substantially different from the original.

In some cases an arranger may create additional material such as lyrics, melody, or vocal parts of a song. Although an arranger may make substantial editions to a composition, he or she does not have any **copyright** status in the material he or she arranges. Further, an arranger will not receive royalties for his or her work from recording sales. In most cases, arrangers are hired by a **producer** or record company on a **work-made-for-hire** basis. The same principle of work-made-for-hire holds true for print editions.

See also: **broadcasting**; **copyright**; **publishing**; **synchronization license**

Further reading: Brabec (2006); Felton (1980); Krasilovsky (2007)

ARTIST

A person who creates or interprets artistic works as an occupation. In music an artist is defined as a person who creates musical compositions as well as interprets works of art, although the term *performer* is the preferred terminology. In **copyright** law the term refers to the identifiable creator or **author** of a work of art.

See also: **AFM**; **AFTRA**; **artist and repertoire (A&R)**; **manager**

Further reading: Barrow (1996); Dannen (1991); Dennisoff (1975), (1986); Halloran (2007); Harvard law Review (2003); Holland (2004); Levin (2004)

ARTIST AND REPERTOIRE (A&R)

A division of a record label that is responsible for the discovery and development of new talent.

The A&R department's principal responsibility is two fold: the discovery of talented **artists** for a record label and the discovery of repertoire for the label's artists to record. The A&R department will scout both new and established talent. Established artists are often under **contract** at other record labels and require negotiations between labels for release. Both roles require the department to negotiate contractual relationships between all parties, schedule recording sessions, and acquire **publishing** contracts with the record label's affiliated publishing company or independent publishing companies. A record label's A&R department supervises various administrative activities. These activities include the planning and monitoring of budgets, often at the approval of the business affairs office. Most budgets deal with studio costs, talent costs, and other expenses such as lodging and travel. The A&R department is often responsible for paying artists union **scale** wages for recording sessions. Finally, an A&R department is responsible for obtaining **mechanical license**s from a publisher or their representative. After an **artist** has agreed to all terms of the contract with a record label, the A&R department will negotiate favorable rates for licensed music, develop ancillary income through merchandising, and the licensing of **copyright**ed material.

See also: **artist**; **independent record label**; **major record label**

Further reading: Dannen (1991); Halloran (2007); Howard-Spink (2000)

ASSIGNMENT

The transfer of property from one party to another for personal or financial gain.

This may include the transfer of property, rights, or interests in property. Other forms of transfer include the assignment to act including corporate voting rights, franchise ownership, or power of attorney. In most recording **contract**s assignment involves the transfer of **copyright** from an **artist** to the record label or **publisher**. When this occurs an artist looses all rights associated with the ownership of a copyright. In an exclusive songwriting contract an artist will assign all rights to the publisher. This includes revenue from receiving **royalties** from a **license**.

See also: **agent**; **author**; **independent record label**; **major record label**

Further reading: Halloran (2007)

ASSOCIATED ACTORS AND ARTISTS OF AMERICA (FOUR A'S)

An umbrella organization consisting of several autonomous music unions.

Membership of the Associated Actors and Artists includes the Actors Equity Association, the **American Federation of Television and Radio Artists** (**AFTRA**), the **American Guild of Musical Artists** (**AGMA**), the American Guild of Variety Artists (AGVA), and the Screen Actors Guild (SAG). Commonly referred to as the Four A's, each member union represents a different area of the performing arts. The New York–based union was established in 1919 to represent the common interests of the members and resolve jurisdictional problems that may arise between members. Although each organization is autonomous in day-to-day operations, their bylaws and constitutions are revised so as not to conflict with each organization's functions and goals. In the event of jurisdiction disputes, the international board of the Four A's may make a final determination. Other affiliates of the organization include international unions such as the Hungarian Actors and Artists Association, the Italian Actors Union, the Polish Actors Union, and the Puerto Rican Artists and Technicians Association.

See also: **guild**; **trade association**

Further reading: Hull (2004); *Monthly Labor Review* (1992)

AUDIO ENGINEER

An experienced technician who manipulates sound through analog or digital means in a controlled environment.

In a recording studio the roles of an engineer include operating sound/ recording equipment, editing mixing and mastering an **artist**'s or **producer**'s creative vision. Within the context of the studio, audio engineers are differentiated according to their role and their creative output. A recording engineer is responsible for the recording of music sessions. Mixing engineers are responsible for organizing prerecorded material into the final master version. **Venue**s make use of live sound engineers who are responsible for the planning, installation, and operation of live sound reinforcement.

See also: **independent record label; major record label; producer**

Further reading: Cunningham (1996); Kealy (1979); Strasser (2004)

AUDIO HOME RECORDING ACT (AHRA)

A 1992 amendment to U.S. **copyright** law that provided blanket protection for private noncommercial audio copying.

This act protected owners of analog and digital home recording devices from prosecution and established rules in the use of audio home recording. Home recording began in 1975 when Sony introduced the Betamax home videocassette tape-recording system. This was followed in 1976 by JVC (Victor Company of Japan) releasing a competing home recording system called the VHS. Although these systems were for recording video images, the advent and success of these systems set a precedence in terms of commercial and legal acceptance of home recording. For the music industry the release of recordable digital audio formats, including DAT (digital audio tape), DCC (digital compact cassette), and the Minidisc, in the late 1980s presented a similar challenge. The recording industry feared that **consumer**s would be able to make perfect multigenerational copies of digital recordings. The recording industry accused the manufacturers of contributing to unlawful copying (**contributory copyright infringement**) of copyrighted recordings. The manufactures cited the U.S. Supreme Court decision in *Sony Corp v. Universal City Studios, Inc.* that found use of recording equipment, albeit Betamax, for private, noncommercial, time-shifting purposes constituted **fair use** and, therefore, exempt for prosecution. In the early 1990s, recording industry and electronic companies reached an agreement that would allow DAT recorders into the United States under the provision that all DAT recorders include anticopying systems and the manufactures pay **royalties** from the sale of recorders and blank media. With support of manufactures and the recording industry, Congress passed the Audio Home Recording Act. The act requires a 2-percent surcharge on the wholesale price of recording equipment and a 3-percent surcharge of the wholesale price of blank media. All royalties are collected by the Copyright Office on a quarterly basis and distributed into two special **fund**s. The sound recording fund would consist of two thirds of the total royalty revenues and the musical works fund would receive the remaining one third of the revenues. The musical works fund is split 50/50 between songwriters (distributed by the **PRO**s) and the publishers. (distributed by the **Harry Fox Agency** (**HFA**) For the recording fund non-featured **artist**s are paid 4 percent through the **American Federation of Musicians** (**AFM**) and The **American Federation of Television and Radio Artists** (**AFTRA**). The remaining amount is split 60/40 with the record labels receiving 60 percent of the funds (distributed by the **Alliance of Artists and Recording Companies**) and featured artists 40 percent. Labels justify receiving the majority of royalty payments due to lower profits from the introduction of this technology.

SOUND RECORDING FUND		MUSICAL WORKS FUND	
Record Labels	38.4%	Music Publishers	16.7%
Featured Artists	25.6%	Songwriters	16.7%
Nonfeatured Artists (AFM Members)	1.75%		
Nonfeatured Artists (AFTRA Members)	0.9%		
Percentage of Total Fund	66.7% (2/3 of total fund)	Percentage of Total Fund	33.3% (1/3 of total fund)

Source: Alliance of Artists and Recording Companies

See also: **circumvention**; **copyright**; **FCC**

Further reading: Hull (2002); Landau (2005); San Diego Law Review (2000); Texas Law Review (2000)

AUDIOVISUAL WORK

A work that consists of a series of related images and accompanying sounds.

The U.S. Copyright Office does not differentiate the nature of reproduction equipment in defining an audiovisual work. Pictorial images may be shown by the use of projectors, viewers, or electronic equipment and expressed via a filmstrip, slides, video tapes, CD-I (interactive compact disc), or DVD. However, sounds in an audiovisual clip, for example, are not defined in **copyright** law as a "sound recording." The Copyright Office requires separate registrations for individual elements, especially in the case of soundtracks. For registration of audiovisual works, the U.S. Copyright Office requires the use of form PA. **Royalty** payments for audiovisual works are via **synchronization license**s.

See also: **broadcasting**; **copyright**; **Harry Fox Agency**; **performing rights organization (PRO)**

Further reading: Schulenberg (2005); Vogel (2007)

AUTHOR

A general term used in the Copyright Act to describe the creator of a work of art such as a musical composition, a literary work, or a computer program.

In **copyright** law the term refers to an identified person who created a work of art. In the case of a **work-made-for-hire** composition, copyright law considers an employer or the commissioner of a work to be an author. In U.S. copyright law, an author is granted a bundle of rights associated with their registered work. These include the right of reproduction, the right of **distribution** by sale or other transfer of ownership, the right to prepare **derivative work**s based on the original copyrighted work, the right to perform "live" in public and by means of digital audio transmission.

Under European copyright law an author is granted a further right of protection against the unauthorized misuse of a work or **moral rights**. This tenant gives an author a series of rights in regard to their intellectual property including the right to refuse publication, the right to be credited for a work, and the right in the integrity of a work.

See also: **copyright**; **work–made–for hire**

Further reading: Brabec (2006); Dennisoff (1975), (1986); Eliot (1993); Frasconga (2004); Frith (1996); Garofalo (1992); Halloran (2007)

AVAILABILITY

Distribution figures associated with **ASCAP**. A **catalog** rate is based on its availability, depending on the number of recognized works or standards in it. The higher the availability the greater the **royalties** for an author.

See also: **copyright**; **independent record label**; **major record label**

Further reading: Frith (1993); Halloran (2007); Krasilovsky (2007); Schulenberg (2005)

BERNE CONVENTION FOR THE PROTECTION OF LITERARY AND ARTISTIC WORKS OF 1886

An international **copyright** treaty that established protection of an author's intellectual property in 60 signatory countries.

Commonly known as the Berne Convention, this agreement established copyright protection for works of art (musical, literary, and visual) among signatory nations. Prior to the Berne Convention, copyright protection was restricted to an author's country of origin. International protection of works required authors and their representatives to obtain copyright protection in each country that a work could be performed or sold. Furthermore, the Berne Convention established minimum standards for copyright law especially in the expression, length, and amount of protection offered to a copyright holder. Specifically, according to the Berne Convention, copyright is established at **fixation** rather than registration. The Convention also instituted a specific duration that a work can be exploited before returning to the **public domain**. Under the Convention all works are protected for 50 years after the death of an author. This figure was calculated as the average lifespan of an author at the time of the Berne Convention, plus two generations. Finally, the Convention established **moral rights** for intellectual property. This allowed an author, even after the transfer of all rights, to claim authorship of his or her work and to object to any distortion, mutilation, or other modification of the said work. In regard to the **fair use** doctrine, the original Berne Convention maintained that what constitutes fair use is to be decided by legislative bodies in an individual country and for special agreements between member states.

Since the original Convention in 1886, the agreement has undergone several revisions, each named after the city in which the revision took place. These include Berlin (1908), Rome (1928), Brussels (1948), Stockholm (1967), and Paris (1971). Both at the Stockholm and Paris meetings member nations in the Berne Union introduced a three-step test that imposed constraints on **exclusive rights** under national copyright law. The three-step rule limited exclusive rights to certain special cases that do not prejudice the interest of the holder. The three steps and their abbreviated titles stipulated that:

1   exemption is limited to a narrow and specifically defined class of uses (certain special cases);
2   exempted use does not compete with an actual or potential course of economic gain obtained from normally exercised use (conflict with a normal exploitation of the work); and
3   the exempted use does not harm a copyright holders interests in light of general copyright objectives (not unreasonably prejudice the legitimate interests of the right holder).

To administer the agreements within the Berne Convention signatory countries established the United International Bureau for the Protection of Intellectual Property (BIRPI) in 1893. This organization was in existence until 1967, when BIRPI became the **World Intellectual Property Organization (WIPO)**. Universal acceptance of the Berne Convention was achieved with the World Trade Organization's passage of the agreement on **Trade-Related Aspects of Intellectual Property Rights (TRIPS)** that accepted the majority of conditions of the Berne convention. The United States became a member and ratified the Berne agreement in 1989. This was partly because U.S. copyright office would need major modifications to the U.S. copyright law, especially in regard to moral rights, registration of copyright, and copyright notification. Thus, to accommodate the change mooted by the United States, the Universal Copyright Convention of 1952 was developed. Although the United Kingdom became a signatory in 1887, large portions of the convention were adopted after the passage of the Copyright, Designs, and Patents Act of 1988.

See also: **Buenos Aires Convention**; **copyright**; **DMCA**; **performing rights organization (PRO)**

Further reading: Koelman (2006); Wallman (1989)

BEST EDITION

A term used by the U.S. Copyright Office to describe the most suitable published edition of a work for archival purposes at the Library of Congress.

The Copyright Office defines quality on specific criteria as expressed via a ranking. For **phonorecord**s the best-edition quality is ranked by delivery system; therefore, a compact disc is preferred over a vinyl disk, which in turn preferred over a tape. For the reproduction of sound the Copyright Office prefers quadraphonic audio over stereophonic audio and prefers stereophonic sound over monoaural sound.

For musical compositions, both vocal and instrumental, the Copyright Office requires a full score over any reduction. In the case of compositions that are published only by "rental, lease, or lending" the Copyright Office insists on a full score only. The Copyright Office also requires that all scores be bound and use archival-quality paper. If the deposit does not meet the standards established by the Copyright Office it will not be accepted for submission.

See also: **collective work**; **copyright**; **publishing**

BIEM (BUREAU INTERNATIONAL DES SOCIÉTÉS GÉRANT LES DROITS D'ENREGISTREMENT ET DE REPRODUCTION MÉCANIQUE)

A semipublic European **mechanical** licensing collection society that represents more than 40 national licensing societies in 43 countries.

Based in Neuilly-sure-Seine, France, BIEM was established in 1923 to represent the interests of individual **authors**. BIEM establishes a **royalty** rate based on the **Published Price to Dealers** (**PPD**). It is a constructed price charged by a record **producer** to a retailer selling directly to **consumer**s. BIEM establishes a percentage, which now is 6.5 percent of the PPD price. This represents the total royalty payable by the record company for all music on that record. The separate compositions are then divided up on a time basis and the 6.5 percent royalty is allocated in that way. Comparison of the European method with the U.S. method usually results in a higher royalty being payable in Europe on a per-record basis. Member societies of BIEM enter into agreements that allow each member to represent the others' repertoire. In this manner, BIEM is able to **license** users for the vast majority of protected works in the world.

BIEM negotiates a standard agreement with representatives of the **International Federation of the Phonographic Industry** (**IFPI**) establishing the conditions for the use and payment of repertoire from representative societies. The royalty rate agreed between BIEM and IFPI for mechanical reproduction rights is 11 percent on the PPD. This rate is only applicable to physical audio products. Two deductions are applied on the gross royalty rate: 9 percent for rebates and discounts and 10 percent for packaging costs. This results in an effective rate of 9.009 percent of PPD. This standard agreement is applied by the member societies to the extent that there is no **compulsory license** or statutory license in their territory. BIEM's role is also to assist in technical collaboration between its member societies and to help in solving problems that arise between individual members.

Rates for audiovisual use of protected works are negotiated on a territory-by-territory basis, as are rates for Internet and other usage. BIEM also represents and defends the interests of its member societies, particularly in forums relating to intellectual property rights such as those associated with the **World Intellectual Property Organization** (**WIPO**), **Trade-Related Aspects of Intellectual Property Rights** (**TRIPS**), and the **World Trade Organization** (**WTO**).

See also: **Harry Fox Agency; mechanical license; statutory rate**

Further reading: Hardy (1990); Lathrop (2007); Mitchell (2007)

BLACK BOX INCOME

Monies collected by **mechanical license** agencies that have not yet been claimed by a publisher or **artist**.

This often occurs as a result of foreign sales where the collection agency has not contacted the publisher with information on revenue. The International Convention for the Protection of Performers, Producers of Phonograms, and Broadcasting Organizations, known as the **Rome Convention** of 1961, required contracting states to develop an equitable remuneration system so that performers can claim dues in signatory nations. With this requirement in place, performers and **producer**s can apply for **fund**s not yet claimed in a foreign country.

There are several forms of income that form black box income, including unallocated income, unclassified income, and unidentified income. These monies may come from a variety of sources including **publishing**, recording, or **broadcasting**. Often mechanical license agencies have income set aside for expenses that where not used, as the organization did not spend its full budget and surplus collections from unallocated incomes. Some income is a result of a surplus from procedures or from income not separately allocated and attributed to specific musical compositions. **Subpublishing** monies are also available. These monies have accumulated as a result of the failure to communicate necessary information on song titles and songwriters. Other accumulated monies available are a result of inaccurate registration or misallocation of funds.

See also: **BIEM**; **foreign royalties**; **Harry Fox Agency**; **performing rights organization (PRO)**

Further reading: Khon and Khon (2002); Schulenberg (2005); Thall (2006)

BLANKET LICENSE

A term that describes a licensing agreement between a **venue** and a **performing rights organization** for a general music licensing fee rather than a system based on a song-by-song usage.

Also known as block licensing, this method of licensing is applied to situations where collecting data is impossible if traditional electronic or personal methods were used. Such circumstances often occur in venues such as night clubs, bars, and restaurants. Similar situations occur in media outlets such as **radio**, television stations, and the Internet where thousands of songs are performed over a period of time. In these cases the use of blanket licenses often minimizes transaction costs for both the **copyright** owner and users. It allows copyright owners to enforce their rights and profit from their works without the prohibitive expense of finding and negotiating with multiple users. Furthermore, it provides users a lawful method of performing music without the difficulty of obtaining permissions from multiple copyright own-ers. All U.S. **PRO**s (**ASCAP, BMI**, and **SESAC**) collect and are responsible for the development of a fee structure for blanket licenses. Blanket licenses issued by the PRO's are divided into two categories based on usage. Live performance blanket licenses may be issued to radio stations, television net-works, and other forms of broadcast music. In certain cases, radio or television broadcasters may use a per-program license. Similar to blanket licenses, per-program licenses required to track all music used and to obtain the rights for the music used in programs not covered by the license.

"General licenses" are issued to concert venues, malls, hotels, office buildings (elevator music), and night clubs (for live performance of bands). In both cases it is the venue owner or **producer** who pays for the license, and not the actual performer of the music. For example, in a night club, for a specific title to be played, the club owner would secure the license and not the band that actually performed the music. For establishing a fee structure PROs negotiate with industry associations of user groups. Fees represent a reasonable approximation of the value of all performances as a group. A venue may also need more than one type of license (e.g., one for the live performance of bands and another for jukebox performance), and they may also need a license from more than one issuer (e.g., for different song **catalog**s). Blanket licenses last no more than five years and infringe-ment includes statutory damages between $500 and $20,000 depending on the nature and circumstances of the infringement.

Each PRO collects blanket licenses in a different manner. For ASCAP and BMI blanket licenses are based on either gross receipts or market size, whereas SESAC calculates blanket licenses on transmission power or hours of operation. Rate negotiations for ASCAP and BMI are assessed via an all-industry committee, whereas SESAC TV **license**s are negotiated directly with the company.

See also: **AFM; independent record label; major record label; publishing; venue**

Further reading: Biederman (1992); Khon and Khon (2002); McCourt (2005); Nye (2000); Schulenburg (2005)

BRANCH DISTRIBUTOR

A **distribution** company owned by a **major record label**.

Typically, a branch distributor will only sell the label's manufactured CDs. However, the parent company may distribute a subsidiary label's recordings or those of another company. In the later case, payment to the branch distributor is often based on a percentage of the total number of recordings sold, a **royalty** percentage, or upfront fees. Each major label has its own branch distributors, including UMVD (Vivendi–Universal), WEA (Warner Music), EMD (EMI), and Sony BMG distribution (Sony/BMG). All branch distributors work with online and traditional retailers.

See also: **mechanical royalties**; **published priced to dealers (PPD)**; **rack jobber**; **retail**

Further reading: Hirsch (1970); Hull (2002); Kalma (2002); Krasilovsky (2007); Levy and Weitz (1995)

BREAKAGE ALLOWANCE

Clause contained in a recording **contract** that allows a record company to deduct a specified amount from an **artist's royalty** payment for goods damaged during **distribution**.

Most record labels include a breakage allowance of 10 percent, even in contracts that only distribute music online. Although music distribution has become electronic, many record labels will still deduct the amount.

See also: **e-commerce**; **one stop**; **packaging cost deduction**; **phonorecord**; **retail**

BROADCAST DATA SERVICE (BDS)

A subsidiary of ACNielsen, Nielsen BDS is a service that tracks **airplay** of songs on **radio**, television, and the Internet.

Using a digital pattern recognition technology, BDS tracks over 1,000 radio stations in the United States and Canada since 1989. Using audio fingerprinting technology, Nielsen allows for real-time monitoring. The system has become an industry standard due to its accuracy in detecting and monitoring songs. Information gathered is utilized by industry executives of radio stations, record labels, **performing rights organization**s (**PRO**), and artist **manager**s.

In a partnership with Philips electronics, Nielsen developed audio fingerprinting, a technology that extracts unique musical features from radio content and audio classification technology that automatically determines whether sampled content is either music or not. This technology replaced the use of call-outs and station reporting, which were inaccurate and usually fraught with error arising out of favoritism in such methods. Trade journals, such as Billboard and Radio and Records, use BDS in determining their radio airplay music **charts**. With the advent of digital radio, BDS now monitors satellite radio, Internet services, and audio networks as well as **music video** channels.

See also: **broadcasting**; **FCC**; **marketing**; **performance rights**; **playlist**; **royalty**

Further reading: Beville (1988); McBride (2007)

BROADCAST MUSIC INCORPORATED (BMI)

A U.S. **performing rights organization** founded in 1939 as an alternative source of music licensing competitor to the **American Society of Composers, Authors and Publishers** (**ASCAP**).

As a performing rights organization, BMI collects **license** fees on behalf of its members and distributes the income as **royalties**. BMI issues a variety of licenses to users of music including television, **radio**, live concerts, and music **venue**s such as nightclubs, bars, and discos. Recently BMI has begun to issue licenses in new media and emerging technologies. This includes satellite radio, Internet, podcasts, **ringtone**s, and ringbacks.

BMI was established by radio broadcasters as a means to represent **artist**s in genres outside of the general mainstream including rock, blues, country, jazz, gospel, and folk. With over 6 million compositions in its **catalog** and serving some 300,000 songwriters, composers, and music publishers, BMI generates income by charging a service fee on all royalties collected. Fees and terms of licenses are negotiated between BMI and industry committees as well as trade organizations or groups representing members affected by music licenses. In general, fees for broadcasters are based on annual revenue less certain deductions. In determining commercial radio fees, BMI uses a sampling system of licensed stations in four categories. Commercial radio stations are sampled every three months. Stations are randomly chosen and represent a cross-section of **broadcasting** activity and area. In addition to the sample, BMI includes data from third-party providers such as MediaBase in its radio distributions.

Royalty payments are based on the license fees collected from each individual station. Members are eligible for up to three distinct royalty payments current activity payments, hit song bonuses, and standards bonuses. Standard current payments are provided on a quarterly basis regardless of how many times each of the works was performed. Any work that is performed more than 95,000 times during a quarter is eligible for a Hit Song Bonus. Any work that has been performed at least 2.5 million times since being released and are performed at least 15,000 times in a quarter are classified as Standards and, as such, become eligible for the Standards Bonus. If a local commercial radio's feature performance is a classical work, all participants will be paid at the minimum rate of 32 cents per minute. The royalty rate paid for performances on National Public Radio (NPR) is based upon license fees received by BMI from the Corporation for Public Broadcasting (CPB), rather than monitored performances of BMI works. College radio stations pay a minimum rate of 6 cents for featured performances. BMI logs college radio stations using the Electronic Music Reporting (EMR) system. The EMR system allows stations to use existing computer programs to create music-use reports that are uploaded to BMI over a secure Internet connection. As of December 2006, almost 60 percent of stations with EMR capability were submitting reports. Television performance royalties are determined via **cue sheet**s (listing the theme, cue, and other musical data) and performance information. Television royalties are calculated on the basis of the time of the performance (morning/daytime, primetime, late night, or overnight) and performance type; there are several categories, including feature performances (performance on camera), background, theme (music identify a program), jingle performances (used in **advertising**), and live performances. Television royalties collected from concert **promoter**s and venues is based on the status of a performer (headliner or opening act) and a credit formula. **Foreign royalties** are collected on a quarterly basis from affiliate PROs plus a 3.6 percent administrative cost.

BMI has developed an international partnership known as FastTrack with four national performing rights organizations: GEMA (Germany), SACEM (France), SGAE (Spain), and SIAE (Italy) to improve the accuracy of collecting royalty data. FastTrack is an electronic data collecting system that improves the accuracy of foreign performance right royalties.

See also: **copyright**; **foreign royalties**; **International Federation of Phonographic Industries (IFPI)**; **payola**; **SESAC**; **synchronization license**

Further reading: Fujitani (1984); Nye (2000); Ryan (1985)

BROADCASTING

The act of transmitting music and programs from a sender to multiple receivers simultaneously.

This term includes many technologies including **radio**, television, subscription cable, satellite television and radio, and the Internet. Legal regulation of the transmission of information is important due to the limitation of frequencies available and the possibility of interference between transmitters. Government agencies, such as the **Federal Communications Commission (FCC)**, can control the number and content of material transmitted through the licensing process. Because broadcasters are **license**d to serve the public interest, it is the responsibility of the FCC to ensure that stations abide by the Communications Act and FCC rules and policies. In general these rules cover a variety of issues including advertising, obscenity, **payola**, and fraud. Furthermore, the FCC limits individuals or corporations from acquiring a certain number of stations. This policy (originally mandated by Congress through the now-defunct "fairness doctrine") provides an opportunity for the presentation of a diverse range of viewpoints over the airwaves and protects individuals from personal attack and political editorializing.

See also: **airplay**; **audiovisual work**; **Broadcast Data Service (BDS)**; **charts**

Further reading: Allen (1987); Armbrust (2004); Bagdikian (1990); Speiss (1997)

BUENOS AIRES CONVENTION

A 1910 international **copyright** treaty that established recognition of copyright among signatory countries.

The convention required that **author**'s assign property rights over their work through the use of the notice, "**all rights reserved**." This requirement was made obsolete, with the **Universal Copyright Convention (UCC)** of 1952 that established the declaration of copyright through the symbol ©. Both the Buenos Aires Convention and the UCC became obsolete when all the signatory countries to both conventions became signatories to the **Berne Convention**, which provides copyright recognition without formal notification. Copyright protection under the convention follows the "rule of the shorter term" principle by which a work simultaneously published in a Convention and nonconvention state will appropriate the term of protection from the convention state.

See also: **fair use**; **GATT**; **Geneva Phonograms Convention**; **moral rights**; **Rome Convention**; **TRIPS**; **WIPO**; **WTO**

Further reading: Koelman (2006); Wallman (1989)

CAPACITY

A quantifiable measurement of a **venue** for a single performance or sequence of events such as a concert series.

There are two forms of measurement used in determining capacity. Physical capacity is the number of places (i.e., seats) available at the venue. Financial capacity is the monetary value of the places to be used within a venue. This measurement takes into account the various published prices for seating. For venues without seating, such as outside events, theoretical physical capacity is often used. This system measures capacity based on the maximum number of places a facility could offer. Operational physical capacity is a measurement that takes into account the total number of seats available in a venue, minus any seats, wheelchair places, and standing places removed for operational reasons, such as the installation of soundboards.

See also: **agent**; **contract**; **four walling**; **IATSE**; **promoter**; **ticketing**

Further reading: Ashton (2007); Kirchner (1994); Leeds (2007); Waddell, Barnet, and Berry (2007)

CATALOG

The collection of songs owned by a music **publisher**.

Catalogs are often owned and administered by publishers, **performing rights organization**s (**PROs**), **mechanical rights societies**, and songwriters other than the original composer. If an external entity administers a catalog they are required to obtain **copyright**s, collect **royalties**, provide accounting information, and audit other organizations. Smaller publishers will rely on large publishing companies to administer their

catalogs for a percentage of gross receipts. Subpublishers represent catalogs in foreign territories. A catalog's worth is valued in terms of its age, the number of earned copyrights, the catalogs past performance, and **subpublishing** agreements.

Other uses of the term include the number of recordings held in stock by a retailer or wholesaler, the number of songs written by a songwriter, and all the recordings made by an **artist**.

See also: **ASCAP**; **author**; **BIEM**; **BMI**; **folio**; **foreign royalties**; **print license**; **publishing**; **SESAC**

Further reading: Smith (2004); Velluci (1998)

CHARTS

A categorized method of ranking top selling or listened CD or song in a given period of time. Therefore, the higher the ranking, the more popular and successful the CD or song.

Charts are used as a **marketing** tool and are compiled using sales, radio play, and downloaded music. Organization charts are compiled based on genre within a specific timeframe, ranging from a week to a year and a specific geographic locale. However, the wider the geographical scope of the chart, the more important the ranking. **Airplay** charts are complied by *Billboard Magazine* and Radio and Records (R&R). Both monitor stations using **BDS**. The service provides these media publications with airplay information on traditional radio formats as well as satellite radio, Internet services, audio networks, as well as music TV stations. Billboard categorizes their charts based on airplay, genre, and radio format. The most important charts cover the most popular genres of the time. Billboard Hot 100 measures standard singles issued weekly using sales and radio reports. Position on the chart is determined by a total point value acquired in a period of time.

R&R tracks the monitoring of current songs by format, station, and audience cumes. R&R charts include Top 40/Contemprorary Hit Radio, Christian AC, and the Hot AC.

Music charts play an important role for various interests in the music industry. For retailers charts are used to establish inventory levels. Thus, in turn, the success of a song or **album** on a particular chart affects manufacturing and **distribution** decisions. Furthermore, demand from retailers influences record labels to produce more of a specific **artist**, album, or genre. For artists and songwriters chart rankings play an important role in contractual negotiations with record labels, artist **manager**s, and record **producer**s. Publishers will use charts to evaluate songwriters and producers. Performance licensing fees can be negotiated on the basis of chart ranking.

See also: **airplay**; **album**; **cue sheet**; **disc jockey**; **performance rights**; **performing rights organization (PRO)**; **synchronization license**

Further reading: Andersen (1980); Cusic (1996); Feihl (1981); Harrison (2007); Negus (1992); Watson (2006)

CIRCUMVENTION

A term used by the U.S. Copyright Office to describe technology or other methods that allow an individual to obtain copyrighted material without permission.

Anticircumvention law is important with the advent of the **Digital Millennium Copyright Act of 1998 (DMCA)** and the **World Intellectual Property Organization (WIPO) Copyright Treaty** as a means to bypass **fair use** laws. The act clearly states that "no person shall circumvent a technological measure that effectively controls access to a work protected under this title (wipo.org)."

The Copyright Office has established six classes of work not subject to the prohibition against circumventing access controls; for example, **audiovisual work**s included in the educational library of a university or college, when circumvention is used to create compilations for educational use in the classroom. Circumventing technology includes the descrambling, decrypting, or, otherwise, the bypassing or deactivation of technological measures with the authority of the **copyright** owner. Furthermore, the DMCA prohibits the manufacturing, sale, or distribution of such circumventing technology to the public. Copyright law does provide exceptions to this rule, including protection under fair use, free speech, and if any part of a technology is integrated into a system, such as a recording function on a tape recorder.

The European Union has similar laws in regards to anticircumvention. Under the European Directive of 2001, member states are required to provide legal protection against circumvention as well as protect against the manufacture, import, **distribution**, and sale of products that are intended for the purpose of circumvention.

There are several international treaties and conventions that deal with anticircumvention. In 1996 an international anticircumvention law was enacted through the WIPO Copyright Treaty and the **WIPO Performance and Phonograms Treaty**. In the United States the Digital Millennium Copyright Act implemented many provisions of the WIPO Copyright Treaty in regard to circumvention of technological barriers to copying intellectual property. The DMCA criminalizes the production and dissemination of technology created to circumvent protected material or **DRM** systems.

See also: **creative commons**; **e-commerce**; **fair use**; **Intentional Inducement of Copyright Infringement Act**; **IFPI**; **peer-to-peer network**; **piracy**; **RIAA**; **sampling**; **TRIPS**

Further reading: Alderman (2001); Brown (2006); Gillen and Sutter (2006)

CISAC (CONFÉDÉRATION INTERNATIONALE DES SOCIÉTÉS D'AUTEURS ET COMPOSITEURS)

An international association of societies representing **author**s and composers.

The goal of CISAC is the increased recognition and protection of a creator's rights especially in regard to **copyright**. Founded in 1926, CISAC has more than 200 members from more than 100 countries worldwide. The aims of CISAC are to strengthen and develop an international network of copyright societies, develop a central database so that societies can freely exchange information and improve national and international copyright laws. Finally, CISAC societies offer reciprocal representation through a contractual relationship.

As a nonprofit organization, CISAC is governed by bylaws and a board of directors elected by the general assembly. Other statutory bodies of CISAC include International Council of Creators, the five Regional Committees (Africa, Ibero-America, Asia Pacific, Canada/United States, and Europe), Legal and Technical Committee, and the CIS Supervisory Board. Members include most of the major performing rights organizations through the world, including **ASCAP**, **BMI**, **SESAC**, and **PRS**.

See also: **contract**; **foreign royalties**; **performance rights**; **royalty**; **statutory rate**

CLEARANCE

The right to perform, record, or use a composition. Permission to perform a **nondramatic** musical work is obtained through a **license**.

The right to clear a song is obtained through a **performing rights organization** (**PRO**). A music clearance is required when selling, making copies of music, and performing music publicly. Music clearance is a process of determining what permissions are needed, discovering the owner of the music, contacting the owner or their representative **publishing** companies, negotiating an appropriate license and fee, and creating a written agreement for the clearance. A network is indemnified against infringement claims made against "cleared" works. Nondramatic performances of compositions are logged and reported by broadcasters.

See also: **advertising**; **airplay**; **ASCAP**; **BMI**; **marketing**; **performance rights**; **SESAC**

Further reading: Butler (2004)

COLLECTIVE WORK

In **copyright** law a work that consists of a number of contributions.

Each contribution within the collective work is considered a separate and independent work. Common collective works include periodicals, anthologies, and encyclopedias as well as a compilation of songs by a single author. Each contribution constitutes a separate and independent work assembled into a whole. Authorship of a collective work as a whole includes the elements of revising, editing, compiling, and similar authorship. An **author** who has contributed to an article or column to a magazine or newspaper may be entitled to a separate registration. This type of work is called a contribution to a collective work. As such the author is entitled to full rights associated with copyright ownership. Registration is, therefore, based on the type of contribution to the collective work. If the publication consists of a series of contributions during a 12-month period, there is a special provision of a group of contributions to a periodical in application form GR/CP of the U.S. Copyright Office.

See also: **Copyright Term Extension Act**; **license**; **public domain**; **publishing**

COMMERCIALLY ACCEPTABLE

A term used in recording **contract**s that allows a label to determine whether a **master** recording is technically and artistically of a high enough standard to warrant commercial **release**.

In many cases, a label may withhold the release of an **album**, stating that the material contained within is not commercially acceptable. Many **artist**s will insist that the term "technically acceptable" replace the more ambiguous commercially acceptable.

See also: **advertising**; **distribution**; **independent record label**; **major record label**; **marketing**; **producer**

COMMISSION

A percentage of income that is given to a worker or artist.

The size of a commission often depends on the value of the goods or services handled. Payments are calculated on a percentage of goods sold or services rendered. In the music industry in particular commissions are often associated with artist management, concert promotion, and talent agents. In these cases the agent's commission is calculated as a percentage of their client's fee. This often ranges from 10 to 20 percent. Often these rates are established by a music **union** representing the **artist**'s profession.

See also: **agent**; **author**; **festival**; **manager**; **venue**

COMPULSORY LICENSE

A **license** authorizing a licensee certain rights under **copyright** law for the use of copyrighted material in a **phonorecord**, **broadcasting**, performance, and so on.

Also referred to as a statutory license, a licensee need not obtain permission from the copyright owner to use their intellectual property as long as certain conditions, restrictions, and fees apply to their use as defined by the Copyright Office. Fees for compulsory licenses are broken down into four groups: phonorecords, jukeboxes, cable systems, and public broadcasting. The rates range greatly depending on the use of the music. For jukeboxes the annual rate is $275 for the first jukebox, $55 for the second through tenth jukeboxes, and $48 for each additional jukebox. For phonorecords the rate is based on the statutory mechanical rate set by the Copyright Office, which currently stands at 9.1 cents or 1.75 cents per minute of playing time or fraction thereof, which ever is greater. In this case, the license is formally referred to as a Compulsory License for Making and Distributing Phonorecords. The license fees charged for secondary transmission by a cable system and public broadcasting are complicated and are set by the **Copyright Royalty Board** (**CRB**). For webcasters, the now-defunct **Copyright Arbitration Royalty Panel** (**CARP**) recommended in 2002 a minimum fee of $500 per year for each licensee or .07 cents for simultaneous Internet retransmission of over-the-air AM or FM broadcasts. On May 1, 2007, the CRB set new webcasting royalty rates for the period of 2006–2012. Under this new law webcasters, both commercial and noncommercial, must pay a minimum annual fee of $500. Commercial webcasters pay a fee based on a per-play and per-listener rate. For 2008 the standard rate is 11 cents, with the rate continuing to rise annually until 2010 when the interest rate will have reached 19 cents. The CRB also set ringtone mechanical rates at 24 cents in 2008. Statutory mechanical **royalties** are paid by the Harry Fox Agency to owners. Royalty payments are accompanied by a monthly statement of account to the copyright owner.

Compulsory licenses are available to anyone as soon as a phonorecord has been distributed to the public, based on the **first-sale doctrine**. Within 30 days after the creation of the recording or before distributing a phonorecord, an individual or company may serve a "Notice of Intention to Obtain a Compulsory License" to the copyright owner. If the owner of a copyright is not found, a notice of intent is filed directly with the Copyright Office. To encourage negotiated licenses, compulsory licenses have stringent liabilities defined by copyright law. In the case of compulsory licenses royalty payments are to be made only a monthly basis, whereas negotiated licenses are paid on a quarterly basis. No license can be granted to works that are identical reproductions of an existing copyrighted recording, as this amounts to a piracy and is subject to criminal penalties.

See also: **album**; **catalog**; **Fairness in Musical Licensing Act of 1998**; **license**; **mechanical royalties**; **performing rights organization (PRO)**; **royalty**

Further reading: Biederman (1992); Khon and Khon (2002); McCourt (2005); Nye (2000)

CONSUMER

An individual who purchases goods or services for their personal use or consumption.

The exchange process involves the trading of something tangible or intangible between two actors, the **producer** (e.g., record label) and the consumer. Consumers are classified by two segmentation indicators: demographic and psychographic profiles. Demographics, psychographics, and behavioral elements are variables created in an attempt to understand consumer's wants. These wants may be based on emotional elements and external influences such as family members, peers, environmental influences, culture, and personal motivations. The goal is to develop a plan that addresses the purchasing behavior of the target consumer so that an **advertising** campaign can be created to address their attitude toward a product prior to purchasing, during the act of purchasing, and postpurchase satisfaction or dissatisfaction. In the entertainment industry the level of consumption is linked to an individual's level of disposable income.

In **broadcasting**, consumers are referred to as an audience and are defined as a group of people assembled at an event, either physically or via a transmission medium such as **radio** or television; thus, the term audience is relevant to market research vis-à-vis market rating and share.

See also: **marketing**; **retail**; **venue**

Further reading: Adorno (1941); Kaplan (1987); Lopes (1992, 1992a); McBride (2007); Napoli (2003); Shuker (1998)

CONTINGENT SCALE PAYMENT

Additional payments made to non**royalty artist**s appearing on recordings that reach certain sales levels in the United States.

According to copyright law, a nonroyalty artist is an artist who appears on a recording as a background singer or session musician. Contingent scale applies to recordings after 1974 that have not been previously **released**. This category does not include greatest hits **album**s. Recordings cease to be eligible for contingent scale payment ten years after the release of the album. For albums released after July 1, 2002, a contingent scale payment of a specific percentage is based on a percentage of the applicable minimum scale for each side on which the artist appears when an album reaches a sales plateau. The **American Federation of Television and Radio Artists** (**AFTRA**) rates range from 50 percent of the minimum scale on album sales, that is, greater than 157,500 units, to 250,000 units. The rate increases to 75-percent minimum scale on album sales, that is, sale of more than 1,000,000 units. According to AFTRA if an album sells between 250,000 units and 375,000 units, the contingency scale is 50 percent. This amount increases to 60 percent after the sale of 650,000 units.

Rates are also established by AFM.

See also: **AFM**; **Associated Actors and Artists of America**; **license**; **record club**; **retail**

CONTRACT

A legal instrument that defines an agreement between two or more parties.

Contracts can be in written and verbal forms or may be implied. For a contract to be valid it must contain five key elements. First, there must be an offer and acceptance between all parties. This may take the form of a written or oral agreement. In certain circumstances, the agreement may not be in either form, but may be implied. This may take place when both parties may have reached an agreement even though they have not expressed so in written or oral form. The second element requires consideration between the parties in the contractual relationship. In general, this element states that all parties benefit from the contractual relationship in some way. This may take the form of payments made for goods received or services rendered. The third stage requires that all parties intend to be legally bound. Fourth, there must be a declaration of legal capacity in the contractual document. Fifth, the agreement must have legal capacity, whether it is written or oral. Most common law jurisdictions have a statute for the type of contract required for certain circumstances. For example, in the United States contracts for the sale of goods over $500 fall under the Uniform Commercial Code. Once an agreement has been reached a contract has a series of obligations that both parties must fulfill. Failure to perform these duties may result in a breach of contract leading to litigation. A breach may occur due to nonperformance, noncompliance, or repudiation. A nonperformance breach occurs when one party fails to perform a specific task as stated in a contract. For example, a band hired to perform fails to show up. Noncompliance includes any hindrance of duty in a contract, such as obstruction or prevention of performance. Repudiation exists when one party renounces their promise and, therefore, fails to comply with a contractual agreement. This often occurs in verbal contracts where specific details of performance are not established. Remedies for breach of contract require the breaching party to pay all costs including attorney fees and court costs. In some cases a party may return all rights assigned if they have been in breach of contract. In most cases damages awarded by the courts are relative to the amount of injury, loss, or harm incurred by the injured party.

In the music business most contractual relationships take place between two parties, often an **artist**/performer and a corporate entity such as a recording label, publishing house, **venue**, or **artist management**. Within the recording, publishing, and artist management sectors, both parties enter into an exclusive contractual relationship for a specified period. For example, in an exclusive songwriting agreement, a songwriter agrees to deliver a specific number of songs over a specified period. During this tenure, the songwriter must not write for any other publisher, without the approval of the company with which he or she is bound in a contractual relationship. In return the publisher agrees to carry out duties associated with a publishing house such as, promoting the songwriter's music, collecting royalties and making payments to the songwriter. In general contractual relationships in the music industry are unique and driven by specific interests of the parties involved.. Structurally, contracts consist of clauses that address specific duties and requirements. In general there are several clauses common to all music contracts. These include clauses that deal with location, date, names, and addresses of contracting parties. This section not only verifies the location and date of the contract, but it identifies the parties involved in the contractual relationship. Another boilerplate provision in music contracts is the geographical territory of operation. This clause denotes the countries in which the publisher, recording label, or artist manager is permitted to exploit an artist, recording, or composition. In most contracts the company will require worldwide coverage. Some artists will limit the rights to specific areas such as the United States and Canada or the United Kingdom. In recent times, however, clauses mostly include the whole world as a territory of operation. This is to ensure protection of music content with the advent of satellite broadcasting and transmission. Contractual duration ranges considerably between artists and the type of production. Most contract durations are structured on a yearly basis with multiple options that may be exercised by a label.

Contracts are structured around clauses that express a specific duty. Duties include payment terms, warranties and indemnities, breach of contract, arbitration, taxation, force majeure, and termination or expiration. In a recording contract there are several clauses specific to the exploitation of recordings. Many include issues associated with copyright ownership, ownership of **masters**, advances, cross-collateralization, recording **release**s, promotion, distribution, accounting, and royalty statements. Each clause has a specific duty that the parties must complete. In a recording contract there are several unique clauses associated with the production of commercial recordings. An option clause gives one party, usually the label, a specified option to renew a contract for a specified period. In many contracts the label will request four consecutive yearly renewal options. In most cases an option clause favors a label's ability to hinder an artist renegotiating royalty rates at a higher level. The recording of masters clause deals with the quality, quantity, and type of masters an artist must record. The length of the recording that constitutes a master will also be established. Related to this clause is an important clause, the ownership of masters clause. In this clause the record label will own the masters fixed in a tangible form. Although the ownership of the masters is a negotiated item, except in the case of work-for-hire contracts where the artist automatically allows the record label to retain ownership of the masters, artists with a substantial recording career may retain the ownership rights to the masters. In these cases, the artist will lease only the manufacturing and distribution rights to the record label and retain all rights associated with owning the masters. Associated with this clause is the assignment of copyright clause. Within this section, the record label is granted the right to acquire all musical compositions authored by the artist. In some recording contracts the artist must assign all rights in copyright to a music publisher the record label designates. In most cases the publisher in question is an arm of the record label and the artist, in effect, is allowing the label to establish royalty rates. Many artists will insist on the inclusion of a release clause. This statement provides for the return of all rights in masters and sound recordings to the artist if certain events do not take place such as the label not commercially releasing an album within a specific period. A common clause included in recording and publishing contracts is the failure-to-release clause. This clause states the remedies if a label or publisher fails to release an **author's** product within a stipulated time. Remedies for such action include the return of all rights to the author, financial reimbursement, and the suspension of all contractual relations. In an age of digital recordings an interesting clause that still persists in recording contracts is the packaging cost deduction clause. This article states the maximum number of packaging deductions allowable. In most cases the deduction is based on the suggested retail price of a recording and is withheld against an artist's royalties.

A songwriter/publisher contract defines the agreement between a songwriter and a music publisher. As with recording contracts, publishing contracts contain general clauses that deal with duration, options, territorial range of operation and exclusivity.

See also: **agent**; **artist**; **development deal**; **independent record label**; **license**; **major record label**; **royalty**

Further reading: Brabec and Brabec; Halloran (2007); Holden (1991)

CONTRIBUTORY INFRINGEMENT

A legal doctrine that protects the owner of intellectual property against those who, with full knowledge of the infringing activity, induce, cause, or contribute to the infringing conduct of others.

This term is not recognized by the **Copyright** Office but has been established by the courts in regards to **P2P** systems such as Napster, Grokster, and Kazaa. In Sony Corp. of America v. Universal City Studios, Inc (464 U.S. 417 (1984))a, general test was established for determining whether a device with copying or recording capabilities violated copyright law. This came about with the commercial introduction of the VCR, which raised the potential for widespread copying. Known as the "Sony standard" the Supreme Court found that as long as technology has "substantial non-infringement uses" it cannot be held liable for contributory liability.

To obtain protection against infringement a record label must not only show ownership of a valid copyright and unlawful copying but it must show that a P2P company had knowledge of the infringing activity and had contributed to this infringement. The Digital **Millennium Copyright Act of 1998 (DMCA)** protects Internet service providers from copyright infringement liability.

See also: **creative commons**; **FCC**; **publishing**; **RIAA**; **royalty**; **TRIPS**; **WIPO**; **WTO**

Further reading: Alderman and Schwartz (2001); Castillo (2006); Flint (2004); Fox (1993); McLeod (2005); Oellet (2007)

CONTROLLED COMPOSITION

A clause in a recording **contract** that reduces the statutory **mechanical royalty** rate on the sale of recorded music.

Record labels reduce the mechanical rate to 75 percent of the **statutory rate** as a means of reducing the inherent risk associated with the music industry and the exorbitant costs of releasing an **album**. Based on the current statutory rate, the reduction equates to 6.82¢ on a 9.1¢ full statutory rate. With the statutory rate linked to the Consumer Price Index, many labels will try to lock in the rate at a certain point in time, with the date of signing the contract, the date of recording, master delivery, or release of the master. Royalty rates may be further reduced for mid-priced albums, record-club sales, international sales, and may be completely elim-inated for free goods and recordings sold below wholesale price. Some record companies will establish a maximum aggregate mechanical penny royalty limit on an album. This rate is in essence a cap on the amount of **royalties** that an **artist** can obtain. Thus, a record label can limit the num-ber of songs in an album, reducing royalty payment to the artist and the publisher, regardless of whether the artist has produced more than the number of songs originally agreed between the label and artist. This cap is normally based on a stated number of songs per album. Labels can also require further reduced rates of up to 50 percent of the minimum statu-tory rate for **record club** or budget record sales. If the mechanical royal-ties are cross-collateralized with the artist royalties, then the artist may find it difficult to obtain a **publishing** agreement.

Coauthored works also fall under this contractual agreement. Complications can arise if one party is not under contract with the record label and refuses to accept a reduced rate. In such cases an artist may need to pay out their royalties, which can amount to an extra 25 percent. Reductions may be based per song or limit the number of songs on which payment will be made and may be based on the point in time at which the calculation will be made, thereby negating the cost of living increase the Copyright Office has established on statutory rates.

See also: **album**; **independent record label**; **major record label**; **recoupable**; **reserves**

Further reading: Butler (2005); Hull (2002); Khon and Khon (2002); Passman (2006)

CONVENTION FOR THE PROTECTION OF PRODUCERS OF PHONOGRAMS AGAINST UNAUTHORIZED DUPLICATION OF THEIR PHONOGRAMS

An international convention that provides protection for a producer's intellectual property expressed in phonograms.

Central to this international treaty is the protection from unauthorized publication of a producer's intellectual property in another contracting state. Ratified in 1971 and administered by **World Intellectual Property Organization (WIPO)** this convention also protects against the illegal importation of duplicated phonograms for public consumption. Protection may be provided as a matter of copyright law, sui generis (related rights) law, unfair competition law, or penal law. Protection must last for at least 20 years from **fixation** or the first publication of the phonogram. However, national laws and the **Berne Convention** more frequently provide a 50-year term of protection. Limitations to this convention include works under the **fair use** doctrine that are used for teaching or scientific research.

See also: **Buenos Aires Convention**; **GATT**; **Geneva Phonograms Convention**; **TRIPS**; **WTO**

COPUBLISHING

A circumstance in which two or more publishers own the rights to a song or composition.

In certain cases, the songwriter may keep a percentage of the ownership of the **copyright** of the composition between their own **publishing** company and split the ownership with a larger publishing house. In such cases the **artist** retains 50 percent of the total **royalty** revenues, while the remaining 50 percent is divided between the two publishing companies. The copublisher is charged with administrative duties such as the collection of royalties, licensing, copyright administration, and, in some cases, the promotion of the song. Larger publishers will charge an additional administrative fee for managing the **catalog** of an artist. Such agreements may last for several years or have a shorter time frame.

For many songwriters a copublishing agreement increases the share of income that would not be available under a standard publishing **contract**. In a standard agreement a songwriter transfers the copyright of a song to a music publisher and is paid 50 percent of all earnings received. In a **subpublishing** agreement a writer transfers a portion of the copyright to the publisher. The writer receives 50 percent of the earnings for the song share and a portion of the 50 percent that is reserved to the music publisher, what is described as the "publisher share of income." Performing rights organizations recognize coownership in a song and make separate royalty performance payments to publishers and songwriters. As such, songwriters receive direct payments from PROs. **Mechanical right**s organizations, such as the **Harry Fox Agency**, will make payments based on instructions received from coowners to publishers. Unlike PROs, **mechanical right**s agencies do not pay writers directly. They receive sound recording royalties directly from their publisher.

Copublishing agreements are available to writers who have a successful track record of past hits, a record deal, a recording contract with a major label, a track record with the publisher, or a leverage to negotiate such a contract with a publisher. A publisher may enter into a subpublishing agreement if they are interested in acquiring a writer and their catalog. Terms of copublishing agreements cover future compositions and in some cases past songs that are not under the control of another publisher. In some arrangements there may be restrictions on the use of material, such as the use of music in **advertising** without the permission of the writer. Contracts range from 1 to 2 years, with a number of successive **option**s to extend the agreements that can be negotiated. Some contracts are tied to the release of a minimum product commitment within a geographic boundary (e.g., United States), such as releasing five sings for a specific period, say, three years. Finally, some contracts are based on the recoupment of all **advance**s paid under the agreement.

Advances are often paid to writers upon the signing of an agreement. These monies are **recoupable** against future royalties. The amount of payment depends on the reputation of the writer, recording artist commitment, the quality and quantity of the songs, and the past success of a writer's songs. Advances may also be applied to option periods. Amounts paid as advances are based on a percentage of prior earning with minimum and maximum amounts provided so advances won't go below or above set limits. Advances may be based on the **release** of commercial recordings released during a specific period. This rate varies on the commercial success of an album, the status of the album on the trade **charts**, sales activity, and the reputation of the label.

See also: **ASCAP**; **BIEM**; **BMI**; **foreign royalties**; **nondramatic performance rights**; **royalty**; **SESAC**; **territorial rights**

Further reading: Flack (1989)

COPYRIGHT

A bundle of **exclusive rights**, which grants an owner of a copyright to publish, produce, or sell musical, dramatic, or artistic works.

Copyright law provides an owner an exclusive right for a limited period to exploit their intellectual property for publication and commercial sale. Other rights associated with a copyright include the right to perform or **display** the work publicly, to make **derivative work**s of the original, and to sell the work overseas with full legal protection. Copyright law provides an owner the right to create derivative works of the original. Registration of copyright requires applicants to record the existence of **author**ed works and the identity of their authors with the U.S. Copyright Office in the Library of Congress. Copyright registration also confers the right of license to an owner and the right to transfer the ownership of their copyright. Exclusive licenses require the consent of the copyright owner. **Compulsory license**s are granted to anyone without the consent of the owner. The licensee must pay **royalties** to the copyright owner. Transfer of a copyright includes **work–made–for–hire**, which gives the new owner full rights to the copyright. Copyright licenses and royalties are collected by several organizations based on the nature of the use. For works that are performed, either via a broadcast or performed, performing rights organizations such as **ASCAP**, **BMI**, and **SESAC** collect royalties and distribute them to the respective copyright owner. The sale of recordings also carries with it a right (**mechanical right**) and the agency that covers it is the **Harry Fox Agency**.

Although copyright protection is automatic, even when there is no formal registration of a copyright, registration acts as prima facie evidence and permits the owner to collect statutory damages and attorney fees from infringement violators. For a work to obtain copyright protection it must fulfill two obligations. The work must be original, and it must be expressed in a tangible medium such that it can be communicated and reproduced. Concepts, ideas, processes, and discoveries cannot be copyrighted, but their expression can be copyrighted if it is in a tangible form. Copyright notification contains three elements in a sequential order. The first element is the symbol © or word "copyright" or its abbreviation "copr." This is followed by the year of first publication and the name of the copyright owner. In the case of **phonorecord**s, the symbol ©, is replaced with the letter P inside of a circle.

Copyright duration varies with the type of work and the form of copyright protection. In the United States standard copyright duration is measured from **fixation** of a work plus 70 years after the death of the author. Duration of unpublished anonymous, pseudonymous works, and a **work–made–for–hire** is 120 years from the date of creation. A **joint work** prepared by two or more authors that is not a work–made–for–hire, duration is 70 years after the last surviving author's death. The United Kingdom has slightly different durations of copyright based on the **Berne Convention** and the 1988 Copyright, Designs and Patents Act. For literary, dramatic, and musical works a copyright expires 70 years after the death of the last remaining author. For **anonymous work**s the duration is 70 years from the date of creation. Sound recordings in the UK copyright duration expires 50 years from the end of the calendar year in which the work was created or 50 years from the end of the calendar year in which the work was first released. Most other countries follow the Berne Convention, which provides 50 years protection from the date of fixation. When a copyright term has expired a work is released into the **public domain**.

A copyright not only provides a bundle of **exclusive rights** to an owner, it also offers legal protection against infringement of those rights. Copyright infringement is the violation of any exclusive right held by the copyright owner. Intentional infringement occurs when an author creates a new work that is an exact reproduction of an existing work, with the intention of selling the copy for profit. Unintentional infringement, often called "innocent infringement," occurs when an author creates a new work that is a reproduction of an existing work, although the author was unaware of the copyrighted work at the time. Indirect infringement is a situation in which a person facilitates another in the action of committing copyright infringement. Vicarious liability is a form of indirect copyright infringement where an operator obtains a financial benefit from the actions of a person in illegally obtaining copyrighted material and has the ability to stop this action. Under the vicarious liability doctrine the person facilitating the illegal act, even if he or she does not have knowledge of it, is liable for copyright infringement. **Contributory infringement** occurs when a person knowingly assists or induces the action of obtaining copyrighted material.

A copyright owner who has been injured by copyright infringement may file a law suit against the infringing party. The owner may request an injunction ordering the offending party to cease all actions against them. Second, an owner may sue for statutory damages against the infringing party. Damages range from $100 for unintentional infringement to $50,000 for intentional infringement. Intentional infringement is also a federal criminal offense (considered a misdemeanor) and is punishable by a fine and/or imprisonment up to a year.

Although copyright provides an owner with a series of exclusive rights, it does not completely prohibit the copying or reproduction of a work. Under the **fair use** doctrine, a person can make copies of a protected work if it conforms to various factorssuch as the purpose of the use, for example, education. The nature of the work used, the amount used, and the effect the usage has on the commercial value of the copyrighted work. This doctrine is not only established in U.S. copyright law but is also found in international laws and treaties.

In 1886, the **Berne Convention** established recognition of copyrights among signatory nations. This replaced bilateral agreements countries had to obtain to protect their citizens' intellectual property in foreign nations. The Berne Convention also established that works do not have to be asserted with the corresponding nation's copyright office but that copyright is granted as soon as the work is expressed in a "fixed" form. Recent copyright treaties have not only incorporated regulations of Berne Convention but have also expanded on the concept of copyright to meet current needs, such as the **World Trade Organization**'s **TRIPS** agreement. There is also the **World Intellectual Property Organization** (**WIPO**), an international agency that promotes the protection of intellectual property through the administration of over 23 treaties, including the Berne Convention.

See also: **audiovisual work**; **best edition**; **collective work**; **compulsory license**; **contract**; **Copyright Arbitration Royalty Panel (CARP)**; **Copyright Royalty Board (CRB)**; **Copyright Term Extension Act**; **creative commons**; **dramatic rights**; **first-sale doctrine**; **IFPI**; **RIAA**

Further reading: Biederman (1992); Frith (1993); Halloran (2007); Holland (1994); Jones (1992); Negus (1992); Passman (2006); Rietjens (2006); Schulenberg (2005); Wallman (1989)

COPYRIGHT ARBITRATION ROYALTY PANEL (CARP)

A panel of three **copyright** royalty arbitrators appointed by the U.S. Copyright Office and the Library of Congress that establish the rates and the distribution of **royalties**.

The CARP system was established in the Royalty Tribunal Reform Act of 1993 that eliminated the Copyright Royalty Tribunal. The Act not only replaced the Tribunal, it established a system of ad hoc Copyright Arbitration Royalty Panels. Each panel adjusts the copyright **compulsory licensing** rates and distribute the royalties collected by the licensing division to the appropriate copyright owners. CARP comprises of three professional arbiters selected from the private sector.

The panel's job is to hear evidence from witnesses, consider legal argument from all parties, and make recommendations to the Librarian of Congress on the appropriate rates that a licensee should pay. The original Copyright Act provided for four compulsory licenses for cable television, musical mechanical licenses, noncommercial **broadcasting,** and jukeboxes. Groups that testify before the panel include organizations representing copyright owners, such as the **Recording Industry Association of America** (**RIAA**), performers, the **American Federation of Musicians** (**AFM**), industry organizations (corporations in all areas of the music industry) musicians, and expert witnesses (legal experts, economists, and professors). The panel has 180 days to make recommendations after the Librarian of Congress directed the formation of the arbitration panel. The Librarian, upon the recommendation of the Copyright Office, may adopt the decision proposed by the CARP, unless CARP's determinations are found to be arbitrary or contrary to copyright law. If the Librarian rejects the proposed changes, he or she could, after an additional 30 days, issue an order establishing them himself. An aggrieved party who is bound by the Librarian's decision has the right to appeal to the U.S. Court of Appeals for the D.C. Circuit. With the passage of the **Copyright Royalty and Distribution Reform Act of 2004** (**CRDRA**), the CARP system was phased out. Under the new system, three copyright royalty judges (CRJ) now establish rates, conditions, and distribution of statutory licenses.

See also: **AFTRA**; **CRDRA**; **Copyright Term Extension Act**; **DMCA**; **trade association**

COPYRIGHT ROYALTY AND DISTRIBUTION REFORM ACT OF 2004 (CRDRA)

A U.S. bill establishing **royalty** rates for **compulsory license**s for digital transmissions of sound recordings in webcasting.

Prior to the CRDRA royalty rates were established by the **Copyright Arbitration Royalty Panel** (**CARP**). In 2002 the U.S. Congress passed the Small Webcaster Settlement Act to resolve the complexity of digital **royalty** rates. On November 17, 2004, Congress passed the Copyright Royalty and Distribution Act (CRDRA). The CRDRA makes extensive changes to procedures for adjudicating compulsory license royalties. Replacing the ad hoc three-person CARP were three full-time Copyright Royalty Judges (CRJ), each appointed for a six-year term by the Librarian of Congress in consultation with the Register of Copyrights. The panel's duties include decisions on royalty rates and terms of specified statutory licenses; the distribution of royalty fees; dealing with royalty claims and rate adjustment petitions; arbitrating disputes if manufacturers, importers, and distributors are required to pay royalties under the Audio Home Recording Act; and to make necessary procedural rulings. The law includes a small claims procedure for distribution of royalties. A small claim is defined as an uncontested amount of $10,000 or less. Unlike the previous act, which had the Librarian of Congress review a case before it could move to a higher court, the CRDRA allows appeals to be taken directly to the U.S. Court of Appeals for the D.C. Circuit.

See also: **ASCAP**; **Audio Home Recording Act**; **BMI**; **mechanical royalties**; **SESAC**; **synchronization license**

COPYRIGHT ROYALTY BOARD (CRB)

A panel of three Copyright Royalty Judges (CRJ) who determine rates, conditions, and distribution of U.S. statutory copyright licenses.

The CRB's primary function is to establish statutory rates, but the panel also distributes royalties from statutory license royalty pools that the Library of Congress must administer. Created from the Copyright Royalty and Distribution Reform Act of 2004, the panel replaced the Copyright Arbitration Royalty Panel (CARP). The CRB establishes rates through hearings and makes adjustments that reflect national inflation or deflation. Apart from setting statutory rates, the CRB's mandate includes several other goals that improve the "availability of creative works to the public," while affording "the copyright owner as fair return for his or her creative work ...under existing economic conditions" (www.loc.gov).

The Librarian of Congress appoints each judge for a period of six years, which are staggered. Furthermore, one judge is appointed Chief Royalty Judge by the Librarian of Congress. Since the CRB became effective in 2005, it has passed several important rules in regard to statutory license rates. On May 1, 2007, the CRB set new webcasting royalty rates for the period 2006-2012. Under this new law a minimum annual fee of $500 is required of each channel or station. Above this fee, a station must pay a rate based on a formula for that year. Commercial webcasters pay a per-play and per-listener rate. For example, a transmission of a sound recording would cost a webcaster 11 cents for every 100 unique listeners. In 2008, the rate rose to 14 cents and is expected to rise to18 cents in 2009 and 19 cents in 2010. Noncommercial webcasters pay an annual fee of $500 up to a total of 159,400 total listening hours (TLH; or aggregate tuning hours [ATH]). After this amount has been surpassed, commercial webcasting rates apply. On October 2, 2008, the CRB established mechanical rate terms for physical products and digital phonograms at 9.1 cents for recordings 5 minutes or less, or $1.75 per minute for recordings over 5 minutes. It also established the first statutory rate for ringtones, setting the rate at 24 cents for mastertones. The board also granted music publishers the right to seek a 1.5-percent late fee calculated monthly.

See also: **AFTRA**; **CRDRA**; **Copyright Term Extension Act**; **DMCA**; **trade association**

COPYRIGHT TERM EXTENSION ACT OF 1998

A U.S. federal law that extends the length of **copyright** protection beyond standards established in the **Berne Convention**.

Often referred as the Sonny Bono Copyright Term Extension Act, the bill is named after Congressman Sonny Bono. The act extends the U.S. copyright term from the lifespan of the author plus 50 years to lifespan of the author plus 70 years for works created after January 1, 1978. **Work-made-for-hire**, originally protected by copyright for 75 years after publication, was extended to 120 years after creation or 95 years after publication. Works published prior to January 1, 1978, were granted a 20-year extension to their protection. However, the act does not revive copyrights of works that have expired. The term endures for life of the author plus 70 years for works that are not published and created before 1978.

The primary reason for the extensions was the synchronization with European Union's term extension, which set similar adjustments. Further justification included the "adequate protection of American works in foreign nations and the continued economic benefits of a healthy surplus balance of trade in the exploitation of copyright works" (Senate Report, pp. 104–315). The CTEA was challenged in the U.S. Supreme Court in 2003. In Eldred v. Ashcroft, 537 U.S. 186, Eric Eldred challenged the constitutionality of the act and its violation of the Constitution's Copyright clause that gave congress the power "to promote the progress of Sciences and useful arts, by securing for limited times to Authors and Inventors the exclusive right to their respective writings and discoveries" (U.S. Constitution, Article 1, Section 8, Clause 8). The Supreme Court held that the CTEA was constitutional by a 7:2 decision.

See also: **Berne Convention; Buenos Aires Convention; creative commons; Rome Convention**

Further reading: Crawford and Mankin (1999)

CREATIVE COMMONS

A U.S. nonprofit organization that offers copyright licenses with certain "baseline rights."

These "baseline rights" cover a range of topics including the right to distribute copyright works without charge and are available in more than 40 countries. Founded in 2001, Creative Commons offers **license**s based on four conditions. First, licensees may copy, distribute, **display**, perform, and make **derivative work**s. This requires the licensee to give proper attribution to the **author**. Second, the licensees may use copyrighted works for noncommercial purposes. Third, derivative works cannot be sold for commercial purposes. Fourth, if a derivative work is created for the purposes of economic gain, it must be under license identical to the license that governs traditionally copyrighted works. Sampling licenses are available with two options. The first type of sampling, what creative commons refers to as Sampling Plus, is a system where parts of a work can be copied or modified for any purpose other than **advertising**. Furthermore, entire works within the sampling plus definition can be copied for noncommercial purposes. The second sampling method, known as noncommercial sampling, is a system that allows for sampling of whole work or parts of a work for noncommercial purposes.

See also: **clearance; license; mechanical royalties; nondramatic performance rights; performance rights; publishing; royalty**

Further reading: Jones and Cameron (2005); Lessig (2004)

CROSS-COLLATERALIZATION

A technique used by recording labels and in some cases **publishing** companies to take monies due to an **artist** from income earned for the sale of a recording and apply them toward any **recoupable advance**s or costs incurred in another recording.

In most cases a record label will pay debts incurred from an **album** with profits earned from another album. An artist, therefore, may not see any earnings from **royalties** until all debts have been recovered. Cross-collateralization pushes royalties further into the future where better selling albums and songs are used to recoup lesser selling songs. The application of cross-collateralization applies not only to royalty payments but also for advances, especially when contractual relationships are based on long-term, multialbum **contract**s.

The application and breadth of cross-collateralization in a contract is often negotiable between parties. For a publisher or record label negotiating this clause is based on the perceived risk, potential success, and the reputation of the artist/songwriter. An artist/songwriter will endeavor to reduce the amount and range of this clause. Many artists will try to reduce the amount cross-collateralized when renegotiating a contract for further work.

See also: **independent record label; major record label; phonorecord**

CUE SHEET

A document that lists all of the musical elements of an **audiovisual** program for collection by a performing rights organizations for the purposes of distributing **royalties**.

This includes audiovisual programming on television, film, commercials, infomercials, and any other audiovisual products that contain multiple musical works. Cue sheets contain information such as song duration, usage, and entitled parties (songwriters, publishers, etc.) that help in distributing royalties equitably among members. For television programs cue sheets are due three months after the original broadcast. Feature film cue sheets are filed before the first foreign theatrical performance. **PROs'** will distribute funds in the quarter that the program was first broadcast. In most cases this is four to six months after the program was aired. **ASCAP** and **BMI** have developed RapidCue, an electronically submitted cue sheet used for the processing of television performances.

See also: **broadcasting**; **music video**; SESAC

DEMO (DEMO VERSION)

A recording used for the purpose of an audition, obtaining a recording **contract**, present ideas or material to **producers**, **managers** and other influential people in the music industry, or for **publishing** or copyright purposes.

Many bands will send out a *demo* (short for "demonstration") in the hope that a label will include them on their roster and produce a professional studio recording. Demos are typically crudely recorded with minimal instrumentation—often a vocalist with guitar or keyboard accompaniment. In publishing, demos are categorized into four groups: (1) demo **masters** that are of high quality and can be converted into a master with little additional recording; (2) writer-made demos are simple recordings of a singer and basic accompaniment. The purpose of writer-made demos is to give a potential publisher the basic melody, harmony, and lyrics. The demo acts as a tool for pitching a song; (3) publisher-made demos are more elaborate than writer-made demos and include more musicians on a recording; and (4) an unsolicited demo is one that is sent without consent of the receiver. In many cases, labels ignore unsolicited material sent to them by mail.

See also: **artist**; **audio engineer**; **contract**; **independent record label**; **major record label**; **producer**; **recoupable**

DERIVATIVE WORK

A work based on a preexisting work which is substantially recast, transformed, or adapted into an original **copyright**ed work of authorship.

A derivative work can be created through an arrangement, abridgement, or condensation of the original work. Essential in obtaining copyright protection as a "new work" the derivative must contain a substantial amount of original material.

An **artist** may be able to negotiate a passive **royalty** on derivative works or trade the grant of the right to create derivative works for more favorable terms in other areas of the development agreement. For non-music-related derivative works (e.g., merchandise) an artist may be able to negotiate a higher royalty rate from the publisher because such products require little or no expenditures on the publisher's part. Publishers typically attempt to control all intellectual property rights to a song, including the right to create derivative works. A publisher may argue that this comprehensive intellectual property ownership is necessary in order to reduce their financial risk. Because a composition can be exploited in numerous ways (sequels, movies, merchandise, etc.), numerous royalty streams increase the chances that the publisher will make a profit on a composition. Duration of a derivative work, as with standard copyright is the life of the author plus 70 years.

See also: **Berne Convention**; **copublishing**; **Copyright Royalty Board (CRB)**; **DMCA**; **fair use**; **joint work**; **TRIPS**; **WIPO**

Further reading: Erickson (2005); Van Camp (1994)

DEVELOPMENT DEAL

An introductory **contract** offered to an **artist** as a promissory for a future contract.

Record labels often invoke a development deal to allow an artist time to prepare before undertaking a master recording. This may include songwriting, performing, vocal coaching, or other area that the label deems necessary. Development deals reduce a label's risk in case the artist does not reach the potential or commercial success expected. Similar contractual agreements are offered by music publishers.

See also: **agent**; **independent record label**; **license**; **major record label**; **recoupable**; **royalty**

DIGITAL AUDIO RECORDING TECHNOLOGY ACT (DART)

A U.S. federal law, called the DART Act (originally passed on October 7, 1992) that requires manufacturers and importers of digital audio recording devices to pay a royalty that is held in a fund for distribution to record labels, publishers, and artists.

Organizations who sell such products in the United States must file an initial notice upon distribution of such devices and media. Companies are expected to pay the appropriate **royalty** fees to the Licensing Division of the Copyright Office. Furthermore, companies must submit quarterly and annual statements of account to the Licensing Division.

DART royalties are s**tatutory license** fees collected by the Copyright Office and are held by two separate funds. The Musical Works Fund distributes one-third of the royalty payment between writers (distributed by **ASCAP**, **BMI**, and **SESAC**) and publishers (distributed by the **Harry Fox Agency**) in a 50:50 split. The remaining two-thirds is distributed via the Sound Recordings Fund to **artist**s and record labels. Featured artists receive 25.6 percent of the Sound Recordings Fund, while nonfeatured instrumentalists and vocalists receive 2.7 percent. Record labels receive the remaining 38.4 percent of the Sound Recording Funds.

See also: **Audio Home Recording Act**; **e-commerce**; **MP3**; **sampling**

Further reading: Blunt (1999)

DIGITAL MEDIA ASSOCIATION (DiMA)

A national trade organization that represents the interests of its members in the online audio and video industries.

Activities that DiMA engages in include industry promotion, public policy, and lobbying for laws made both in the United States and internationally on issues affecting its membership. DiMA focuses on three issues: **copyright** modernization, antipiracy, and net neutrality. According the organization's Web site, DiMA "promotes legislation to modernize the scope and application of music copyrights in order to create a business environment where digital services can deliver exciting offerings to consumers and compete against pirate networks" (www.digmedia.org). Examples of this philosophy include "fair competition" for radio services, especially in regard to royalty rates and programming rules for Internet, satellite, and cable radio stations. Tangible examples of DiMA testifying in Congress regarding copyright modernization include various hearings in regard to the Section 115 of the Reform Act of 2006. A second area in which DiMA actively represents its members is anti**piracy** policy. DiMA not only lobbies in U.S. Congress for developing antipiracy law enforcement but is also actively involved in public education. Finally, DiMA is involved in issues surrounding net neutrality, especially the right of consumers and creators in regard to the selection and creation of information and content on the Internet without financial limits. Not only does DiMA work with U.S. organizations and legislators but also coordinates with other international organizations on digital media issues, including the European Digital Media Association (EDiMA), the **World Intellectual Property Organization (WIPO)**, the International Telecommunications Union (ITU), and the **World Trade Organization (WTO)**.

The organization was established in 1988 and its board of directors comprises of five companies: America Online, Apple, Live365, RealNetworks, and Yahoo!. Other members of the organization include Amazon, Microsoft, Muzak, Napster, and YouTube.

See also: **Berne Convention; Buenos Aires Convention; Copyright Arbitration Panel (CARP); Copyright Royalty Board (CRB); CRDRA; Digital Performance Right in Sound Recording Act of 1995; e-commerce; RIAA; TRIPS**

DIGITAL MILLENNIUM COPYRIGHT ACT (DMCA)

A 1998 U.S. **copyright** law that implements two 1996 **World Intellectual Property Organization (WIPO)** treaties and addresses copyright-related issues in regard to online music **distribution**.

The two WIPO treaties include the WIPO Copyright Treaty, an international treaty that deals specifically with information technology and the **WIPO Performances and Phonograms Treaty**, which is deals with the application of anti**circumvention** copyright protection systems

The DMCA is divided into five titles:

1　The WIPO Copyright and Performances and Phonograms Treaties.
2　The Online Copyright Infringement Liability Limitation Act, which creates limitations on the liability of online service providers for copyright infringement.

3   Computer Maintenance Competition Assurance Act, which provides no litigation for the copying of computer programs for the purposes of maintenance and repair.
4   Miscellaneous provisions, including the function of the Copyright Office, distance education, exceptions in the Copyright Act for libraries, and for keeping copies of sound recordings and provisions that deal with the transfer of movie rights.
5   Vessel Hull Protection Act that protects the design of boat hulls.

Of the five provisions, the first two are of particular importance to the music industry. The WIPO Copyright and Performances and Phonograms Treaties deals directly with anticircumvention provisions. Section 103 provision makes it illegal to "circumvent a technological measure that effectively controls access to a work" (Section 1201). It is also illegal under this provision to manufacture, import, or sell to the public a device or service that is primarily intended to circumvent protection technology. This section does not, however, prohibit the act of copying a work under appropriate circumstances using the **fair use** doctrine.

DMCA title II, the Online Copyright Infringement Liability Limitation Act, protects an Internet Service Provider (ISP) from copyright liability. This is granted if the providers block access to infringing material if they receive notification from a copyright holder or their agent. Furthermore, the ISP is protected by the DMCA takedown provisions that provide a safe harbor if the ISP promptly removes content when notified by the copyright holder. This safe harbor is enacted if the ISP had no knowledge that the material was placed on the system or network, did not receive financial benefit directly from the infringing activity, or has a designated agent registered with the U.S. Copyright Office to receive notification of claimed infringements. The DMCA amends the **Digital Performance Right in Sound Recordings Act of 1995 (DPRA)** by expanding the statutory license for subscription transmissions to include webcasting as a category of "eligible non-subscription transmissions."

The DMCA mandated a **royalty** payment of 50 percent to the copyright holder, 45 percent to the featured **artist**, and 5 percent to the non-featured musicians and vocalists for noninteractive webcasting. Interactive serves are negotiated between the artist and the label.

See also: **Berne Convention; Buenos Aires Convention; Copyright Arbitration Royalty Panel (CARP); Copyright Royalty Board (CRB); CRDRA; Digital Performance Right in Sound Recording Act of 1995; e-commerce; TRIPS**

Further reading: Angwin (2006); Carlin (2007); Elkin-Koran (2007); Kao (2004)

DIGITAL PERFORMANCE RIGHT IN SOUND RECORDING ACT OF 1995 (DPRA)

An amendment that provides an exclusive right to perform sound recordings publicly by means of digital audio transmission.

This right not only gives **copyright** holders the right to perform a copyrighted work publicly but to collect **royalties** from digital "performances" of sound recordings. This act was the first attempt to create a law that dealt with musical performances on the Internet. The bill allowed recording labels to collect royalties from digital performances on the Internet. Provisions within the DPRSA permit labels to negotiate exclusive **license** agreements with webcasters.

Terms and rates may be determined by voluntary agreement between the affected parties, through compulsory arbitration. Rates are set for a two-year period through this process, unless otherwise agreed upon. For interactive services owned by record labels, royalty payments are determined in the **artist**'s recording **contract**. Furthermore, the DPRSA contains provisions for labels to negotiate exclusive license agreements with webcasters. The scope of the **compulsory license** was expanded in the **Digital Millennium Copyright Act of 1998**.

See also: **Berne Convention; Buenos Aires Convention; Copyright Arbitration Royalty Panel (CARP); Copyright Royalty Board (CRB); CRDRA; Digital Performance Right in Sound Recording Act of 1995; e-commerce; TRIPS**

Further reading: Blunt (1999)

DIGITAL RIGHTS MANAGEMENT (DRM)

An all-encompassing term that refers to the management and control of digital intellectual property.

This includes the right to use technology that permits content owners to control user access to digital content, including the issuing of **license**s and decryption systems from a client's device as well as individuals and organizations from accessing material. Copyright holders justify the use of DRM to protect copyrighted material against duplication for unauthorized resale or **distribution**. The advent of digital recording allowed for the unlimited reproduction of music recordings. Personal computers combined with the Internet and popular file-sharing tools, made unauthorized distribution of copyrighted digital files extremely easy.

Laws that permit companies to use DRM as a means of copyright protection include the WIPO Copyright Treaty. This treaty requires signatory nations to enact national laws against DRM **circumvention**. In the United States the **Digital Millennium Copyright Act (DMCA)** criminalizes the production and dissemination of technology that allows users to circumvent copy-restricting methods. In 2001, the European Union passed a similar law through the EU Copyright Directive. Although these international treaties have provided a legal platform for the use of DRM technology, the application of this technology has been controversial. In 2005, Sony/BMG installed DRM software without notification on audio CDs. When customers tried to play the CDs on their computer, the CD downloaded a rootkit that left the computer venerable to viruses. After several class action suits filed against Sony/ BMG, the company was forced to recall affected CDs and offer cash payouts to customers. Nonetheless, other companies have continued to use DRM systems. ITunes makes use of FairPlay built into the MP4 files that prevent users from playing files on unauthorized computers. However, in 2007 iTunes gave customers the option of downloading DRM-free music.

See also: **ASCAP**; **BMI**; **DMCA**; **e-commerce**; **IFPI**; **MP3**; **RIAA**; **TRIPS**; **WIPO**

Further reading: Alderman (2001); Angwin (2006); Blockstedt (2006); Burkart and McCourt (2006); Carlisle and Chandak (2006); Gillespie (2007)

DIRECTIVE HARMONIZING THE TERM OF COPYRIGHT PROTECTION

A European Union directive ensuring a single **copyright** duration and related rights across all member states.

Established by the European Council in 1993 and implemented in 1995, the directive has as its principle goal the establishment of a new term length for copyright protection. Unlike the previous term limit of a copyright in Europe, established in the **Berne Convention** of 50 years from the death of the **author**, this directive extended the term to 70 years from the death of the author or 70 years after the work is lawfully made available to the public. The minimum term of protection established by the Berne Convention (life of the author plus 50 years) was intended to provide protection for the author and the first two generations of the author's descendants. Because the average lifespan in Europe grew, the current term did not sufficiently cover two generations. In the case of a work of joint authorship, the term is calculated from the death of the last surviving author. For anonymous or pseudonymous works, the term of protection runs for 70 years after the work is lawfully made available to the public. Under the directive the rights of performers expires 50 years after the date of the performance. Likewise, the rights of producers of phonograms also expire 50 years after **fixation**.

See also: **Berne Convention; Buenos Aires Convention; Copyright Arbitration Royalty Panel (CARP); Copyright Royalty Board (CRB); CRDRA; Digital Performance Right in Sound Recording Act of 1995; e-commerce; TRIPS; WIPO**

Further reading: Blunt (1999)

DISC JOCKEY (DJ)

A person who selects and plays prerecorded music either on the **radio** or at live **venue**s such as clubs, discos, and private events.

DJ's use a variety of techniques to mix or blend prerecorded music. These include cueing, mixing, and equalizations. The manner in which this is done depends on the setting in which a DJ is working. Radio DJs are less concerned with mixing music than club DJs who rely on creating a smooth transition between songs. DJs of hip-hop select, play, and create musical accompaniments through scratching, beat juggling, and other manipulations as accompaniment to one or more MCs. Radio DJs play music that is broadcast across radio waves on either AM, FM, or Internet radio stations. In syndicated radio and larger radio stations, the DJ does not choose the music to be performed. This is often done by the program or music director in consultation with the DJ. In many respects this was done in a effort to reduce the possibility of **payola**. The scandal that erupted in the 1950s has forced station management to have tighter control over the choice of music selection on the radio. With larger syndicated radio stations, DJs are known more for their individual style and personality rather than their ability to select music.

See also: **airplay; album; playlist**

Further reading: Cooper (2007); Flandez (2006); Killmeier (2001)

DISPLAY

The exclusive right, under **copyright** law, to exhibit a work or its copy directly or by means of a device.

This includes the display of copyright material in the physical sense, such as a score in a journal or magazine or the intangible sense, the performance of a recording via a **broadcasting** medium such as radio or television.

DISTRIBUTION

The act, process, or business of disseminating goods and services from a point of origin to the final buyer.

Distribution includes the transportation, storage, merchandising, promotion, selling, and packaging of goods and services. Distribution is also one of the four aspects of the **marketing** mix. The others are product management, pricing, and promotion. From the perspective of the physical movement of tangible goods, such as CDs, **distribution** deals with logistics of moving goods from the manufacture to the customer. The various stages may include the movement of goods through a wholesaler or retailer. This may be an exclusive, selective, or extensive relationship. The process also includes the various distribution channels. In a simple system the channel is the direct transaction between producers and **consumer**s. This is often known as direct mail selling and is seen in the music through **record club**s. Where production is highly concentrated and consumers are widely diffused, a number of different channels may develop and coexist with a variety of agents, distributors, wholesalers, retailers, and other intermediaries acting as the channel though which goods flow. The first step in the supply chain begins with the manufacturer supplying a distributor with products. If a **major record label** owns their own distribution system, the product will be sent to a **branch distributor**. If the manufacturer presses the recordings for an independent label they may deliver the recordings either to a branch distributor that the **independent record label** has entered into an agreement with or send it to an independent distributor. These distributors are not owned by the major labels, may handle promotion or sales activities, and may have distribution relationship with major label distribution companies and service-independent labels. Another form of independent distribution is the one stop. **One-stop** distributors carry a variety of titles from multiple manufacturers and sell to independent as well as larger retailers and jukebox operators. Once a distributor has received the products they will sell directly to **retail** outlets, before it finally reaches the consumer or end user. Each of the elements in this chain will have their own specific needs, which must be taken into account. A number of alternate "channels" of distribution may be available including direct selling through mail order, the Internet, and telephone sales. In this distribution model, the distributor will acquire a license to sell the product.

See also: **advertising**; **album**; **Audio home Recording Act**; **breakage allowance**; **ERA**; **GERA**; **GATT**; **Harry Fox Agency**; **IFPI**; **minimum advertised price (MAP)**; **NARAS**; **Published Price to Dealers (PPD)**; **rack jobber**; **RIAA**

Further reading: Kalma (2002); McLeod (2005); Pachet (2003)

DRAMATIC RIGHTS (GRAND RIGHTS)

A term referring to the rights of a **copyright** owner whose work is considered dramatic in nature (a "dramatico-musical work") under which the owner has the exclusive right to perform, **display**, or present such copyrighted work publicly.

Frequently called grand rights, examples include, but are not limited to, plays, ballets, operas, operettas, oratorios, pantomime, revues, musical comedies, sketches, and dramatic scripts designed for radio and television broadcast. A dramatico-musical work may encompass the performance of an entire composition, such as the performance of an opera or the performance of sections of a dramatico-musical work, for example, the concert version of an opera, where the singers perform various arias of an opera on stage with orchestral accompaniment. The right to obtain a grand rights **license** is obtained directly from the copyright owner or the publisher.

See also: **Harry Fox Agency**; **nondramatic rights**; **ticketing**; **venue**

Further reading: Hon and Khon (2002)

E-COMMERCE (ELECTRONIC COMMERCE)

Business transactions conducted on the World Wide Web. E-commerce consists of the **marketing**, **distribution**, buying and selling of music, products and services over the Internet.

As with traditional business models, e-commerce involves the application of transactions, albeit via electronic funds transfers, e-marketing, online transaction processing, electronic data interchange (EDI) automated inventory systems, and automated data collection systems. E-commerce companies have an advantage over traditional businesses in the relationship to their customers and their ability to construct customer-oriented models.

E-commerce is heavily dependent on an easy and secure method of transaction. In most cases the use of credit cards allows for electronic transfer of funds for online purchases. Transactions are conducted via a payment gateway that provides a secure method for the transfer of funds. For example, many music e-companies will use PayPal as their preferred payment gateway. Security for e-commerce companies is provided by firewalls, information encryption systems, and fail-safe technology.

Distribution can be either tangible (order online and receive the product in the mail) or electronic (the transmission of electronic material directly to the **consumer**'s computer). Transmission of music electronically is achieved by one of several methods. Permanent downloads are transfers of music for permanent retention on either a computer, **MP3** device, or mobile telephone. Limited downloads are similar to permanent downloads but restrict the use of the copy through an encryption system, such as **DRM** or associated technology that makes the download unusable when a subscription ends. Continuous music streaming provide music to a consumer's device with no copy remaining. On demand streaming permits the consumer to stream music for a subscription fee. In **contract** webcasting is a stream of preprogrammed music chosen by the service provider. For a consumer to have greater access to music, they would need to obtain premium webcasting or special webcasting sites that provide greater interactive content.

E-companies derive revenue from one of three methods. Direct payment by the consumer for a specified amount of music. Subscription by the consumer for a specified amount of music or an unlimited amount of streamed music. Finally, many e-commerce companies obtain revenue through advertisements or sponsorships from third parties.

See also: **circumvention; contributory infringement; DART; DMCA; Digital Performance Right in Sound Recording Act of 1995; EICTA; EUCD; GERA; GATT; Intentional Inducement of Copyright Infringement Act; RIAA; TRIPS; WIPO; WTO**

Further reading: Alderman (2001); Bhattacharjee (2006); Blockstedt (2006); Diese (2000); Fellenstein (2000); Hill (2003); McCourt (2005); McLeod (2005); Ouellet (2007); Rifkin (2001); Terranova (2000)

ENTERTAINMENT RETAILERS ASSOCIATION (ERA)

A U.K. trade forum for entertainment producers, **retail**ers, and wholesalers.

Established in 1988 by several music **distribution** companies, ERA allows for dialogue between distributors, record labels, industry associations, such as the British Phonographic Industry and government departments. Furthermore, ERA monitors legislation affecting its members and negotiates with government agencies on behalf of its members. Recently, this has included advocating for the enforcement of **antipiracy** laws. Decisions are conducted via a council of 18 elected members from the association's members. ERA is affiliated with the **National Association of Record Merchandisers** and other overseas retail Associations, including the **Global Entertainment Retail Association**.

See also: **album; Audio Home Recording Act (AHRA); breakage allowance; EICTA; GERA; GATT; Harry Fox Agency; IFPI; Minimum Advertised Price (MAP); NARAS; Published Price to Dealers (PPD); RIAA**

EUROPEAN INFORMATION, COMMUNICATIONS AND CONSUMER ELECTRONICS TECHNOLOGY INDUSTRY ASSOCIATION (EICTA)

A European trade group that represents the telecommunication and electronic industries.

EICTA was formed in 1999 to represent members at the European Commission in areas of legislation affecting the digital technology industry. EICTA is located in Brussels. The main function of EICTA is to ensure that digital technology functions in the European single market. To achieve this, the EICTA develops policies that encourages innovation and provides advice on issues dealing with data protection, digital rights management, and information security. The organization is governed by an executive board consisting of 12 to 20 technology industry leaders

See also: **Audio Home Recording Act; breakage allowance; GERA; GATT; Harry Fox Agency; IFPI; Minimum Advertised Price (MAP); NARAS; Published Price to Dealers (PPD); RIAA**

Further reading: Blunt (1999)

EUROPEAN UNION COPYRIGHT DIRECTIVE (EUCD)

An EU copyright directive that deals with digital issues associated with European copyright law.

This internal treaty implements aspects of the **WIPO Copyright Treaty** into European Union intellectual property law. The directive was designed to deal with rapid changes in technology that affect copyright protection in Europe, while providing a high level of protection of intellectual property. Established in 2001, the directive's intention was provide clear legal boundaries for online **distribution** of intellectual property. The EUCD is similar in scope to the U.S. **Digital Millennium Copyright Act of 1998 (DMCA)** and provides protection of technological systems as well as limits **circumvention** technology. The EUCD asserts that member states must provide "adequate legal protection" against the deliberate circumvention of technological measures, regardless of whether such an act infringed any copyright. Similarly, member states must provide legal action against copyright infringement for vicarious and **contributory infringement**. As with the DMCA, the EUCD grants Internet service providers (ISPs) protection from litigation, even if they vicariously infringe a copyrighted work. Like the DMCA, the EUCD protects the **fair use** doctrine in five areas: (1) teaching and scientific research, (2) use by disabled persons, (3) news reporting, (4) criticism or review, and (5) caricature or parody. Unlike the DMCA, EUCD does not give protection to certain groups (such as security researchers) against liability for circumvention offences. Furthermore, the EUCD upholds **moral rights** established in the WIPO Copyright Treaty and the WIPO Performance and Phonograms Treaty.

See also: **circumvention; contributory infringement; DART; DMCA; Digital Performance Right in Sound Recording Act of 1995; e-commerce; GERA; GATT; Intentional Inducement of Copyright Infringement Act; RIAA; TRIPS; WIPO; WTO**

Further reading: Kirkham (2002); Schneider and Henten (2004)

EXCLUSIVE RIGHTS

A legal right that grants a person to perform an action or acquire a benefit and to permit or deny others the right to perform the same action or to acquire the same benefit.

Copyright law denotes the rights of an **author** to exploit his or her intellectual property. A copyright provides an author six exclusive rights:

1 Right to reproduce a copyrighted work in copies or **phonorecord**s.
2 Right to prepare **derivative work**s based on the copyrighted work.
3 Right to distribute copies or phonorecords to the public for sale, lease, or transfer of ownership.
4 Right to perform copyrighted work publicly.
5 Right to **display** the copyrighted work publicly.
6 Right to distribute copyrighted material by means of digital audio transmission. This includes the right to perform sound recordings by means of digital transmission including satellite, cable, and broadcast transmission.

Exclusive rights also extend to digital performances. For a digital performance to qualify for this exclusive right it must meet certain criteria. First, three months must have passed since the first public performance by means of digital transmission or four months from the first sale to the public, whichever comes first. Second, the purpose of the transmission must not be to enable reproduction of the recording. Third, the transmission must not exceed the specified sound recording performance complement. Finally, transmission must be accompanied by any encoded information identifying the sound recording or underlying work.

See also: **agent; artist; development deal; first-sale doctrine; independent record label; license; major record label; royalty**

FAIR USE

In **copyright** law this term refers to the free use of copyrighted material for purposes that are beneficial to the public and do not cause financial harm to a copyright owner.

First defined in the Copyright Act of 1976, the doctrine is often applied for the purposes of education, criticism, comment, news, scholarship, and research. The purpose of fair use is to stimulate creativity for the general public or advance knowledge or the progress of the arts. The Copyright Act established four factors to be considered when determining whether usage constitutes fair use:

1 The purpose and character of the use, including whether such use is of a commercial nature or is for nonprofit educational purposes.
2 The nature of the copyrighted work.

3   The amount and substantiality of the portion used in relation to the copyrighted work as a whole.
4   The effect of the use upon the potential market for or value of the copyrighted work.

Although the amount a work protected by the fair use doctrine is not clearly defined, fair use may be regarded as the reasonable use of a work. In 1975 a Congressional Copyright Subcommittee tried to establish guidelines in regard to what constitutes the minimum standards of educational fair use. Passed in the Senate in 1976, H.R. 2223 established a series of guidelines that are stated in Section 107 of the Copyright Revision Bill. For example, emergency copying to replace purchased copies that are not available for an imminent performance is protected under fair use. It is, however, expected that the educational institution purchase a replacement copy in due course. For academic purposes, multiple copies can be made provided the excerpts do not exceed 10 percent of the whole work. A single recording owned by an educational institution or an individual teacher for the purpose of constricting aural exercises or exams.

Another area that is protected by the fair use doctrine are parodies and satire. In Campbell v. Acuff-Rose Music (510 U.S. 569, 1994), the U.S. Supreme Court distinguished parodies from satire, which they described as a broader social critique not intrinsically tied to ridicule of a specific work, and so not deserving of the same use exceptions as parody because the satirist's ideas are capable of expression without the use of the other particular work. The case also established that income from the parody should not be a factor in determining fair use. Rather the courts state that it is merely one of the components of a fair use analysis.

The fair use doctrine has also been applied to numerous international copyright conventions, most noticeably the Agreement on **Trade-Related Aspects of Intellectual Property Rights** (**TRIPS**). Article 13 of TRIPS states, "members shall confine limitations or exceptions to **exclusive rights** to certain special cases which do not conflict with a normal exploitation of the work and do not unreasonably prejudice the legitimate interests of the right holder."

See also: **audiovisual work**; **best edition**; **collective work**; **compulsory license**; **contract**; **Copyright Arbitration Royalty Panel (CARP)**; **Copyright Royalty Board (CRB)**; **Copyright Term Extension Act**; **creative commons**; **dramatic rights**; **first-sale doctrine**; **IFPI**; **RIAA**

Further reading: Bunker (2002); Castillo (2006); Das (2000); Gomes (2000); Hull (2002); Kempema (2008); Stover (1990)

FAIRNESS IN MUSICAL LICENSING ACT OF 1998

A revision of **copyright** law that expanded the exemption from infringement for the public performance of broadcasted music in restaurants and other merchants.

Under this revision, transmission of **nondramatic** musical works by means of broadcast, cable, satellite, or other methods are exempt from performance licenses or infringement under the following conditions:

1   The rooms or areas within an establishment where the transmission is intended to be received is less than 3,500 square feet, excluding space for customer parking.
2   The areas exceed such square footage limitation, but only a limited number of speakers or audio visual devices are employed.
3   No direct charge is made to see or hear the transmission.
4   The transmission is not further transmitted beyond the establishment where it is received.
5   The transmission is licensed.

The act sets forth conditions under which landlords, organizers of conventions, or others making space available to another party are exempt from liability under any theory of vicarious or **contributory infringement** with respect to an infringing public performance of a copyrighted work by a tenant, lessee, or other user of such space. If the general user and a **performing rights organization (PRO)** are unable to agree on the appropriate fee to be paid for the user's past or future performance of musical works in the society's repertoire, the user is entitled to binding arbitration. This arbitration process is carried out by the American Arbitration Association in lieu of any other dispute mechanism or judgment.

The **World Trade Organization (WTO)** ruled that the amendment did not comply with treaty obligations under the **Berne Convention** and WTO rulings. The WTO's objections are based on the number of establishments exempted from performance license requirements.

See also: **audiovisual work; best edition; collective work; compulsory license; contract; Copyright Royalty Arbitration Panel (CARP); Copyright Royalty Board (CRB); Copyright Term Extension Act; creative commons; dramatic rights; first-sale doctrine; IFPI; RIAA**

Further reading: Delchin (2004); Hull (2004); Krasilovsky and Schemel (2007)

FEDERAL COMMUNICATIONS COMMISSION (FCC)

A U.S. government agency established by the Communications Act of 1934 as the successor to the Federal Radio Commission.

The agency is charged to regulate nongovernment radio and television **broadcasting**, and interstate telecommunications including cable and satellite transmission and international communications emanating from the United States. The FCC is governed by five commissioners appointed by the President of the United States for a period of five years. Of the five members, the President designates one of the members to serve as chairperson. The chairperson delegates management and administration responsibility to the managing director. The President can only elect three commissioners of the same political party, thereby granting him or her a majority in the governing body. To diminish any conflict of interest none of the commissioners may have financial interests in commission-related business. The organization is divided into seven operating bureaus and ten staff offices whose individual responsibilities include the granting of **license**s, investigation and analysis of complaints to the FCC, the development of regulations in the communications field, and the participation in congressional and other hearings of importance to the communications industry. As the primary licensor for broadcasting in the U.S., the FCC may use this power to fine organizations or revoke licenses of broadcasters who violate federal laws. Short of that the FCC has little leverage over broadcast stations

Structurally, the FCC is divided into several offices that administer certain aspects of the Communications Act. The Office of General Counsel serves as the chief legal advisor to the Commission and its various bureaus and offices. It represents the FCC in federal courts and assists the commission in its decision making. The Office of Legislative Affairs (OLA) is the FCC's liaison to the U.S. Congress, providing lawmakers with information about FCC regulations. OLA also prepares FCC witnesses for Congressional hearings and helps create FCC responses to legislative proposals and Congressional inquiries. In addition, OLA is a liaison office that works with other Federal agencies as well as state and local governments. The Consumer and Government Affairs Bureau (CGB) is responsible for the development of an implementation of **consumer** policies. The bureau is also responsible for the investigation of consumer complaints as well as working with state and local government on issues concerning communications, use, and maintenance of emergency frequencies and coordination of issues that have overlapping jurisdiction.

See also: **airplay**; **album**; **Copyright Royalty Arbitration Panel (CARP)**; **Copyright Royalty Board (CRB)**; **DMCA**; **Digital Rights Management (DRM)**; **FTC**; **radio**; **RIAA**

Further reading: Armbrust (2004); Block (2007)

FEDERAL TRADE COMMISSION (FTC)

A U.S. Federal government commission that regulates and promotes fair competition in interstate commerce.

The commission's mandate is the protection of **consumer**s and the creation of an equitable business environment by eliminating anticompetitive business practices. The FTC consists of five commissioners who are nominated by the President and confirmed by the Senate. No more than three commissioners are from the same political party. The tenure for the commissioner position is seven years, but terms are aligned such that in a given year at most one commissioner's term expires. Established in 1917 under the Federal Trade Commission Act, the FTC works toward promoting consumer protection and eliminating anticompetitive business practices. Since its inception, the FTC has enforced antitrust legislation established in the Clayton Antitrust Act of 1914.

FTC carries out its missions by investigating issues raised by reports from consumers and businesses, congressional inquires, and reports from the media. The FTC may investigate one company or an entire industry. If a company is found guilty the FTC may seek voluntary compliance through a consent order or initiate federal litigation. The FTC's Bureau of Consumer Protection's mandate is to protect the consumer against unfair or deceptive acts or practices . Bureau attorneys enforce federal laws related to consumer affairs. The bureau investigates and enforces laws disseminated by the FTC. Areas of principal concern are **advertising**, financial products, privacy, identity protection, and telemarketing fraud. For example, the FTC was instrumental in requiring the **major record label**s to discontinue their "**Minimum Advertised Price**" (**MAP**) programs. The FTC found that the major record labels had illegally modified their existing cooperative advertising programs to induce retailers into charging consumers higher prices for CDs. According to complaints to the FTC, companies required retailers to advertise CDs at or above the MAP set by the **distribution** company in exchange for substantial cooperative advertising payment, even if the advertising was entirely funded by the retailer. The commission vote unanimously found that the five largest distributors of prerecorded music violated antitrust laws by facilitating horizontal collusion among the distributors and that the distributor's arrangement constituted an unreasonable vertical restraint of trade.

See also: **e-commerce**; **FCC**; **GATT**; **RIAA**; **WTO**

Further reading: Heinauer (2001); Peers and Evan (2000)

FESTIVAL

An event that provides entertainment to a large audience for an extended period of time.

Criteria for categorizing festivals include music genre (such as jazz, folk, classical, or rock) and type of event (charitable or social conscience that promotes a social cause of event). Audiences to festivals differ according to demographic factors (age, race, gender, etc.) and personal interests. Festivals that try to attract a broad target group will offer a variety of genres or entertainment that appeal to a wide audience. At a festival, usually several groups ranging from a star to multiple-starrer supporting-acts perform. Other factors critical to a festival's success include ticket pricing, location, budget, and the theme of the festival. Festivals are usually held outdoors and during summer months without reserved seating. Although most festivals takes place in one location there are several examples of traveling festivals (warped **tour**, Lilith Fair and Ozzfest).

See also: **artist**; **artist and repertoire (A&R)**; **capacity**; **IATSE**; **performance rights**; **performing rights organization (PRO)**; **ticketing**; **venue**

Further reading: Duffy (2000); Lim, Hellard, Hocking, and Aitken (2008); Schowater (2000)

FIDUCIARY DUTY

A duty that obliges an agent or trustee (the fiduciary) to act with loyalty, honesty, and in the best interest of a client (the principal).

In this relationship, the fiduciary agent must not place their own personal interests before their duty to the principal. Furthermore, the agent must not profit from their position beyond what has been agreed to by both parties. Throughout their relationship, an agent's behavior is highlighted by good faith, loyalty, and trust toward the principal. Within the music industry the most common fiduciary relationship exists between a **manager** and **artist**, members within a band, and partnerships within a business endeavor. In all of these relationships, there must not be a conflict of interest between the various parties. However, due to financial needs, managers are permitted to represent other clients without breaching their fiduciary duty to an artist.

Fiduciary duty arises under a broad array of laws in the United States, including a variety of federal statutes, state statutes, and the common law. Should there be a breach of fiduciary duty the courts have tended to find that benefit gained by a fiduciary relationship should be returned to the principle. The type of damages and compensation differ between proprietary remedies (dealing with property) and personal remedies (dealing with monetary or pecuniary compensation).

See also: **artist and repertoire (A&R)**; **author**; **contract**; **territorial rights**

FIRST–SALE DOCTRINE (FIRST RECORDING RIGHT)

An exclusive right granted through the Copyright Act of 1976 to an **artist** to, "dispose of, or authorize the disposal of, the possession of that **phono-record**, by rental, lease or lending or by any other act or practice. . . ." (17 U.S.C § 109)

This right grants the owner of the **copyright** the ability to create the first commercial recording of the copyrighted work. The law allows for future disposition in the form of resale lease, license, or rental without the consent of the owner. The Record Rental Amendment of 1984 prevented all owners from renting or leasing phonorecords, except nonprofit libraries or educational institutions. In 1998, the **Digital Millennium Copyright Act (DMCA)** addressed the question of whether to expand the first-sale doctrine to permit digital transmission of lawfully made copies of works. In revising Section 109, proponents argued that transmission of a work would foster the principles of the first-sale doctrine. Thus, the transmission of a work that was deleted from the sender's computer is the digital equivalent of giving, lending, or selling a physical copy of a phonogram. Those opposed to this principle argued that the DMCA states that the first-sale doctrine is limited to the **distribution** right of copyright owners but it never implicated the reproduction right. The doctrine is limited to off-line world by virtue of geography and the degradation of books and analog works.

See also: **contract**; **development deal**; **independent record label**; **license**; **major record label**; **royalty**

Further reading: Biederman (1992); Klinefetter (2001); Pike (2007)

FIXATION

The physical existence of intellectual property embodied in a tangible medium of expression.

Fixation of ideas is required to obtain protection under **copyright** law. The embodiment of a work must be created by or under the authority of the **author** and must be sufficiently permanent or stable to permit it to be perceived, reproduced, or communicated for more than a brief duration. If a musical work is broadcasted, the sounds must be fixed simultaneously with the transmission. In December 1994, the U.S. Congress changed the law concerning unrecorded music performances when it passed the Uruguay Round Agreements Act. This act included a new provision, which prohibited the recording of live musical performances even when there was no other "fixation" of the work. Furthermore, the provision includes separate prohibitions against the **distribution** and transmission of bootleg copies. In fact, the prohibition against transmission does not even require that a physical copy of the performance ever be made. While this act appears to create an exception to the fixation requirement for copyright, it is best described as a right similar to the requirements found in a copyright, but not a copyright itself.

See also: **Berne Convention**; **Buenos Aires Convention**; **DMCA**; **DART**; **first-sale doctrine**; **TRIPS**; **UCC**; **WIPO**

Further reading: Biederman (1992); Donat (1997)

FOLIO

A collection of songs in a single edition by an **artist** or group of artists.

Royalty rates for the sale of folios are negotiated between a songwriter and a publisher. Rates are calculated on the amount of copies sold based on plateaus reached. For example, typically **royalties** are 10 percent of the wholesale sale price for the first 200,000 copies sold, 12 percent of the wholesale sale price for 200,000 to 500,000 copies sold, and 15 percent of the wholesale sale price for 500,000 or more copies sold. As the folio is usually composed of several songs (often with different writers involved), the gross amount would be divided by the number of songs in the folio and each song would receive a proportionate share payment. Foreign royalty payments for sums received by the publisher from sources outside the United States and Canada are normally 50 percent of all foreign gross receipts.

See also: **author**; **collective work**; **copublishing**; **publishing**

FOREIGN ROYALTIES

Royalty monies available to a music publisher, record label, artist, or other entity from international sales.

With the music industry becoming an international business and the growing influence of American culture, foreign sales of music have become an important source of income for songwriters and **artist**s around the world. In most **contract**s, foreign **royalties** are an important source of income, especially for companies outside of the United States and Canada who can gain financially by entering the U.S. market. Traditionally foreign royalty rates are normally 50 percent of all gross national receipts collected on a quarterly basis.

Performing rights organizations around the world cooperate in the process of licensing and collecting royalties for members in their territory through the International Confederation of Performing Rights Organizations (CISAC). In the United States, **ASCAP** operates an International Monitoring Unit (IMU) that makes use of a database (EZ-MAXX) to verify the accuracy of television performance statements received from affiliated foreign societies.

Mechanical rights organizations maintain reciprocal representation agreements with affiliated foreign collecting societies and the territories they represent. The reciprocal agreements provide **author**s and publishers collection, monitoring, and payment services in their home territories. In most territories, the royalty rate is a percentage of the record companies' **PPD (Published Price to Dealer)** for a particular recording, with the per-track royalty determined on a pro-rata basis according to the number of **copyright**ed compositions contained on the recording.

See also: **ASCAP; BIEM; BMI; TRIPS; WIPO**

FOUR WALLING

A method of renting a **venue** that only includes the physical space.

The rental fee does not include the box office, **ticket** collectors, security, ushers, and so on. In such arrangements the financial risk is placed on the performing **artist** or **promoter** rather than the venue. A promoter must fill the venue to cover the rental cost and pay for other requirements of operating a venue. In most contractual arrangements the venue will continue to operate concession stands, which may generate greater income than ticket sales.

See also: **agent; IATSE; papering the house; rider; road manager**

FUND

Monies or other resources held for present or future purposes by an external entity.

In the **Home Recording Act, royalties** collected by the Copyright Office are held in two separate funds to be distributed to members of specific groups. The Musical Works Fund distributes royalties to writers and publishers through the three U.S. **PRO**s and **Harry Fox Agency**. The Sound Recordings fund distributes royalties through the **AFM** and **AFTRA** to nonfeatured musicians and vocalists.

AFM also collects monies held in two funds for its members. The Music Performance Trust Fund (MPTF) is a trust established for the presentation of free live instrumental performances in connection with a patriotic, educational, and civic occasion in the United States and Canada. The source of this fund are record sales collected on a semiannual basis. The Phonograph Record Manufacturers' Special Payment Fund are monies collected as a percentage of income earned from record sales distributed to musicians based on their **scale** wages.

See also: **ASCAP; BMI; contract; license; nondramatic performance rights; scale; SESAC; weighting formula**

GENERAL AGREEMENT ON TARIFFS AND TRADE (GATT)

An international trade agreement signed in 1947 to promote trade between member nations through the reduction of trade barriers by eliminating tariffs, import quotas, and subsidies.

The formation of GATT and its subsequent amendments led to the founding of the **World Trade Organization (WTO)**. This took place at the third general meeting, known as the Uruguay Round, between 1986 and 1994, which extended the agreement to include areas such as intellectual property and to comply with provisions of the **Berne Convention**

GATT special section that deals with intellectual property, the **Trade-Related Aspects of Intellectual Property Rights (TRIPS)** Agreement required industrialized countries to implement provisions within one year of the WTO agreement taking effect. Less developed countries were given a five-to-ten-year period to comply with most provisions depending on their state of economic development. Under GATT, **fair use** was limited to "certain special cases that do not conflict with normal exploitation of a work." This provided minimum rights for the protection of performers, producers of phonogram, and **broadcasting** organizations on an international basis. GATT also required signatories to provide geographical indications of origin and that damages awarded for infringement of an intellectual property must be "adequate to compensate for the injury" suffered. Finally, GATT required countries to develop procedures by customs authorities at national boundaries to intercept pirated **copyright**ed goods. This was an attempt to curtail the ever-growing **piracy** of digital music.

See also: **copyright**; **DMCA**; **EUCD**; **Geneva Phonograms Convention**; **IFPI**; **royalty**; **UCC**; **WIPO**

Further reading: Adeloye (1993); Blunt (1999); Maskus (2000)

GENEVA PHONOGRAMS CONVENTION

An international treaty adopted in 1971 to deal with **piracy** of recorded music.

The **Convention for the Protection of Producers of Phonograms against Unauthorized Duplication of their Phonograms**, commonly known as the "Geneva Phonograms Convention," protects copyright holders against unauthorized duplication of sound recordings and against unauthorized import and **distribution** of such copies. With the development of the cassette tape during the 1970s there was a concern that the widespread use of new technology would damage the interests of **author**s, performers, and producers of recorded music. The convention required signatories to provide protection from the use and distribution of illegal copies within their territorial boundaries. Nonetheless, legal remedies are based on local **copyright** laws rather than on international standards. The convention also required that individual phonograms or their containers bear the notice consisting of the symbol (P), accompanied by the year-date of the first publication and the name of the **producer** or the exclusive licensee. Finally, the convention recognized the **fair use** doctrine principle only if duplication is used solely for the purposes of teaching or scientific research.

The Geneva Convention is conceived so as not to interfere with the work of the United Nations Educational, Scientific and Cultural Organization (UNESCO), the **World Intellectual Property Organization (WIPO)**, and the **Rome Convention** of 1961 and includes protection for performers and broadcasting organizations.

See also: **DMCA**; **EUCD**; **Geneva Phonograms Convention**; **IFPI**; **royalty**; **UCC**; **WIPO**

Further reading: Blunt (1999)

GLOBAL ENTERTAINMENT RETAIL
ALLIANCE (GERA)

An international association of entertainment retailers established to develop a coherent approach to the global electronics industry.

GERA was established in 2000, and its founding members include representatives from Australia, Canada, Germany, Mexico, the Netherlands, New Zealand, the United Kingdom, and the United States. The association deals with issues concerning its members, including disintermediation, competition, and **consumer** privacy and choice. GERA lobbies governments in areas of consumer privacy, fairness in trade practices, and greater uniformity in **copyright** law treatment of sales through digital **distribution**. The organization also encourages dialog between record companies, government bodies, **trade association**s, and consumer groups. Established in 2000, the GERA-Europe acts as the European arm of the GERA. GERA-Europe acts as a representative for all European members on commercial and legislative matters affecting their business.

See also: **advertising**; **Audio Home Recording Act**; **branch distributor**; **consumer**; **ERA**; **FTC**; **retail**

Further reading: Ferguson (2002)

GUILD

A formal association of professionals within a specific business who have similar interests and goals.

Originally structured around a group of craftsmen, guilds were established as a means of protecting and enhancing members livelihoods through the control of instructional capital of members from apprentice to grandmaster as well as furthering a particular trade. In the middle ages guilds were given a patent protection that allowed them to hold a monopoly on a trade both within the city and exports in a cartel fashion. Today guilds function as business associations and as guides to industry behavior. Most guilds set standards within a particular industry, such as standard pricing, self-regulation, cultural identity, and methods used by practitioners. Often the function of a guild is similar to that of a union. The Screen Actors Guild is a guild in name only. It functions vey much as a trade union, in respect to collective bargaining on behalf of its members, industrial action, and membership and jurisdiction policies that include radio, television, the Internet as well as movies.

See also: **AFM**; **AFTRA**; **Associated Actors and Artists of America**; **ERA**; **FTC**; **GERA**; **NARAS**; **RIAA**; **trade association**

HARRY FOX AGENCY (HFA)

A U.S. **mechanical rights** agency founded by the National Music Publisher's Association as an information source, clearinghouse, and monitoring service.

Since its founding in 1927, HFA has provided services for publishers, licensees, and a broad spectrum of music users. With its current level of publisher representation, HFA **license**s the largest percentage of the mechanical and digital uses of music in the United States for the sale of CDs, digital services, records, tapes, and imported phonorecords. HFA also offers licensing for various digital formats, including full-length permanent digital downloads (DPD's), limited-use digital downloads, and on-demand streaming. Although HFA issues licenses under the **statutory rate**, it does not procure master use rights that must be obtained from the copyright owner of the sound recording. For its services, HFA charges a **commission** based on the **royalties** collected and certain fees. For mechanical reproduction, HFA's commission is 3.5 percent. For music used on **broadcasting**, including background music and **radio** broadcasting, HFA charges a commission of 10 percent.

Similarly, HFA charges a 10-percent fee for TV commercials and music used on movies. However, TV commercials have a ceiling of $2,000, while movies have a ceiling of $150. Licenses are due from major sources on a quarterly basis. Likewise, **mechanical license**s are distributed on a quarterly basis. HFA distributes royalty payments at the full statutory rate. A licensee may negotiate this rate with their record company.

HFA also represents U.S. publishers in collecting mechanical licenses in foreign countries. By maintaining working relationships with various foreign mechanical rights licensing societies, HFA is able to collect funds for writers who have acquired **subpublishing** agreements with foreign publishers. HFA collects royalties based on gross earnings, minus the local society's fees and a 3.5-percent HFA commission.

See also: **AFM**; **AFTRA**; **artist**; **author**; **dramatic rights**; **ERA**; **GERA**; **NARAS**; **RIAA**; **synchronization license**

Further reading: Butler (2007); Lichtman (2000)

INDEPENDENT RECORD LABEL

An autonomous record label that functions without the direct funding of a **major record label**.

Although definitions vary greatly on what constitutes an independent label, certain characteristics exist that differentiate an independent record label from a major record label. A trait found in most major labels is the control of the **distribution** channels. In the case of a major record label, all aspects of music production, including manufacturing, distribution, and, in some cases, publishing, are controlled by the label. This vertical integration is important for obtaining funds and controlling costs while reducing the risks in bringing a new product to market. In the case of independent record labels most of these functions are handled by outside companies.

This reduces the overall management cost for the label, allowing them to concentrate on record production. Due to the close synergies and the vertical integrations, many majors won wholly or partially acquired independent labels.

As with a major label an independent label is structured for the sale of recording products. Departments are planned on functionality. Therefore, an independent label will comprise of an **A&R** department, whose function is the acquisition of new talent, and the Artist Development department, which oversees the overall career growth of **artist**s signed to the label, **marketing** and sales department, and business and legal affairs department.

See also: **AFM**; **AFTRA**; **agent**; **ASCAP**; **BMI**; **copyright**; **development deal**; **IFPI**; **license**; **NARAS**; **one stop**; **phonorecord**; **RIAA**; **royalty**; **trade association**

Further reading: Andersen (2006); Fabrikant (1996); Kalma (2002); Kirkham (2002); Strachan (2007)

INFRINGEMENT

The act of violating a law, right, or **contractual** relationship.

Copyright infringement is the unauthorized use of copyright material or the violation of a copyright owner's **exclusive rights**, such as the right to reproduce, distribute, and sell their intellectual property. Infringement in a contractual relationship includes breach of contract (one party has not fulfilled their obligation as stated in the contract), fraud, or failure to perform specific duties as stated in a contract. For works registered with the Copyright Office, statutory damages are available as an option for monetary relief in infringement cases. This also includes recovery of attorney fees. Furthermore, copyright registration is a prerequisite for U.S. **author**s seeking to initiate suit for copyright infringement in the federal district courts. If an infringement is constituted a criminal misdemeanor, the case may be prosecuted by the U.S. Department of Justice.

See also: **all rights reserved**; **Buenos Aires Convention**; **Copyright Arbitration Royalty Panel (CARP)**; **Copyright Royalty Board (CRB)**; **DMCA**; **Digital Performance Right in Sound Recording Act of 1995**; **Digital Rights Management (DRM)**; **RIAA**; **TRIPS**; **UCC**; **WIPO**; **WTO**

Further reading: Castillo (2006); Harvard Law Review (2005); Kempema (2008); Radcliffe (2006); Stern (2000)

INTELLECTUAL PROPERTY

Any product of the human intellect that has a value and can be exchanged in the marketplace.

This may be in the form of a tangible or intangible object. Tangible assets include objects that can be perceived with the senses such as buildings, musical instruments, and equipment. Intangible assets have no material substance. This includes intellectual property, such as **copyright**s, patents, and **trademark**s including names, brands, and logos. For recording companies an **artist**'s intellectual property is a high-value asset, as it can be **license**d for use in numerous platforms. Furthermore, effective IP management enables music companies to use their assets to improve their competitiveness and strategic advantages. IP management is more than protecting an enterprise's copyright; it involves a label's ability to commercialize its IP through effective licensing and joint ventures, while adding value to the enterprise. International IP and the development is protected by several treaties, such as the ones established by the **World Intellectual Property Organization (WIPO)**, and the **Trade-Related Aspects of Intellectual Property Rights (TRIPS)** established through the **World Trade Organization (WTO)**.

See also: **audiovisual work; best edition; collective work; compulsory license; contract; copyright; Copyright Royalty Arbitration Panel (CARP); Copyright Royalty Board (CRB); Copyright Term Extension Act; creative commons; dramatic rights; first-sale doctrine; IFPI; RIAA**

Further reading: Adeloye (1993); Dutfield (2005); Kretschemer (2000); Kretschmer, Michael, and Wallis (1999); Schur (2006); Shadlen (2007); Wallis et al. (1999)

INTENTIONAL INDUCEMENT OF COPYRIGHT INFRINGEMENT ACT OF 2004

A federal law developed with the intention of clearly defining vicarious and **contributory infringement** within the Copyright Act.

The passing of this act eventuated in the addition of a new subsection (g) to Section 501 of the Copyright Act. This subsection clearly states that anyone who "intentionally induces any violation of subsection (g) shall be liable as an infringer." Libraries and other organizations opposed this bill, as it would introduce the concept of intentional inducement and limit **fair use** especially through the Internet. Under the terms of this act, a jury can infer that a manufacturer intended to induce infringement even in a situation where the technology is capable of a substantial noninfringement use.

The act was designed as a measure aimed at reversing a federal district court decision in the Ninth Circuit called MGM et al. v. Grokster et al. (545 U.S. 913(2005)). Due to the growth of **peer-to-peer** (**P2P**) services, courts have struggled to apply existing common-law doctrines to new P2P services. Central to this situation are **contributory infringement** and vicarious liability. Contributory infringement occurs when one party, often a P2P service, has knowledge of an infringing activity and either induces or contributes to this behavior by providing material. Vicarious liability occurs when a controlling party receives financial benefit from an infringing activity. The Copyright Act of 1976 did not contain any express provisions on secondary liability, thus courts were left to interpret these laws on a case-specific basis. In most cases the courts have relied on a Supreme Court decision known as the Sony Betamax case to determine whether the application of a technology has the potential to induce copyright infringement.

See also: **all rights reserved**; **Buenos Aires Convention**; **Copyright Royalty Arbitration Panel (CARP)**; **Copyright Royalty Board (CRB)**; **DMCA**; **Digital Performance Right in Sound Recording Act of 1995**; **Digital Rights Management (DRM)**; **RIAA**; **TRIPS**; **UCC**; **WIPO**; **WTO**

INTERNATIONAL ASSOCIATION OF THEATRICAL AND STAGE EMPLOYEES (IATSE)

A United States and Canadian union for stagehands, lighting technicians, box office treasurers, and ushers.

The IATSE represents technician, artisan, and craftpersons in the entertainment industry including theater, film, and television production and trade shows. More than 500 local unions in the United States and Canada are affiliated the union. Within this structure, local organizations have autonomy in collective bargaining agreements. Nationwide agreements for film production personnel are negotiated with the Alliance of Motion Picture and Television Producers (AMPTP). The strength of the IATSE comes from the "complete coverage" of all the crafts involved in the production of theater, film, and TV products from conception through production and exhibition. During the 1990s, West Coast members of the National Association for Broadcast Employees and Technicians (NABET) merged with the IATSE to strengthen both organizations members involved in the film, **broadcasting**, and television industries.

See also: **AFM**; **AFTRA**; **agent**; **manager**; **promoter**; **road manager**; **ticketing**

Further reading: Ruling (1999)

INTERNATIONAL FEDERATION OF PHONOGRAPHIC INDUSTRIES (IFPI)

An international trade organization that represents the interests of recording labels and producers.

Founded in 1933, it represents more than 1,000 record companies in 75 countries on issues dealing with **copyright** protection, legislation, and establishing guidelines for negotiations of **contract**s between copyright owners and performers. This includes the protection of legal conditions, and anti**piracy** enforcement and technology such as the adoption of **DRM**. The IFPI also lobbies governments to adopt effective copyright legislation that are in the interest of recording companies. This includes the reduction of sales taxes and the adoption of legislation that offers protection to intellectual property rights of its members. On an international level, the IFPI is influential in the development of international treaties dealing with intellectual property. In 1961, the IFPI lobbied at the **Rome Convention** for the Protection of Performers and Producers of Phonograms to establish an international standard for the protection of **phonorecords**. In 1971, the IFPI was successful in initiating the creation of the **Convention for the Protection of Producers of Phonograms against Unauthorized Duplication of Their Phonograms**.

Any company or person producing commercial sound recordings or **music videos** is eligible for membership with the IFPI. Members are represented at three levels: international, regional, and national. The international secretariat in London works directly with industry committees on legal policy, performing rights, and technology. Regional branches are divided into Asia, Europe, and Latin America. The IFPI is headed by a board of directors comprising of leaders from the recording industry who are responsible for implementing IFPI strategies and coordinating political lobbying efforts for national legislatures. IFPI also recognizes 48 affiliate groups, including British Phonographic Industry (BPI), **Recording Industry Association of America** (**RIAA**), Australian Recording

Industry Association (ARIA), and the Argentine Chamber of Phonograms and Videograms Producers).

See also: **artist**; **DMCA**; **independent record label**; **major record label**; **WTO**

Further reading: Breen (1994); Garofalo (1993); Harker (1997); Mitchell (2007); Negus (1992); Sanjek (1991)

INTERPOLATION

The process of composing or recreating an original melody for use in a new composition.

This technique is applied in rap and hip-hop, when an **artist** will use a melody for recording purposes. Instead of using the original recording of the work, an artist will record the melody rather than a **sample** of the original recording. There are several advantages for an artist to do this. First, the interpolated melody is easier to **clear** through legal channels. Second, **royalty** payments are made directly to the original songwriter or owner of the publishing rights rather than a label or owner of the original recording. Third, if an artist creates a melody with enough difference from the original, the artist may apply for **copyright** protection of the melody as a **derivative work**.

See also: **author**; **ASCAP**; **BMI**; **copyright**; **license**; **mechanical royalty**; **SESAC**

JOINT WORK

A work prepared by two or more **author**s who are coowners of the **copyright** in the work.

The Copyright Act offers limited guidance to who may qualify as a joint author. In most cases a prerequisite for joint authorship is a mutual understanding between the contributors that they are to be regarded as joint authors. Because authors of a joint work are coowners of the copyright, their individual contributions are considered inseparable parts of a united whole. However, joint owners may independently **license** any of their rights in a work. These licenses are nonexclusive unless all of the joint owners join in the grant of license. Coowners' may grant a different record company to distribute the sound recording, and it is common practice that all rights are assigned to a single record label. Each coauthor has the independent right to terminate a grant of rights. Termination of the grant may be effected by a minority of the authors who executed it. Thus, if three members of a five-member band were to sign a single transfer agreement, the minority members would be bound by the decision of the majority to terminate and would receive a proportionate share of the reverted right. Duration of a joint work in the United States is 70 years after the death of the last surviving author.

See also: **Berne Convention**; **copublishing**; **Copyright Royalty Arbitration Panel (CARP)**; **Copyright Royalty Board (CRB)**; **derivative work**; **DMCA**; **fair use**; **TRIPS**; **WIPO**

LICENSE

Contractual permission to perform specific acts granted by one party to another.

In the music industry, a license is a specialized **contract** that provides legally authorized use of **copyright**ed material by an copyright owner or their agent. A licensor (the party who licenses a right) will grant a licensee (the party to whom a right is licensed) permission to use a copyrighted work in a particular way for a specified period of time in a defined territory in return for some kind of compensation. The licensor is, therefore, granted all rights normally reserved for a copyright owner, including the right to make copies of a work and sell the copies for profit. Furthermore, a licensor has the right to exhibit a work and collect synchronized royalties from the broadcast. Performance licenses are granted to a licensor for the performance of a work publicly. This not only includes the live performance of music at a music **venue**, but the transmission of recorded music via **radio**, TV, satellite, or the Internet. Radio stations pay a **blanket license**, covering all music performed at the station or a monthly per-program license rate calculated on periodical audits of music performed, revenue generated from **advertising**, and the station's blanket license fee. These fees are paid to one of the three main **performing rights organization**s **(PRO)** such as **Broadcast Music Incorporated (BMI)**, the **American Society of Composers, Authors and Publishers (ASCAP)**, or **SESAC**. **Mechanical license**s are rights given by a copyright holder for the manufacturing and **distribution** of music on a **phonorecord** to the public. This license requires a record label to pay a music publisher the full statutory **royalty** rate for each phonorecord manufactured and sold. In many cases, a record label will negotiate a lower royalty rate than the statutory amount for items such as budget alums, international sales, and phonorecords sold through **record club**s.

The concept of **compulsory license**s is associated with mechanical licenses. Unlike other licenses that are contractually negotiated, compulsory licenses are statutory grants of permission for music to be used in a specific manner, providing certain conditions are met, such as royalty payment. Furthermore, a license may be granted without the permission of the copyright owner. Although commonly associated with mechanical licenses, compulsory licenses fall under four categories: music recordings, cable TV, noncommercial public broadcasting, and jukeboxes. As with the previous licenses, print licenses are rights given to a licensee for the manufacture and distribution of sheet music, such as fakebooks or songbooks. As with the other licenses, this is contingent upon a print publisher meeting certain criteria, such as prescribed royalty payments.

See also: **ASCAP**; **author**; **BIEM**; **BMI**; **catalog**; **folio**; **performing rights organization (PRO)**; **publishing**; **RIAA**; **royalty**; **WIPO**

Further reading: Biederman (1992); Jones (2005); Khon and Khon (2002); Kwok and Lui (2002); McCourt (2005); Nye (2000); Speiss (1997)

MAJOR RECORD LABEL (MAJORS)

A term that refers to large record labels and entertainment conglomerations as opposed to the Indies or independent record labels.

Although most **author**s do not provide an exact definition of a major label, most agree on several principles when classifying such an organization. First, most major record labels have in-house **distribution**. This not only provides direct manufacturing of recordings of the label's **artist** roster, but assists the major label in controlling all aspects of the management, production, distribution, and sale of recorded music through vertical integration. In theory, the greater the vertical integration, the less vulnerable the label to outside forces, such as competition. Another feature that most major record labels posses is that they are part of multinational conglomerates. A conglomerate is a company that owns a large number of divisions or companies, often in the same sector. These businesses may be related to the parent company in regard to the business sector or they may be in unrelated areas. By diversifying its interests, a company can reduce risk in one sector. However, many companies that diversify in areas not related to the parent company have failed due to the complexities of managing a company in a different sector. Companies that have subsidiaries in the same sector do so to reduce manufacturing costs. Often the subsidiary business runs independently of the other companies and has ties to the parent company in upper management. In the recording industry many of the major labels are owned by parent companies outside of the United States. Therefore, these conglomerates are known as multinational conglomerates. Finally, all major record labels have similar organizational structures. Apart from typical management hierarchies consisting of president, chief executive officer (CEO), chief financial officer (CFO), and divisional vice presidents, a major record label will also contain specific departments devoted to the production and sale of recorded music. Although there is no standard structure for a major record label, most contain several essential divisions to the creation and dissemination of recorded music. The **artist and repertoire (A&R)** division is responsible for finding (scouting), acquiring, and developing new artist talent. The promotion division is in charge of obtaining exposure, often through **radio** and video **airplay** for the label's artistic roster. Similarly, the sales, **marketing**, and promotion divisions work to ensure that an artist's work reaches it designated target market. The marketing division is often the largest division of a label that may also serve smaller labels associated with the major. Often this division is in charge of product conception, development, manufacturing, and distribution. The sales division, a subdivision of the marketing department, is responsible for supplying retailers (**retail** chains, **rack jobber**s, and one stops) on a local, regional, and national level. Business and legal affairs, often outsourced by smaller labels, is in charge of negotiating contracts between a label and an artist or **producer**. The department also deals with licensing, both on a national and international level, for TV, film, and use through sampling.

Other divisions important to the functioning of a major record label are the accounting division and the international division.

See also: **AFM**; **AFTRA**; **agent**; **artist**; **ASCAP**; **BMI**; **copyright**; **development deal**; **IFPI**; **license**; **NARAS**; **one stop**; **phonorecord**; **RIAA**; **royalty**; **trade association**

Further reading: Andersen (2006); Barnett (1994); Holden (1991)

MANAGER

A representative who assists an **artist** in the development and administration of their musical career.

In developing an artist's career, a personal manager is not only responsible for developing a day-to-day strategy for an artist but also for the selection of other representatives such as an agent, attorney, business manager, and publicist. In serving an artist, a personal manager performs numerous functions. First, a personal manager is responsible for engaging in and consulting with agencies for the purpose of securing employment, engagements, and **contract**s on behalf of the artist. These agencies include talent agents, booking agents, and theatrical agents. In certain states, a manager cannot procure employment for an artist without the proper **license**. In states such as California, Florida, and Illinois legislation requires that agents be governed by the labor code. Apart from obtaining a license, agents in these states are required to submit contracts to the Labor Commissioner for approval, maintain a separate artist trust account, and act within state and federal laws. Although a manager cannot procure employment for an artist in certain states, they closely work with agencies to sell an artist's image (publicity).

One of the most important tasks of a manager is to obtain a recording contract with a bona fide label. This requires a manager to act on behalf of the artist and in his or best interests. An artist will often give power of attorney to the manager in regard to contracts as well as to act on his or her behalf in all areas of the entertainment field. Once a recording contract is obtained, a manager will coordinate with a label in promoting the artist and **release** of new **album**s. This includes ensuring that the recording is marketed and promoted especially in regard to the exploitation of an artist's personality, name, likeness for publicity, merchandising, and **advertising**. A manager will also coordinate with a record label on an artist's **tour** schedule and oversee the coordination of the tour to album releases. Manager will coordinate on all aspects of the tour with a tour **promoter**. Apart from duties associated with the procurement of recordings and touring, a manager has numerous roles in regards to an artist's career, business interests, and publicity. Services include advice and counseling in the selection of musical and artistic material, selecting publicity materials, and developing strategic plans of an artist's long-term viability. In most cases a manager will be granted power of attorney to act on behalf of an artist, without the artist being present

A personal manager is compensated for services rendered on a **commission** basis. This rate is typically based on the gross earnings of the artist. Commissions range from 10 percent to 25 percent of gross revenues. As such, a manager is paid when income is received, or, in some arrangements, compensation may be paid at the conclusion of a specific intervals, such as at the end of month or at the completion of an engagement. Commissions are derived from salaries, **advance**s, bonuses, and **royalties**. A manager may also earn money from ancillary income from an artist. This includes monies from film, television, and merchandise. Amounts vary according to the level of experience of the artist and the networks, and the resources and the experience of the manager.

Duration of a management contract is usually two to three years, but a one- or two-year option is also in practice.

See also: **AFM**; **AFTRA**; **independent record label**; **major record label**; **producer**; **RIAA**

Further reading: Seifert and Hadida (2006)

MANUFACTURER'S SUGGESTED RETAIL PRICE (MSRP)

A suggested retail price that manufacturers' recommend retailers set to sell products.

Although intended to standardize pricing among retailers, stores may sell at or below the MSRP. In many countries resale price maintenance is illegal, especially when tied to requirements by the manufacturer. Such is the case in the United States where five of the largest music distributors of recorded music illegally modified their cooperative **advertising** programs to induce retailers into charging **consumer**s higher prices for CDs. The **FTC** ordered recording labels to discontinue their "**Minimum Advertised Price**" (**MAP**) programs for a period of seven years. Recent trends show that manufactures set the MSRP closer to the "street price." This is certainly the case with the growth of "deep discounters" who are able to sell products substantially lower than the recommended MSRP.

See also: **advertising**; **album**; **consumer**; **e-commerce**; **ERA**; **first-sale doctrine**; **GERA**; **Published Price to Dealers (PPD)**; **rack jobber**; **retail**; **SoundScan**; **trade association**

Further reading: Fox (2005)

MARKETING

The process of analyzing, planning, implementation, and control of products designed to bring a voluntary exchange in a target market.

Marketing involves designing the company's offerings to meet the target markets' needs and desires, using effective pricing, communication, and distribution to inform, motivate, and service specific markets. To successfully reach a target audience a company will undergo a series of performance actions, commonly known as the "marketing mix" (Known colloquially as the "four Ps"). The first element, product, consists of the tangible and intangible attributes of a product, service, or **artist**, including the brand-name packaging, services, and so on. A second element is price, which includes activities of setting a value to a product's goods and services. The third element, place (**distribution**), is concerned with the movement of goods from the producer to the **consumer**. The process of strategically moving music from an artist to the consumer is known as supply chain management. The final element, promotion, includes all communication between the various channel partners in the supply chain. In most definitions *promotion* refers to the communication between the manufacturer and the consumer. The three components of promotion include **advertising** (paid personal communication), promotion (nonpaid promotion), and **public relations** (**PR**) (communications to build good will or prestige). In an effort to elicit a traceable, measured response many companies have begun using interactive marketing techniques, such as direct marketing, buzz marketing, or word-of-mouth marketing. These methods make use of a variety of media including catalogs, postcards, as well as direct marketing techniques in traditional media such as TV (via telemarketing), radio, magazines, and the Internet. The technique requires the consumer to take specific action by contacting the manufacturer, visiting a Web site, returning a response card, or completing a survey. Results from direct marketing are measured against costs incurred without reference to revenue. The widespread use of databases and data-mining techniques has stimulated the growth of direct marketing. Communications can be targeted at specific individuals with customized messages. In an effort to develop a message for a specific audience, marketing companies will divide potential consumers into specific groups or demographic profiles. Populations are grouped into categories based on demographic variables. The most common variables include age, sex/gender, race/ethnicity, socioeconomic status, educational attainment, marital status, religion, and life cycle. Marketers often combine several variable to develop a demographic profile. Therefore, a profile may consist of features such as single, male, middle-class, with a college degree, age 18 to 24, and other demographic information.

An important aspect of the marketing mix is branding. Brands are a clear set of characteristics that differentiates an artist, product, or service from competing products. The most common characteristics adopted by companies and artists are names, logos, terms, slogans, characters, or designs. Not only do brands establish a product within a market but they also provide a guarantee to the customer of product quality as well as intangible benefits such as social status, symbolism, and value. The value associated with a specific product is known as brand equity. Awareness of a brand is measured in terms of tangible and intangible attributes including recall and recognition, brand image (overall brand association), and price. Products that have a high brand equity can be sold at greater prices than generic products. However, valuation of brand equity is one of approximation rather than science. The extent consumers of a particular brand intend to repurchase a product is known as brand loyalty, a consumer's loyalty to a product even when attractive incentives, such as lower price, are offered by other manufacturers of similar products. Loyalty is determined by usage rates, market types, and usage levels, even if alternatives, such as a lower-priced product, are offered. In order to better understand customers, marketing department collects data about consumers, markets, and other organizations, and analyze this data using market research techniques to support future decisions. Marketing is a a collective of several functions and includes demand forecasting, price setting, and copy testing. Data collection procedures include focus groups, in-depth interviews, surveys, and experiments. Audience research is the science of measuring consumer numbers exposed to a particular media. This has implications for advertising rates, success of a campaign and potential sales. Audience research may involve demographic or psychographic data. In the music industry, there are several companies that measure audience response to a particular media. AC Nielsen measures Internet usage through telephone and Internet surveys. **Arbitron** makes use of an electronic devise, the Portable People Meter to track audiences on radio, television, or the Internet. Other research methods found in the music business include techniques such as focus groups, surveys, and callout research. Call-out is primarily a market research method used in the radio industry whose purpose is to track listeners' preferences. Often a radio station will induce listeners to call in their favorite songs for inclusion on a particular radio show. A radio station will randomly select listeners to obtain information on song selection, programming, and listening habits.

See also: **FCC**; **FTC**; **GERA**; **IFPI**; **merchandising rights**; **Ofcom**; **trade association**

Further reading: Aaker (1998); Bayler (2006); Beville (1988); Hemphill (2002); Jefkins (1998); Nexica (1997)

MASTERS

An original multitrack recording either on tape, disc, or computer file from which productions are developed for later mixing.

Due to the importance of the master recording, copies are made in case of damage. Because the master is considered intellectual property, possession entitles the owner to certain rights under **copyright** law. Therefore, the value of a master is inherently determined by the cost of production and its potential to sell albums. For an **artist**, the cost of producing the recording is **recoupable** against all incomes earned from **royalties**. In a contractual relationship with a record label, the artist will receive an **advance** to produce the master. In certain circumstances, such as an independent artist or production deal, if the artist finances the production of the master, he may own all rights in it. **Major record label**s have an interest in owning a master as it gives them the ability to control the production of music over a long period of time, thus increasing the potential profit from their initial investment and reducing the risk involved in producing the recording. Even if album sales do not cover the cost of producing the master, a record label can **cross-collaterize** this cost against an artist's future record sales to recoup initial funds.

Income generated by the ownership of master is usually obtained from the sale of CDs through **mechanical royalties**. Although mechanical royalty rates in the U.S. are set by statute, record labels will negotiate the rate at which artist's royalties are paid, in many cases this is no greater than 75 percent of the statutory rate. The ability of a recording label to sell CDs adds value to a master. Often when an **independent record label** has a successful **album**, a major label will endeavor to control the masters from the independent label for several hundred percent greater than the initial investment in producing it.

See also: **audio engineer**; **first-sale doctrine**; **Harry Fox Agency**; **MP3**; **piracy**; **RIAA**

MASTERS CLAUSE

A clause contained in a recording **contract** that sets out the quality and quantity of the master recording that an **artist** must produce.

Most clauses state that the master must be **commercially acceptable** with the material chosen by the record label. Often, in a separate clause, a record company will assert that a master will be owned by the record label, unless otherwise stated. If an artist is under a **work–for–hire** contract, ownership of the **masters** will be automatically granted to the recording label.

See also: **audio engineer**; **first-sale doctrine**; **Harry Fox Agency**; **MP3**; **piracy**; **RIAA**

MECHANICAL LICENSE

Under the U.S. Copyright Act of 1976, a mechanical license gives the right to use **copyright**ed, nondramatic musical works in the manufacturing of **phonorecord**s for distribution to the public for private use.

However, the Copyright Act provides that once a copyright owner has recorded and distributed a work in the United States, others may obtain the right to record the work through a compulsory mechanical license. This **license** is available to anyone else who wants to record and distribute the work in the United States upon the payment of license fees at the statutory "compulsory" rate as set forth in Section 115 of the Act. In the United States the **Harry Fox Agency** is responsible for the distribution and collection of mechanical license fees.

See also: **first-sale doctrine**; **Harry Fox Agency**; **MP3**; **piracy**; **RIAA**

Further reading: Halloran (2007)

MECHANICAL RIGHT

An exclusive right granted in **copyright** law to the owner of a musical work for the authorized use of his or her intellectual property in a fixed **phonorecord**.

Section 106 of the U.S. Copyright Act of 1976 states that a copyright holder "has the exclusive right … to reproduce the copyrighted work in … phonorecords." U.S. law also provides, in the case of nondramatic works, the exclusive right to distribute phonorecord to copyright holder, and these phonorecords are subject to **compulsory license**s. This **license** is only for the purpose of making a commercial recording for private use. For commercial licenses a copyright owner will issue a negotiated or modified **mechanical license**. Compulsory licenses are not granted for a musical recording used for public use such as a **radio** or television transmission.

However, in 2006, the Register of Copyrights in the United States ruled that **ringtone**s are subject to compulsory licensing.

See also: **first–sale doctrine**; **Harry Fox Agency**; **MP3**; **piracy**; **RIAA**

Further reading: Halloran (2007)

MECHANICAL ROYALTY

Royalties earned by a **copyright** holder for the sale of music through "mechanical" devices such as **phonorecord**s.

In the US, a recording is **license**d by an agent to a record manufacturer at a certain per-unit price or rate known as the mechanical rate. A manufacturer produces the recordings and makes periodic payments to the copyright owner. This mechanical royalty equals the total number of recordings sold during a particular period for a particular rate known as the mechanical or **statutory rate**. The current statutory rate for the United States is 9.1 cents per copy or 1.75 cents per minute whichever is greater. Although this is a statutory rate, there is a practice of manufactures to withhold a certain percentage of **mechanical royalties** as "**reserves**" for returned recordings. Lower statutory rates may also apply for a variety of recordings sold at the **retail** level such as budget **album**s, cutouts (albums dropped from a manufacturers catalog), overruns (overproduced albums when a manufacturer anticipated a greater demand), and **record clubs** where companies will often pay 75 percent of the statutory rate.

The major **mechanical rights** agency in the United States is the **Harry Fox Agency** (**HFA**). It issues licenses and collects royalties under a publisher's specific instructions. Royalties are paid at the full statutory rate minus a **commission** of 3.5 pecent for administration costs incurred from collecting and distributing royalties. In Europe, **BIEM**, a semipublic mechanical collection society, collects mechanical royalties on behalf of its members throughout Europe. BIEM establishes a royalty rate, which is based on the **Published Price to Dealers** (**PPD**), a constructed price somewhere between the wholesale and retail price. BIEM establishes a percentage, which now is 6.5 percent of the PPD price. This represents the total royalty payable by the record company for all the music on that record. Separate compositions are then divided up on a time basis and the 6.5 percent royalty is allocated in that way. Comparison of the European method with the US method usually results in a higher royalty being paid in Europe on a per record basis.

See also: **first–sale doctrine**; **MP3**; **piracy**; **RIAA**

Further reading: McCourt (2005)

MERCHANDISING RIGHTS

The rights associated with the commercialization of an **artist**'s name, image, or likeness in promotional material and other products such as t-shirts, posters, **advertising**, motion pictures, and the like.

Often a standard clause in a recording **contract** a record label will claim ownership of commercialization rights to promote an artist and his or her recordings. However, many artists retain as many of these rights as possible, aiming to control their image and negotiate better deals with outside sources for the sale of goods, including clothing, perfumes, video games, and commercial tie-ins. Licensing for merchandising are usually negotiated between the merchandise manufacturer and the party that owns the merchandising rights. The scope of these agreements cover exclusivity, territorial boundaries, and the length of term of the **license**. Often, merchandising agreements are linked with other contractual relationships, such as recording contracts, **distribution** agreements, and so on. Payments for the right to obtain a merchandise license are based on royalty payments as well as **advance**s. Royalty payments by licensee will range from 1 percent to 50 percent. Royalty payments may also be expressed as a specific flat rate (e.g., $1,000 per year) or rate per unit (e.g., $.50 per unit sold) or a percentage based on net or gross receipts, minus a deduction for overheads such as manufacturing costs, shipping costs, and advertising and promotion expenses.

See also: **copyright**; **festival**; **license**; **retail**; **WTO**

Further reading: Halloran (2007); Passman (2006); Schulenberg (2005)

MINIMUM ADVERTISED PRICE (MAP)

A method in which manufactures and distributors obtain an agreement from retailers to sell CDs at a specific price in return for cooperative **advertising** funds.

These rules prevent retailers from competing too fiercely on the price of CDs, thereby reducing profits from their sale. Opponents to MAP insist that the technique unreasonably restrains competition. This policy requires retailers not only to set prices according to the instructions of the labels but to also observe MAP conditions in all media advertisements, even in advertisements funded solely by a retailer, such as in-store signs and displays.

Failure to adhere to these provisions subjects a retailer to a suspension of all cooperative advertising funding often for a period of 60 to 90 days.

Prior to the adoption of MAP, new retailers, especially **consumer** electronic chains, had sparked a **retail** "price war" that had resulted in significantly lower CD prices, with some prices for popular CDs falling as low as $9.99, and lower margins for retailers. Some retailers, who could not compete with the newcomers, asked the distributors for discounts or for more stringent MAP provisions to take pressure off their margins. In 1992, all five major distributors adopted MAP policies generally required adherence to minimum advertised prices in advertisements paid for by the distributors. By 1995 all five distributors expanded the restrictions in their MAP programs to require adherence to minimum advertised prices in advertisements regardless of the funding source. Although the distributors' actions were effective and retail prices stabilized, soon after, all distributors began to raise their wholesale prices.

In 1997, the **Federal Trade Commission (FTC)** began an investigation of the MAP policies of the five largest distributors of recorded music (Sony Music Distribution, Universal Music & Video Distribution, BMG Distribution, Warner-Elektra-Atlantic Corporation, and EMI Music Distribution) In 2000, the FTC accepted agreements containing the proposed consent orders from the corporate parents of the distributors. The agreements settled charges by the FTC that these five companies violated the FTC Act by engaging in practices that restricted competition in the domestic market for prerecorded music. The settlement prohibited all five companies from linking any promotional funds to the advertised prices of their retailer customers for the next seven years. And these five companies are prohibited for a further 13 years from conditioning promotional money on the prices contained in advertisements they do not pay for. The agreements also prohibited the companies from terminating relationships with any retailer based on that retailer's prices.

See also: **contract; major record label; marketing**

Further reading: Fox (2005)

MORAL RIGHTS

A right granted to **author**s to protect their personal interests independently from the economic rights that might exist in a work.

Unlike economic rights granted under **copyright** law, moral rights are inherent in a work even after the transfer of all rights. Although the scope of a creator's moral rights differs with cultural conceptions of authorship and ownership, moral rights fall into three categories: (1) The right of paternity gives the owner of a copyright the right to be identified as the author. Therefore, a work must carry visible notice of an author, even after the sale of a work; (3) The right of integrity requires that all works have a right not to be subject to "derogatory treatment" by a third party. This includes the adaption, arrangement and parody of a work; (3) Moral rights protect a work being falsely attributed. This right addresses a situation in which a third party has sought benefit from the reputation of a creator by attributing there name to a particular work in order to make a work commercially attractive.

This concept, though established in the **Berne Convention** and extended in 1996 with the **WIPO Performance and Phonogram Treaty**, many countries, such as the United States refuse to acknowledge it. A narrow interpretation of moral rights is recognized in the United States through the Visual Arts Rights Act (VARA) of 1990, which provides visual **artists** the right to protect their works against mutilation, alteration, and discredit. The concept is an inherent element in **creative common** licenses. In the United Kingdom, moral rights were introduced in the Copyright, Designs and Patents Act of 1988.

See also: **copyright**; **Copyright Term Extension Act**; **EUCD**; **TRIPS**; **WIPO**

Further reading: Einsenschitz (2006); Joffrain (2001); Landau (2005); Lea (1999); Masiyakurima (2005); Oppenheim (1996); Rajan (2002); Reder (1940); Westmacott (2006)

MP3 (MPEG-1 AUDIO LAYER 3)

A digital audio encoding format used for **consumer** audio storage.

It has become the de facto standard encoding for the transfer and playback of music on portable digital audio players. Developed by several engineering teams from Germany and the United States, MP3 became an international standard in 1991. MP3's ability to greatly reduce the amount of data required for transmission while maintaining audio fidelity has made it an important tool in the development of the music industry on the World Wide Web.

Considering the extent of data compression possible, MP3 files can be transferred with relative speed on the Internet, especially on **peer-to-peer** (**P2P**) file-sharing sites. The size of the file or bit rate not only reduces the original size of the file, thus making it easier to transfer, but also has an effect on quality of the play back. The lower the bit rate used the faster a file can be downloaded; however, this will result in lower audio quality.

In 1999, Napster, the first large **P2P** file-sharing network, began to allow individuals to share MP3 files ripped from compact discs. The ease of creating and sharing MP3s resulted in widespread **copyright** infringement. Furthermore, the ability to recreate an infinite number of copies, without degradation, led the recording industry to accuse individuals and companies of copyright infringement for the unauthorized sharing of intellectual property. Organizations such as the **Recording Industry Association of America** (**RIAA**) began filing lawsuits against Napster and individual uses engaged in file sharing. As a consequence, many companies began to use encrypted MP3s as a means of deterring individuals from unauthorized use of recorded music. **Digital Rights Management** (**DRM**) tools not only limit users the ability to copy downloaded music to their computers and distributing it through the Internet, but they also prevent users from playing purchased music on different devices. Many online companies have now removed their DRM tools on files in an effort to allow for greater interoperability among various devices. Nonetheless, organizations such as the RIAA continue to file litigation against those who download and share music without permission.

See also: **Audio Home Recording Act**; **breakage allowance**; **GERA**; **GATT**; **Harry Fox Agency**; **IFPI**; **Minimum Advertised Price (MAP)**; **NARAS**; **Published Price to Dealers (PPD)**; **RIAA**

Further reading: Alderman (2001); Angwin (2006); Bockstedt (2006); Goodman (1993); Haring (1996); Levin (2004); McCourt (2005); McLeod (2005); Mann (2000); Rifkin (2001); Strauss (1999)

MUSIC CONTROL AIRPLAY SERVICES

A music broadcast monitoring system owned and operated by Nielsen, Inc.

Also known as Nielsen Music Control, the system monitors over 700 **radio** and television stations across 18 countries worldwide. Nielsen Music Control uses an electronic fingerprinting technology called Medicor to track broadcasters. As with **BDS**, Nielsen's North American Music Monitoring service data are used by the music industry for chart development and reports ranging from individual radio stations to market share performance. Reports are available through the Nielsen Web site in real time, daily, weekly, or any other period requested.

See also: **Arbitron**; **radio**; **SoundExchange**; **SoundScan**

Further reading: McBride (2007)

MUSIC VIDEO

A short film complete with a song used as a **marketing** device to promote the sale of singles and albums.

The term first came into popular usage during the 1980s, when MTV's format was solely based on the music video. Music videos come in a range of styles including animation, live action, and nonnarrative approaches such as abstract film. With the advent of easy-to-use video recording equipment, many **artists** began to see the potential of promoting their music via a visual medium. Although the amateur philosophy became the norm for early video production, soon professional videos were using movie-standard 35 mm film. According to Vernallis (2004), "music videos are nonnarrative and follow a song's cyclical and episodic form rather than present a chain of events. In most cases, viewers are faced with a deliberate ambiguity, "... if there is a story, it exists only in the dynamic relation between the song and the image as they unfold in time."

With the decline in MTV using the video as its central format and the development of broadband, the music video has gained a wider audience through the World Wide Web. The advent of social networking sites, such as YouTube, and the relative ease of uploading content, "do-it-yourself" music videos have almost become the norm. Due to the unauthorized use of record label property, namely, uploading unauthorized content, the **Recording Industry Association of America (RIAA)** has issued several cease-and-desist letters to YouTube to prevent single users from sharing videos.

See also: **advertising**; **ASCAP**; **BMI**; **broadcasting**; **FCC**

Further reading: Angwin (2006); Banks (1996); Gillet, Essid, and Gael (2007); Gow (1992); Laing (1985); Vernallis (2004)

NATIONAL ACADEMY OF RECORDING ARTS AND SCIENCES (NARAS)

A U.S. organization that recognizes, represents, and rewards **artist**ic achievements within the recording field.

Established in 1957, the Recording Academy's membership comprises of songwriters, musicians, **producer**s, photographers, and art directors who are actively engaged in the recording field. Eligible members have voting rights in electing prizes of merit for the organization's main awards for achievement in the recording industry, namely, the Grammy Awards. Members cast nomination votes in four general categories: Record of the Year, Song of the Year, **Album** of the Year, and Best New **Artist** within select genres. Other awards are given for arranging, engineering, producing, and other record-related activities. Special awards are presented for life-time achievement to the recording industry. Membership qualifications require an individual to have contributed creatively to at least six commercially released tracks. Recording Academy members belong to one of 12 regional chapters throughout the United States. Each chapter represent the Academy at the local level by working directly with local recording community, addressing issues on education, advocacy, and professional development. The activities of the local chapter is administered by a Board of Governors.

See also: **AFM**; **audio engineer**; **author**; **phonorecord**; **trade association**

Further reading: Watson (2006)

NATIONAL ASSOCIATION OF RECORDING MERCHANDISERS (NARM)

A U.S. **trade association** that represents the music **retailing** business.

Established in 1958, the organization serves the music retailing industry by representing members in areas of advocacy, information, networking, education, and promotion. Membership comprises of music and other entertainment retailers, wholesalers, distributors, record labels, multimedia suppliers, and suppliers of related products and services, as well as individual professionals and educators in the music business field divided into two categories: general and associate. General membership is open to businesses actively involved in record retailing including brick and mortar stores and electronic retailers and any company whose business activity is wholesale, such as jack robbers and **one stop**s. Associate membership comprises of distributor members (**distribution** and supply), entertainment software suppliers (record label or multimedia supplier), and supplier of related product and services (CD manufacturers and digital suppliers). NARM holds a major annual conference for its members, presents regional meetings and conferences, and sponsors educational programs in music industry. The organization is also actively involved in lobbying government agencies in areas of digital distribution, marketplace competition, and censorship. NARM collaborates internationally with the **Global Entertainment Retail Alliance** (**GERA**) to facilitate anti**piracy** efforts and issues associated with digital distribution of music and video.

See also: **album**; **ERA**; **trade association**

Further reading: Watson (2006)

NONDRAMATIC PERFORMANCE RIGHTS

Rights associated with the performance of a single song.

Unlike **dramatic rights**, which are part of a musical or opera, the **grand rights** associated with nondramatic performances are only part of a story; hence there are limitations compared to dramatic rights that have a greater degree of freedom. Small rights include the right to perform music via broadcast and at live-performance venues, as long as it is not presented as part of a dramatic work. **Copyright** owners grant to **performing rights organization**s (**PROs**) the nonexclusive right to **license** nondramatic performing rights. In the United States, nondramatic performances are licensed via PROs such as **ASCAP**, **BMI**, and **SESAC**. Under U.S. Copyright law after a **phonorecord** has been distributed to the public any person may obtain a **compulsory license** to arrange, make, and distribute the work by phonorecord.

See also: **BIEM**; **blanket license**; **compulsory license**; **license**; **performing rights organization (PRO)**; **royalty**

Further reading: Khon and Khon (2002)

OFCOM (OFFICE OF COMMUNICATIONS)

An independent regulator of the communication industry in the United Kingdom.

The Office of Communication or Ofcom was established in 2003 as the administrating organization of the Office of Communication Act of 2002. Ofcom replaced five regulatory bodies, including the Broadcasting Standards Commission, the Independent Television Commission, and the Radio Communications Agency. Ofcom is responsible for the management, regulation, and **assignment** of media licensing, the development of policies, the addressing of complaints, and evaluating competition in the marketplace. In this regard, Ofcom's main goal is the development of a communications industry that protects **consumer**s against monopolistic tendencies and offensive material. Ofcom operates in an open and accountable manner and is receptive to public and industry comments.

The process of evaluation begins with the publishing of issues in a specific area. After a period of ten weeks organizations and individuals may respond to the report. A summary of the responses is used to assist the organization in making a decision. After the consultation has closed, Ofcom will prepare a summary of the responses and may use this as a basis for some of its decisions.

Ofcom is responsible for administration of TV, **radio**, mobile phone, and private communication licensing. The process of licensing varies depending on the type of usage required. Some **license**s simply require payment and filing of the appropriate application form, whereas others are subject to a bidding process.

See also: **advertising**; **broadcasting**; **FCC**; **marketing**; **public relations (PR)**

Further reading: Ashton (2007); Smith (2006)

ONE STOP

A wholesale subdistributor that buys recordings from a variety of manufacturers for resale to **retail** stores.

Traditionally, one stops sold recordings to jukebox operators. The convenience of purchasing singles from one wholesaler, rather than multiple manufacturers, became ideal not only for jukebox operators but also for small retailers and **rack jobber**s. Eventually one stops expanded their range of products to include **album**s and other items. Retailers pay a slightly higher price for goods purchased from one stops in comparison to local distributors.

See also: **advertising**; **album**; **Audio Home Recording Act**; **breakage allowance**; **ERA**; **GERA**; **GATT**; **Harry Fox Agency**; **IFPI**; **Minimum Advertised Price (MAP)**; **NARAS**; **Published Price to Dealers (PPD)**; **RIAA**

OPTION

A **contract** clause that expresses a privilege that one party may or may not exercise.

Typically, in a recording contract an option refers to the length of time in which a contract may be exercised beyond the initial period of the agreement. This period of time is established in a contractual agreement and is renewed at the conclusion of a predetermined event or time. An option period may run for a specific period from 90 days, 6 months, or 1 year. In some cases, the duration of the term may be determined by the performance of a recording or by the delivery of the **masters** to a record label within a specified time period. Other provisions in exercising an option include the payment of money, specific sales of a previous recording, or national **distribution**. The right to exercise an option may be revoked for several reasons. The most common of these reasons is the failure of one party to meet the expressed requirements of the option within a specific period. However, due to the level of investments involved, both monetarily and creatively, in creating a recording, parties often require compensation upon the conclusion of the initial period. In some cases, an **artist** may request the return of the masters to obtain future recording agreements or for commercial **release** through another medium. Record labels may request an artist to recuperate recording costs and/or **advance**s.

Record labels may also resort to describing **development deal**s in which the label will "test" a potential artist through a temporary exclusive agreement before getting into a permanent contract that in turn allows the artist to negotiate with other companies.

See also: **agent**; **development deal**; **independent record label**; **license**; **major record label**; **manager**; **override**; **promoter**; **royalty**

ORIGINALITY

The application of an **author**'s independent skill and labor in the creation of an artistic work.

The 1976 Copyright Act provides that **copyright** protection "subsists . . . in original works of authorship fixed in any tangible medium of expression, now known or later developed" (17 U.S.C.A. § 102(a)). Apart from **fixation**, originality is the most important quality needed in a work for it to receive copyright protection. For the purposes of obtaining copyright protection, originality is not dependent on a work meeting any standard of aesthetic or artistic quality. This low level of originality contrasts to the novelty requirement under patent law, which requires a patentable invention to be new and not otherwise seen before. This requirement is not only designed to prevent the creation of works similar to original copyrighted works but also to prevent authors from appropriating elements of an original work that is considered inherently unoriginal, hence un-copyrightable. Thus, the Copyright Act explicitly excludes from protection "any idea, procedure, process, system, method of operation, concept, principle, or discovery."

The Copyright Act also recognizes **derivative work**s as original only to the extent of the original contribution of the author who prepares the derivative work. This means that the contribution to an underlying work must meet the standard for copyright as an independent work, not restatements of the original work. Thus, the contributions to a derivative work must be substantially different and "nontrivial" in nature from the original.

Originality is also a prerequisite for copyright protection under the UK Copyright, Designs and Patents Act of 1988. In order to qualify for copyright protection literary, artistic, dramatic, and musical works must be original. As with U.S. Copyright Law, the requirement of originality imposed by UK law has a low threshold for protection. Thus, UK Copyright Act protects the expression of a work rather than the ideas contained within the expression.

See also: **Berne Convention**; **Buenos Aires Convention**; **DMCA**; **DART**; **TRIPS**; **UCC**; **WIPO**

ORPHAN WORKS

A **copyright**ed work in which the owner is not known or cannot be found.

Orphan works pose problems for **author**s trying to **license** or sample older works. The cost of finding the owner of an orphan work can be so high that creators of derivative works cannot obtain a license and may abandon the new composition. A work may fall into this category for a number of reasons, such as corporate mergers, sales, and consolidations, authors' failure to renew works in a timely manner, or there is confusion about the ownership of a particular work. With the elimination of copyright registration formality, namely, the registration and mandatory renewal of registration, many authors have copyright protection without registration. In an effort to remedy this problem, the members of the U.S. Congress have proposed the "Orphan Works Act of 2008." The proposed bill allows for use of works for which the copyright holder can't be found and limits liability for those users who perform and document "a qualifying search, in good faith, for the owner of the infringed copyright." Because this legislation is in violation of Article 5 of the **Berne Convention** (which states, "the enjoyment and the exercise of these rights shall not be subject to any formality") and fails the three-step test of the **Trade-Related Aspects of Intellectual Property (TRIPS)**, its passage is highly unlikely.

Unlike the U.S. laws, which do not address accounting of orphan works, the Canadian copyright law authorizes the Copyright Board of Canada to issue licenses for use of orphan works. Applicants must show that all efforts have been made to identify the owner of the copyright before the right to use an orphan work may be granted. **Royalty** payments are deposited with the Copyright Board in a **fund** held for the author if he or she is eventually found. Although this legislation was established as early as 1997, not many licenses have been granted thus far. EU members have not established so far a legislation dealing with the collection of royalties from the use of orphan works.

See also: **BIEM; black box income; foreign royalties; Harry Fox Agency; performing rights organization (PRO)**

OVERRIDE

A fee paid by a new record label to an **artist**'s old label when they sign that artist in order to buy him or her out of his or her old **contract**s. Often this is a sequence of payments based on sales or success rather than a single check.

See also: **agent; development deal; independent record label; license; major record label; manager; promoter; royalty**

PACKAGING COST DEDUCTION

A recording **contract** clause that states a record label can deduct from an artist's royalties the production of packaging or container of a recording.

Often known as "container charges" or "jacket charges," the amount deducted is calculated against the suggested **retail** price of a recording before the artist's royalty rate is calculated. The reduction is often 20 to 25 percent of the suggested retail price of CDs. These charges are also applied to **record club** sales, foreign sales, and other categories with reduced royalties. A contentious issue related to packing charges is how such charges should be dealt with when it comes to recordings delivered through electronic transmissions; since there is no physical container, there should be no packing charge.

See also: **album**; **breakage allowance**; **distribution**; **Published Price to Dealers (PPD)**

PAPERING THE HOUSE

A term used in **venue** management to describe the act of providing free **tickets** to give the impression that a venue is well attended.

A house is "papered" when ticket sales have reached a plateau within a week or two of the performance date. This technique is used by **managers** and **promoters** when invited guests, such as **A&R** representatives, record label executives, publishers, and the media, especially critics, will be present in the audience.

See also: **agent**; **capacity**; **four walling**; **public relations (PR)**

Further reading: Ashton (2007)

PAYOLA

The payment or inducement by a record label to broadcasters for preferential treatment of the label's recordings on a specific show.

Although illegal, the practice of paying **radio** stations for preferential treatment is allowed if the payment is disclosed as sponsored airtime. The act of payola came to head in a 1959–1960 U.S. Congressional probe into the practice of **disc jockey**s receiving monies for playing specific record-ings on the radio. Hearings by the House of Representatives Special Subcommittee on Legislative Oversight began on February 8, 1960, and included disc jockeys from Boston and Cleveland. Focus of the investiga-tion was on the disc jockey Alan Freed (1922-1965) and, Dick Clarke (b. 1929), the host of American Bandstand of the ABC network. Freed lost his radio and television shows, having refused to sign an affidavit stating that he had not taken payola for playing records. Eventually, Freed did not appear before the committee.

On May 19, 1960, a grand jury in New York City charged 8 disc jockeys with having received $116, 580 in payola payments. Freed was subpoenaed to appear before the grand jury, but pleaded his constitutional right to not testify. He was later charged with 26 counts of bribery and, at a trial in 1962, he pleaded guilty to two counts of bribery. He was fined $300 and given six months suspended sentence. He was later indicted for having evaded taxes in 1962, but was never brought to trial due to his death in the same year.

Dick Clark did appear before the Congressional Subcommittee on May 2, 1960. Clarke testified that he had interests in recordings that appeared on Bandstand. It was reveled that Clarke's music interest included 27% interest in the songs/records that were performed on Bandstand and that he had partial or full interests in 33 different music-related businesses including publishing, recording, and manufacturing plants. Before he testi-fied, Clarke had divested himself of all these business connections due to pressure from ABC. At the conclusion of the trial, Chairperson Oren Harris said of Clarke, "You are obviously a fine man . . . I do not think that you are the inventor of the system; I do not think that you are even the architect of it, apparently. I think you are the product that has taken advantage of a unique opportunity."

Payola scandal spread to other areas of the industry. The Chairperson of the **Federal Communications Commission** could not deny that he had enjoyed a six-day junket in Florida with all expenses paid by the Storer Broadcasting Company. Under pressure from President Eisenhower he was forced to resign his post.

The consequence of the payola investigations eventuated in Congress enacting a law in 1960 that made payola a criminal offense punishable by a $10,000 fine and/or a year in jail. Nonetheless, record labels bypassed federal law by paying a third party or independent record **promoter**s who "promoted" the label's songs to radio stations. Offering the radio stations "promotion payments," independent record promoters paid an "induce-ment" to obtain radio play. Because these inducements did not fall under payola rules, radio stations did not have to report them as promotions. In 2005 New York Attorney General, Elliott Spitzer, began investigations into practices by Sony Records and several radio stations in New York and nationwide. The consequence of this investigation led to Sony BMG, Warner Music Entertainment, and Universal Music Group settling with the New York State Attorney's Office to the sum of $10 million, $5 million, and $12 million, respectively.

See also: **advertising**; **album**; **ASCAP**; **BMI**; **fund**; **major record label**; **promoter**

Further reading: Kronemyer (1987); McLeod (2005); Russell (2005); Segrave (1994)

PEER-TO-PEER NETWORK (P2P)

A computer network system in which music files are transferred between users without the use of a centralized management source.

Most P2P networks are used for connecting individuals (commonly known as peer nodes) via large ad hoc connections for the sharing of content files containing audio or video information. An advantage of P2P networks is that all clients provide the necessary resources for the system to operate. These resources include bandwidth, computing power, and storage space. As the system increases in user size, so does the total capacity. With the advent of **MP3** files, P2P networks have become conduits for legal and illegal digital music **distribution**. P2P structures are classified according to the interaction between members and clients. Some networks such as Napster use a client-server structure for some tasks (e.g., searching) and a P2P structure for others. Networks such as Gnutella use a P2P structure for all purposes and are sometimes referred to as true P2P networks, although Gnutella is greatly facilitated by directory servers that inform peers of the network addresses of other peers. **File sharing** in most systems usually follows similar or identical methods for storing and exchanging information; the files are stored on and served by personal computers of the users. Most people who engage in file sharing on the Internet both provide (upload) files and receive files (download).

The speed at which P2P networks have been adopted on the World Wide Web presents new challenges from a legal perspective. Current national **copyright** laws are not attuned to this rapid growth, especially within the music industry. The fact that P2P networks operate on an international level makes it difficult to litigate infractions in various countries, especially in those whose legislation is not able to meet the needs of this changing environment. In an effort to curtail piracy, representatives of the music industry opposed to open P2P networks have requested that legitimate P2P systems adopt **Digital Rights Management (DRM)** tools as a means of curtailing **piracy**. However, adding DRM systems would inevitably reduce the interoperability of music files on various systems. Further challenges have arisen because of the need to balance self-protection against **fair use**. Some P2P networks are able to encrypt the traffic flows between users, thereby allowing P2P networks to hide content from ISPs and other protective organizations.

See also: **distribution; e-commerce; FCC; MP3; RIAA; TRIPS; WIPO; WTO**

Further reading: Angwin (2006); Evans (2003); Kwok and Lui (2002); Levin (2004); McCourt (2005); Michel (2006); Rietjens (2006); Rifkin (2001); Schwartz (1995)

PERFORMANCE RIGHTS

The exclusive right to a public performance of a **copyright**ed work.

Under U.S. Copyright Law, "the owner of (a) copyright ... has the exclusive ... right to perform the copyrighted work in public." (title 17, www.loc.gov) Performance is defined by the Copyright Act as the recitation, rendering, playing or, acting directly or indirectly through mechanical means. Public performances are expressed either as performances in a place open to the public for a substantial number of people outside of a normal circle of family and social acquaintances or a transmission of a performance by means of a device or process in which the public can perceive the performance. However, there are exceptions to the exclusive right of public performance. Nonprofit public performances are exempt for the need to acquire authorization. This rule includes performances in the course of educational activities, performances of works of a religious nature, performances that have no commercial advantage (i.e., no payment of any admission fee) and performances within establishments of a particular size. Under the "Fairness in Music Licensing Act" of 1998, establishments such as **retail** stores and restaurants are exempt from performance licenses for the use of **radio**s and televisions. **Performing rights organization**s **(PROs)** collect performance licenses for nondramatic or small rights performances. Dramatic works, or **grand rights**, are licensed directly from a writer or publisher.

See also: **ASCAP**; **BIEM**; **BMI**; **Digital Performance Right in Sound Recording Act of 1995**; **SESAC**; **weighting formula**

Further reading: Nye (2000)

PERFORMING RIGHTS ORGANIZATION (PRO)

An organization that administers performing rights associated with a musical work on behalf of composers, songwriters, lyricists, and music publishers.

Typically, a PRO has three functions. First, they grant **copyright** owners the nonexclusive right to **license** nondramatic (dramatic licenses are negotiated on an individual basis) public performances of their compositions. Second, they issue performance licenses to individuals and organizations for the public performance of nondramatic works. Third, PROs administer performing rights by monitoring, logging, and accounting for performances of members' works. Finally, PROs distribute license fees (performance royalties) to writers, publishers, and affiliates of the organization in an equitable fashion. Because PROs handle the majority of music licenses, music publishers use them as clearinghouses for music licenses, thereby preventing duplication and misappropriation of royalties

In the United States, there are three important PROs: **ASCAP**, **BMI**, and **SESAC**. Although membership to PROs is voluntary, songwriters may join only one of the organizations, whereas a publisher may join or be affiliated with all three organizations. This arrangement allows publishers to accept songwriters who are members of any organization. However, a songwriter must assign the ownership his or her performing rights to a publisher that is a member of the writer's organization. PROs pay songwriters and publishers separately.

PROs also collect international **royalty** dues on behalf of their members. All U.S. performing rights organizations have reciprocal agreements with foreign organizations for the collection of royalties performed in a foreign country. This mitigates the need of a songwriter to join international PROs to collect royalties from their respective country. Foreign PROs calculate payments based on their own distribution rules before remitting payments to a national PRO. After administration fees are deducted, a national PRO will be distributed to the organization's members. As this process may take up to a year, many publishers will enter into **subpublishing** agreements with foreign publishers throughout the world.

PROs allocate monies earned from public performances by monitoring public performances. For example, television revenues paid by ASCAP are determined by either a sample or a census method. The sampling method of determining funds is carried out by a random sampling of criteria/ demographics related to broadcasters, such as the media, community (rural or metropolitan) geographic location, and size/revenue generated via annual licensing fees. Surveys are created via a mathematical formula based on a random check of broadcasters. The census method relies on the use of **cue sheet**s and program log primarily supplied by the major television networks. Licenses collected from other television broadcasters use a combination of sample and census methods.

See also: **BIEM**; **Digital Performance Right in Sound Recording Act of 1995**; **weighting formula**

Further reading: Ehrlich (1989); Fujitani (1984); McCourt (2005); Nye (2000)

PHONORECORD

A material object in which sounds are fixed and can be perceived, reproduced, or otherwise communicated directly or with the aid of a machine or device.

Phonorecords include cassette tapes, LP , CD, or other means of storing audio. A phonorecord does not include those sounds accompanying a motion picture or other **audiovisual** work.

A digital phonograph is a nonanalog phonorecord fixed in a digital medium. Because digital phonorecords are a new concept for **copyright** law, there is no exact legal definition of the term. The Copyright Act of 1976 has a broad definition of phonorecords that includes technology from that period as well as all technology "later developed." As a musical work requires **fixation** for copyright protection, a digital recording (**MP3**) may be fixed in a material object, such as a hard disk drive or some memory storage device. Much like tangible phonorecords, digital phonorecords must allow a user to perceive, reproduce, and communicate the material held within. A further delimiter between analog phonorecords and digital phonorecords is the ability of unlimited reproduction in the digital realm. Generational copies of traditional analog systems have the tendency to decline in audio quality over a period of time and thus are not cost-effective. Digital copying is cost-effective, as multiple copies can be made and distributed simply utilizing a computer's copy and paste function. This provides an accessible platform for illegal copying and **piracy** on a large scale. Finally, the divide between digital and analog phonorecords is the ease of instant and widespread **distribution** of copies. Currently, the **first-sale doctrine** does not allow for the disposal of digital phonorecords through **distribution**, as there is no transfer of ownership when there is a transfer of possession. Furthermore, in a digital phonorecord, there is no disposal of a phonorecord in a transaction; the sender still has the original copy.

See also: **artist**; **author**; **Buenos Aires Convention**; **Convention for the Protection of Producers of Phonograms against Unauthorized Duplication of their Phonograms**; **TRIPS**; **WIPO**; **WTO**

Further reading: Cunningham (1996); Stover (1990)

PIRACY

The illegal copying, **distribution**, and sale of recorded and printed music by individuals or organizations.

Illegal copying can be divided into three categories: bootlegging, counterfeiting, and piracy. Bootlegging refers to the practice of unauthorized recordings of live performances for sale. Counterfeiting is the illegal act of duplicating recordings, including packaging for sale.

Piracy is often a generic term for the act of producing for sale illegally recorded music. Nonetheless, piracy is a problem that extends throughout the music industry. The unauthorized reproduction and sale of **copyright**ed and printed music has been a widespread problem for over a hundred years. Today the printed music industry has faced the problem of unauthorized copying of material in fakebooks. These manuscripts can contain hundreds of songs, and melody-line arrangements have become abundant with the advent of photocopying. Recently, the development of peer-to-peer sharing and transfer of **MP3** files over the Internet has increased the ability for individuals to download and transfer files. Traditionally, pirated music took the form of bootlegged recordings of physical recordings, such as cassettes or CDs. The use of the Internet as a means of distributing digital music has increased on an international level as countries with less-than-strict copyright laws or enforcement history have opened the possibilities of piracy on a global level.

Protection against piracy exists on three levels: international, national, and state. In the United States, all states have enacted antipiracy statutes making piracy a felony punishable by the law. In the Copyright Act of 1976, willful infringement of **copyright** in a sound recording for the purpose of monetary gain is considered an offense punishable by imprisonment and a fine. International laws against piracy often require member states to close manufacturing plants that produce pirated goods and arrest those involved in such action. Organizations such as the **World Trade Organization (WTO)** and the **World Intellectual Property Organization (WIPO)** offer members the opportunity to hear cases against piracy practices in other member states. Action may include sanctions against countries that allow piracy to take place. In an effort to reduce piracy, WIPO provides member nations a range of activities in an effort not only to stop piracy but also to educate governments and individuals on the effect of piracy on the economy. Activities include providing member states legal and technical assistance to establish effective enforcement mechanisms, providing a forum for discussion and information, working closely with intergovernmental organizations and nongovernmental organizations (NGOs) in reducing piracy, and developing educational programs to enhance public awareness on the economic damages of piracy.

See also: **broadcasting**; **copyright**; **DMCA**; **DRM**; **payola**; **RIAA**; **TRIPS**; **WIPO**

Further reading: Angwin (2006); Barrett (2001); Das (2000); Flack (1989); Flanagan (1994); Fox (1993); Heylin (1996); Marshall (2003); Mitchell (2007); Morton and Koufteros (2008); Ouellet (2007); Schwartz (1995)

PLAYLIST

A **radio** or television station's fixed selection of music that forms the basis of its programming for a period of time.

The term originates from radio stations that would devise a limited list of songs to be played. Today the term refers to the **catalog** of songs that a radio station plays regularly. Similarly, the term is used by music television stations (MTV, VH1, etc.) for the number of **music video**s played regularly. Often radio stations will use a tiered listing system for their playlists. The criteria for this listing is the amount of time a song will be played during the day. Therefore, songs on an A list will be played X number of times, the B list slightly fewer times, and the C list still fewer. Playlists are often adjusted based on time of day. The reason why songs are placed into a category is based on several factors, including the popularity of a song, the commercial success of a song based on record sales and market research, and the process of formatting the radio according to the time of day, known as dayparting.

See also: **broadcasting**; **SESAC**

Further reading: Andersen (1980); Barnes (1988)

POOR MAN'S COPYRIGHT

The practice of obtaining **copyright** protection without filing the appropriate documentation via the U.S. Copyright Office.

This technique is most commonly performed by **authors** who send their work through the postal service or by a notary public to themselves and using a time stamp to valid a date of creation. In the event of the intellectual property being misused by a third party, a date of creation can be established by the postal mark in a court of law. Currently, there is no provision in copyright law regarding such type of protection. Furthermore, courts have rejected such cases as the method is susceptible to tampering. U.S. courts will award damages only for those works registered at the copyright office.

See also: **audiovisual work**; **best edition**; **collective work**; **compulsory license**; **contract**; **copyright**; **Copyright Royalty Arbitration Panel (CARP)**; **Copyright Royalty Board (CRB)**; **Copyright Term Extension Act**; **creative commons**; **dramatic rights**; **first-sale doctrine**; **IFPI**; **RIAA**

PRINT LICENSE

Specific Rights granted to reproduce a **copyright**ed work in print.

Print rights are administered by music publishers for sheet music, songbooks, **folio**s, lyrics printed on liner notes, and so on. Unlike **compulsory license**s, an **author** is not obliged within a recording contract to allow reproduction in print form. Under copyright law, a composition may be licensed to third parties or retained or not used at all.

Most publishing companies will enter into agreements with specialized music printing companies to perform most of the functions mentioned above. In most cases the terms of the agreement will cover the print rights to a particular song or a publisher's **catalog**. Compensation is usually based on a **royalty** payment often at 10 to 15 percent of the **retail** selling price for each copy sold. Revenue generated from print sales are obtained from large sheet music retailers and educational dealers that supply music to school bands, orchestras, and choral groups. For songwriters income from print licenses is usually a fixed cent rate for each sheet music or print-type music sold that range from 5 cents to 20 cents for each sale.

See also: **ASCAP**; **author**; **BIEM**; **BMI**; **catalog**; **folio**; **performing rights organization (PRO)**; **publishing**; **RIAA**; **royalty**; **WIPO**

PRODUCER

A person who is involved in the creation of a musical recording, often based on their artistic vision.

This person has multiple functions during a recording session that culminates in the production of a recording. These functions include the overall control of a recording session; the organization and scheduling of resources based on specified budgets; the supervision of recording, mixing, and mastering of the recording session; and the training, arrangement, and guidance of musicians and singers during the recording. A producer will also work with a sound engineer to record, mix, and master the records. Record producers are categorized into two groups: in-house and independent. In-house producers are employed by record labels to produce a signed **artist**'s recording. As employee of the label the artist may receive a salary for his or her work or be entitled to royalties. **Royalty** rates range from 1 percent to 5 percent of **retail** price. Independent producers work on a nonexclusive basis. Often they are paid on an **advance**-against-royalty basis with a higher return on royalties than an in-house producer. If a producer agrees to act as a **manager** for an artist, they will often receive a royalty that includes the artist's royalty. In such cases the royalty rate may range from 10 percent to 20 percent of the retail price of a recording with the producer paying the artist a royalty rate of 5 percent to 10 percent. Often an independent producer will receive a royalty fee independently from an artist. Rates in these cases average 1 percent to 3 percent of the retail sales of a recording.

Today a producer is responsible for writing, performing, and arranging the music in a recording. If this is the case, a producer will often establish a production company that not only deals with the production of recordings but may also deal with issues associated with publishing and personal management.

See also: **arranger**; **audio engineer**; **independent record label**; **major record label**; **phonorecord**

Further reading: Andersen (1980); Brooks (2004); Brophy-Warren (2007); Cunningham (1996); Holland (2004); Moorefield (2005); Zager (2005)

PROMOTER

Individuals or companies responsible for the organization and management of live performances.

Promoters, also known as concert or tour promoters and/or talent buyers, will organize a range of live performances, from special event performances to international concert **tour**s. In this **capacity**, a promoter will often book acts at **venues**, often working closely with an **artist**'s **agent** and **manager**; arrange publicity for the events; and coordinate the various components of an event such as security, insurance, and management of the box office. A promoter will work within a specific territory and will cooperate with other promoters and companies if a tour moves beyond their territory. For this reason the concept of national promotion companies came into being in the 1960s to meet the needs of international artists and national tours. National promoters can offer artists and venues higher percentages of gross **ticket** sales due to the scale of economies associated with managing multiple performances.

A promoter also assists in pricing events with venues. The price charged includes the cost of travel, the venue, and the potential of the venue to attract **consumer**s. In a bid to increase attendance a promoter will oversee **advertising** for a performance. Advertising requirements include the production of a press kit as well as traditional advertising placements in various media outlets including **radio**, television, Internet, and print media. The promoter will also coordinate travel and accommodation for the tour. **Contract**s for performers follow the **American Federation of Musicians** (**AFM**) contract format, commonly known as the AFM Performance Agreement.

Compensation for a promoter is based on a variety of methods. Most common is a flat fee (guarantee) plus a percentage of the box office receipts. Payment or revenue distribution is negotiated between the promoter and venue based on gross or net receipts. Another method of compensation is the guarantee split. In this system a promoter is paid an upfront guarantee and a percentage of the net box office. After the guarantee and expenses are deducted from box office receipts, the promoter receives a percentage, usually 20 percent, while leaving the remaining percentage for the performers. Promoter/performer percentages are most commonly 80/20, 85/15, and 90/10. Actual rates are determined by location and size of a venue and the success of the performance.

See also: **independent record label**; **major record label**

Further reading: Ashton (2007); Brooks (2004); Kalma (2002); Kirchner (1994); Waddell, Barnet, and Berry (2007)

PUBLIC DOMAIN

A term indicating that a **copyright**ed work is not owned or controlled by the creator and is thus public property.

This status indicates that the public can freely use the intellectual property for any purpose. Public domain laws associated with the scope of proprietary rights vary greatly from country to country. This is the case with the length that a work may be protected by copyright law. All copyrights have a finite term, after which a work enters the public domain. Copyright in a published work expires when the last surviving **author** died at least 70 years before January 1 of the current year. Unpublished anonymous and pseudonymous works and works made for hire expire 120 years from the date of creation. A **joint work** prepared by two or more authors that was not a "**work-made-for-hire**," the copyright enters the public domain 70 years after the last surviving author's death. The United Kingdom has a slightly different duration of copyright based on the **Berne Convention** and the 1988 Copyright, Designs and Patents Act. For literary, dramatic, and musical works, a copyright expires 70 years after the death of the last remaining author. For **anonymous work**s, duration is 70 years from the date of creation. Sound recordings in the U.K. copyright duration expires 50 years from the end of the calendar year in which the work was created or 50 years from the end of the calendar year in which the work was first released.

Under Section 203 of the U.S. Copyright Act, an **author** of a work has the right to cancel "the exclusive or nonexclusive grant of a transfer or **license** of copyright or of any right under a copyright" 35 years later, unless the work was originally a work-made-for-hire. A holder of a copyright could in theory release a work into the public domain.

There are some rare exceptions to the rules associated with a work entering the public domain. Although highly uncommon, perpetual copyrights do exist. For example, "Peter Pan" is protected in the United Kingdom by special legislation that allows the Great Ormond Street Hospital to collect **royalties** in perpetuity, even though they do not have creative control over the work. Works created by an agency of the U.S. government are public domain at the moment of creation.

As with copyrights, patents have specific timeframe for intellectual property protection, after which they enter the public domain. Unlike copyrights and patents, **trademark**s can be maintained indefinitely. However, a trademark may enter the public domain if they lapse due to disuse, negligence, or misuse.

See also: **Berne Convention**; **Buenos Aires Convention**; **creative commons**; **Rome Convention**

Further reading: Bishop (2005); Therien (2001)

PUBLIC RELATIONS (PR)

The deliberate, planned, and sustained effort to establish and maintain a mutual understanding between an organization and its target audience.

Public relations, through the direct management of communication, seeks to create and maintain a positive image of a product (tangible or intangible) or a concept or a service for its targeted audience. To achieve this goal PR individuals and companies use a variety of techniques and media, which range from press releases and press kits to the use of wire services and the Internet. Other direct means of PR include press conferences, media seminars, photo ops, and in-person appearances and performances. Traditional tool for PR in the music industry has been the press kit. Standard press kits include material such as **artist** histories, news clips, and other media-related materials such as tour plans. (add a section on electronic Press kits) Most of the information that is transmitted involves the popularization of successes, downplaying of failures, and announcements of changes or, in other words, the selective presenting of facts and quotes that support a specific position in a biased manner. Often seen as disingenuous and deceptive, this PR method involves the careful choice of timing in the release of information to take advantage of events that may affect the artist.

The process of creating a PR campaign begins with identifying a target audience and tailoring an appropriate message to appeal to that audience. Most companies will use a demographic profile to identify a particular market. Apart from economy-driven demographics, PR firms will group individuals according to psychographic groupings, generic titles (soccer moms) or stakeholders. As there is often multiple constituencies for a single product, several distinct but still complementary messages must be created. The outcome is a particular response from a particular public that essentially benefits both parties. Public perception measured through market research and situation analysis. Data is then used to verify that original goals and objectives have been met.

Apart from influencing individuals from an economic perspective, PR is used as a tool in lobbying government organizations especially in influencing policy. Most organizations that are involved in lobbying represent a particular interest. For example, the recording industry is represented by the **Recording Industry of America Association (RIAA)**.

See also: **FCC**; **FTC**; **GERA**; **IFPI**; **merchandising rights**; **Ofcom**; **trade association**

Further reading: Jefkins (1998)

PUBLISHED PRICE TO DEALERS (PPD)

The highest price charged by a record manufacturer or distributor to a retailer.

The rate is calculated by **BIEM** and only concerns physical audio products sold within the European Union. The PPD is important for the establishment of **royalty** rates within the European Union. In a recording **contract** a major label will pay 15 percent to 19 percent of the PPD to an **artist**. Two deductions typically are applied on the gross royalty rate. A 9 percent deduction for rebates and discounts and 10 percent for packing costs. (9.009 percent of PPD). Most record labels will offer as little discounts as possible. The reason for this is that **royalties** paid to artists are tied to the PPD and not to the net price paid by retailers.

Audiovisual use of protected works are negotiated on a territory-by-territory basis, as are rates for the Internet and other usage. Currently the royalty rate agreed between BIEM and the **International Federation of Phonographic Industries (IFPI)** for mechanical reproduction rights is 11 percent on the PPD. The PPD is often announced when a record label presses recordings. Royalties on imports is 6.25 percent of the **retail** price or 10.6 percent of PPD.

See also: **album; Audio Home Recording Act; breakage allowance; ERA; GERA; GATT; Harry Fox Agency; IFPI; Minimum Advertised Price (MAP); NARAS; rack jobber; RIAA**

Further reading: Spahr (2004)

PUBLISHING

The **marketing**, sale, and administration of music **copyright**s and **catalog**s.

Although primarily concerned today with the sale of intangible rights associated with **intellectual property**, the music publishing industry began with the sale of sheet music. With the growth of the music industry into divergent fields of entertainment, music publishers have expanded to meet the needs of the music industry environment. Today music publishers are categorized according to several variables including size, music genre, and organizational structure. Publishers range in size from self-publishing companies established by artists to large multinational corporations. It is common for a songwriter to establish or purchase their own publishing company to reduce the sharing of **royalties** with a publishing company. Another category includes independent publishers and those that are directly associated with a recording label, motion picture companies, or advertising agencies. Often, independent publishing companies will enter into an administration agreement with other publishing companies to carry out copyright and business administration. Despite the presence of a plethora of small independent publishing companies, few large corporations dominate the music publishing industry, as is the case with the recording and live performance industries. Many of these large companies are subsidiaries of **major record label**s and service their artistic roster. Publishers are also categorized by the type of music they represent. Publishers associated with classical music derive most of their income from print music sales and rentals rather than licensing music to secondary sources.

Music publishers derive their income or royalties directly from the exploitation of copyrights from various sources. To maximize earnings, publishers will exploit a song through as many avenues as possible. This is done through **license**s, which permit the licensee to use intellectual property for a desired purpose as long as an appropriate fee has been paid. A music publisher will pay royalties to the copyright owner, after deducting administrative costs and fees. Royalties collected by a publishing company are determined by the use of the intellectual property. Music publishers earn most of their revenue from **synchronization license** fees, public performance dues and sale of recorded or sheet music. **Performance royalties** are obtained from performances of music either nondramatic performances and dramatic rights. In the United States, **performing rights organization**s (**PROs**) acquire nonexclusive rights to license public performances from songwriters and music publishers. As the publisher and songwriter must belong to the same PRO, most publishers will be affiliated with all three PROs to accommodate a songwriter. Works comprising of multiple compositions joined in a coherent whole (dramatic performances) are licensed directly with a publishing company (**ASCAP** administers copyrights for a fee of approximately 15%). **Mechanical royalties** are collected from the sale of recorded music. Most labels prefer to obtain negotiated licenses from publishers. In a recording contract, the record label will have a **controlled composition** clause that reduces the statutory compulsory license rate paid by 25 percent. Most songwriters share mechanical royalties in a 50/50 split with the publisher after administrative fees have been deducted by a mechanical collection organization. Synchronized royalties are collected from the use of music in a motion picture, in television shows, and other types of televised media. In the case of motion pictures, a license fee is negotiated between the film producer and the publisher. Therefore, licenses are highly individualized according to use and negotiations between the various parties. Print royalties are collected for the sale of printed editions, which take the form of sheet music; folios; songbooks; and arrangements for orchestras, choruses, and bands. On average, a print publisher will pay a music publisher approximately 40 to 60 cents per copy of sheet music. Finally, ancillary royalty revenues are obtained from a variety of sources, including adverting, greeting cards, and video games. The exploitation and administration of music copyrights go well beyond the national boundary of a publisher. U.S. publishers obtain funds through subsidiaries of their own company in foreign countries or through subpublishing agreements. A foreign publisher will collect all revenue earned in its territory and transmit it to the U.S. publisher after making deductions for its negotiated share.

Typically, a songwriter will assign a song's copyright to a publisher under a "**copublishing** agreement," essentially making the publisher a coowner of a composition. The publisher's role is to promote the music to recordings, arrangements, and performances, thereby generating income. The goal is to create a hit record, thereby generating large sales and **airplay**.

This not only includes the country where the publisher resides but also organizations and sources with an international presence. Once these royalty monies are collected, they are distributed to the appropriate owner of the copyright. Traditionally, after deducting administration costs, music publishing royalties are split fifty/fifty between publisher and the songwriter. Such agreements are codified within contractual relationships; the most basic contractual relationship between a publisher and songwriter is the single-song agreement. This contractual relationship has the publisher acquiring the copyright to a song. By assigning all copyrights, the songwriter allows the publisher to fully exploit the work in as many avenues as possible. Though terms in this agreement are negotiable, they are often contingent on the publisher acquiring a recording contract for the songwriter or having the song recorded or published within a specified period of time. Any grant of copyright is subject to the Copyright Act's termination right, and a songwriter may negotiate a contractual right to be returned to the songwriter if the publisher fails to obtain a recording contract or have the songs recorded or published within a specified period of time. Another standard publishing contract is the exclusive songwriter agreement. Similar to the single-song agreement, especially in regard to royalty payments and duration, this contract requires a songwriter to work exclusively for a specific publisher. Under such agreements, a songwriter may also be required to complete an assigned number of songs within a specific timeframe.

Structurally a music publisher is very similar to any other music industry company, with the organization separated into creative and administrative divisions. Departments are designed along a functional role, with each department undertaking a specific role in the publishing process. The most critical areas for operating a publishing company include the acquisition of copyrights, copyright administration, and exploitation. Copyright administration includes the preparation of copyright applications and documents for the transfer of copyright ownership. A music publisher also registers songs with performing rights organizations, both in its country of origin and internationally. A publisher is also responsible for the preparation and issuance of licenses. This includes the negotiation of licensing terms with a songwriter or their agent, if the publishing company is not the representing company. An important administrative function is the accounting of collected royalties and license fees, the distribution of advances, the preparation of financial statements, and the auditing of record companies and other licensees or self-auditing. From a creative perspective, a music publisher is responsible for the acquisition of songs as well as the development of potential songwriters. Furthermore, the creative division is in charge of promoting the company's catalog of songs (song plugging) to potential users, including successful recording artists, recording companies, and ancillary users of music, such as movie and television producers.

See also: **author**; **best edition**; **Berne Convention**; **copublishing**; **license**; **performance rights**; **subpublishing**

Further reading: Flack (1989); Garofalo (1999); Morton and Koufteros (2008)

RACK JOBBER

A wholesaler who purchases space in a **retail** store to install, stock, and replenish selected recordings.

Typically, rack jobbers placed racks in nontraditional music outlets such as department and grocery stores, pharmacies, and gas stations, and replenish the stock on a regular basis. Recently rack jobbers have expanded into the retailing industry, especially big-box retailers, such as Wal-Mart. Unlike mass merchants, which have 60,000 to 80,000 stocking-keeping units, big-box retailers will only stock approximately 5,000 units of top selling titles. A rack jobber would either rent the space from the retailer and keep all proceeds or pay the retailer a percentage of the sales. The latter case is often advantageous for large chains as it may be more cost-effective and less risky to sub**contract** its music sales to a third-party vendor.

A rack jobber is responsible for all record sales activity within the chain store, including inventory management, sales and **marketing**, and returns. As most rack jobbers operate on a consignment basis, they will often only carry a limited selection of titles, mostly top 100 **artists**. This improves the prospect of sales and reduces returns from stores, which are often at a rate of 100%. At the conclusion of a specified period, the rack jobber will present the store manager with a copy of the inventory control sheet, which indicates the amount of merchandise sold.

Although contractual relations between a store and a rack jobber are highly individual, there are three standard contracts. First, a rack jobber rents space from the retailer for a flat monthly fee. In this scenario, the rack jobber retains all of the money collected from sales. Second, the rack jobber pays the store a percentage of sales, thereby reducing the rack jobber's initial start-up costs. The final version occurs when a rack jobber's lease is based on sales. If sales in a specific period is higher than an agree-upon amount, the rack jobber pays the retailer a percentage of the additional funds.

See also: **album**; **breakage allowance**; **distribution**; **ERA**; **GERA**; **GATT**; **Harry Fox Agency**; **IFPI**; **Minimum Advertised Price (MAP)**; **NARAS**; **Published Price to Dealers (PPD)**; **RIAA**

Further reading: Cort (1958); Gubernick (1989)

RADIO

The wireless transmission and reception of audible signals encoded in electromagnetic waves.

As an important media tool for the music industry, radio is important in the promotion of **phonorecord**s for sale. Record labels depend on the **broadcasting** of recordings to expose new **album**s to the general public. The greater the **airplay** of a song, the higher the sales.

During the 1930s, 1940s, and 1950s, radio in the United States was dominated by four major networks: NBC, CBS, ABC, and Mutual-Don Lee. Although the 1950s saw the networks move toward television, radio remained a major entertainment medium due to three factors. First, the emergence of rock and roll, which became the basis of Top 40 radio programs. Second, the expansion of the teen market. Third, the creation of the transistor radio, which provided a cheap, portable product that allowed teens to listen to radio. Although 50 percent of the radio market was still using AM radio in mid-70s, FM radio had begun to erode AM radio's dominance and by the late 1970s FM radio was the dominant format. Deregulation of the radio industry in the 1980s and into the 1990s led to a loosening of ownership limits, thus allowing big national chains to dominate individual radio markets. In the new millennium, traditional radio faces a new challenge in the form of Internet and satellite radio. Today satellite radio is becoming a dominant format in the radio market.

The organization of a radio programming is based on the listener market segmentation and content. As radio stations earn their income through advertising, a radio station endeavors to reach the greatest audience within a period of time. Thus, a station's format relies on programming elements such as **playlist**s, **charts**, airplay, and the input from **disc jockey**s. Most radio stations concentrate on a particular genre of music within a specific time, usually for a week. To enhance the listenership, stations will divide the day into several time slots or what is commonly known as dayparting. Each slot is designed toward a specific demographic and what they engage in at that time. Therefore, during weekdays early morning, between 6:00 a.m. to 10:00 a.m., programming is designed attract adult commuters traveling to work. Within this structure, radio stations will create playlists of music to be broadcasted. Playlists are created by the program director with recommendations from the music director and with the aim to reach a specific audience through a rotational system. The most popular songs get the most airplay on a radio station, in what is known as heavy rotation or high rotation, as frequently as every 5 minutes.

All music performed is accounted for in logs that provide information to sponsors, including government organizations, such as the **Federal Communications Commission** (**FCC**), for regulation purposes, and performing rights organizations (PROs), for licensing and **royalty** payments. Several publications track song rotation on radio.

A new trade publication that emerged in the 1970s was *Radio & Records* (R&R). The magazine became influential in its focus on airplay charts, as opposed to Billboard, which mixed sales and airplay to create their charts. R&R's biggest influence on the industry, perhaps, has been coining and defining radio formats and assigning reporter status to radio stations that report airplay of current music. The magazine, for example, changed top 40 to "contemporary hit radio," middle of the road to "adult contemporary," and soul to "urban." Top 40 programming pioneers of the 1950s through 1980s tended to command huge shares in major markets. In the 1990s, the rise of alternative radio signaled confirmation of the album format, once offered mainly by rock stations. This led to the acceptance of many specialty formats that were usually hybrids of the established pop, rock, soul, and country formats, which had already begun splintering and merging with crossover music in the 1980s. Even jazz returned as a popular format via pop and soul hybrids.

Because radio stations transmit on public airwaves, broadcasters in the United States are regulated by the FCC. The role of the FCC in radio is to **license** frequencies to companies and to monitor their use, and assign frequency, poser, and call signs to radio stations. Radio broadcasting is categorized into two frequencies: AM and FM. AM (amplitude modulation) occupies the space between 535 and 1,605 kilohertz while FM (frequency modulation) is a high-fidelity sound in the VHF radio spectrum between 87 to 108 megahertz. High power is useful in penetrating buildings, diffracting around hills, and refracting for some distance beyond the horizon. A 100,000 watt FM station(s) can regularly be heard up to 100 miles (160 km) away from the source and even farther (e.g., 150 miles, 240 km), if there are no competing signals.

See also: **Arbitron**; **ASCAP**; **BMI**; **Ofcom**

Further reading: Barnes (1988); Beville (1988); Harwood (2004); Killmeier (2001); Pease and Dennis (1995); Sklair (1984)

RECORD CLUB

A method of direct sale from a record label to a **consumer**.

Record Clubs were established in 1955 as an experiment to test **marketing** music through the mail by Columbia Records and proved to be highly successful with consumers. The business model for a record club is predicated on consumers agreeing to purchase a minimum number of recordings at regular prices over a period of time, usually a month. An incentive for consumers to join the record club consists of several recordings sent to a consumer below **retail** price. Although consumers agree to purchase a specific number of recordings during a set timeframe, they are incentivized through a points system, where recordings result in "points" that can be used for future purchases. If a consumer does not pay for merchandise sent or is delinquent in payment, a credit card number, deposited upon commencing membership in the club, will be charged. This **retail** practice is known as negative option billing and is widely used in other retail sectors. Membership in the record club can usually be terminated after a subscriber has purchased the required number of CDs specified in the **contract**. If a consumer fails to contact the record club, usually in writing, they will continue to receive the monthly recordings.

Although the more successful record clubs are owned by the major labels, some smaller companies do exist. Though record clubs associated with record labels had unparallel access to manufacturing, **distribution**, and marketing avenues, other companies are required to enter into licensing agreements with labels. Most manufacturing **license**s state that a recording for the record club must be the same quality as that sold by the recording company. If the record club negotiates for a separate manufacturer for the recordings, a license will require the record label to provide the **master** to the external manufacturer. The record club will assume the responsibility and costs incurred for the manufacturing of recordings. Most licensing agreements permit a nonexclusive right to manufacture, distribute, and sell recordings within a specified region. Furthermore, this contract may stipulate that the record club may not market new **release**s before a specified period, usually after the release of a new album. Record clubs typically pay an **advance** to a licensor for the right to manufacture and sell recordings. This advance is often nonreturnable and is **recoupable** from royalties payable to the licensor under the agreement.

Key to the success of record clubs has been the convenience of receiving merchandise at home without the need to travel to brick-and-mortar stores. However, the advent of Internet has changed how record clubs function. Most Internet music retailers sell **MP3** files of music or offer subscriptions to member for use on electronic devices. Record clubs have seen their market share drop considerably. This may be in part due to the way consumers' purchase and use music or the heavily discounted prices offered by **retail** chains. In both cases, for many, the record club may be entering the end of their presence in the music retailing business.

See also: **album**; **AARC**; **breakage allowance**; **distribution**; **e-commerce**; **major record label**

Further reading: Bloom (2008)

RECORDING INDUSTRY ASSOCIATION OF AMERICA (RIAA)

A **trade association** made up of companies that manufacture and **release** recorded music.

The RIAA was founded in 1951 for companies engaged in the production and sale of recordings in the United States. As a trade association, the RIAA is not only involved in promoting the goals and interests of its members but is also actively involved in the protection of intellectual property rights in the United States and internationally, with the aim to reduce **piracy** and counterfeiting. The RIAA is also actively involved in the monitoring and review of laws, regulations, and policies that affect the interests of its members.

Throughout its history, the RIAA has been actively involved in curtailing piracy, bootlegging, and counterfeiting. Recently, the organization's efforts have focused on illegal music file sharing via **P2P** networks and home recording through the ripping of music CDs to portable players and computers. In an attempt to curtail unauthorized file sharing of recorded music, the RIAA has undertaken high-profile lawsuits against file-sharing service providers and individuals suspected to be involved in file sharing. The RIAA has also begun a campaign against Internet-based piracy companies in foreign countries. In 2006, the RIAA attempted to sue AllOfMP3. com, a Russian Web site operating from Moscow, claiming damages to the extent of $1.65 trillion. Although the suit did not come to court (the RIAA has no jurisdiction in Russia), U.S. trade negotiators warned Russia that the continued existence of AllOfMP3 could jeopardize Russia's entry into the World Trade Organization.

The RIAA is also actively involved in lobbying the U.S. Congress in developing legislation that prevents **copyright** infringement. As a trade association, the RIAA promotes the achievements of participants in sound recording by auditing and certifying gold (500,000 units sold), platinum (1,000,000 units sold), and diamond (10,000,000 units sold) for **album** sales in the United States. Between 2004 and 2006, the RIAA included digital sales and **ringtone** sales to their awards designation. As a nonprofit organization, a board of directors elected by RIAA members governs the RIAA. The RIAA is also affiliated with the **International Federation of the Phonographic Industry (IFPI)**.

See also: **copyright**; **DART**; **DMCA**; **IFPI**; **license**; **royalty**; **TRIPS**; **WIPO**; **WTO**

Further reading: Angwin (2006); Kao (2004); Tavani (2005)

RECOUPABLE

Costs and **advance** payments that are collected at a future date.

In a recording **contract**, recoupable costs are often associated with the production of a recording paid by a label and collected from an **artist**'s **royalty** income. As a means of "sharing" the risk inherent in the music industry, record labels will endeavor to include a range of items that can be recouped in negotiating a recording contract. These recoupable items range from advances paid to an artist as a signing bonus for recording expenses and **producer** fees. As recording contracts are highly negotiable, many artists will insist that advances be nonreturnable, which, in effect, means the advance is not recoupable and not to be paid from the artist's royalties. Other recoupable fees are often associated with the **marketing** of an album, including promotion, **music video** production, and **tour** costs.

Record labels justify passing these costs to an artist as a means of mitigating the upfront risk associated with the sale of recorded music. If an **album** is financially successful, the record label can regain its initial investment and will be keen to invest in future projects. Those opposed to this practice state that the financial burden of a recording is unfairly placed on an artist, who, for the most part, has no control in how an album is marketed or sold. Furthermore, those opposed to the practice point to the fact that recoupable expenses are often cross–collateralized against future albums, further indebting the artist to the recording label.

See also: **black box income**; **breakage allowance**; **controlled composition**; **distribution**; **mechanical rights**; **packaging cost deduction**; **reserves**; **statutory rate**

RELEASE

The **distribution**, sale, or publication of recorded music to the general public.

The establishment of a specific date allows a label to develop strategies and campaigns for the promotion and sale of a recording. In most recording contracts, a label is not obliged to release a recording. A record label may require contingencies to this agreement before releasing a recording: different formats of musical work that is sold; various market territories including new, unexplored regions; and promotional expenditure, which could high or low, corresponding to the type of territory where the product is intended to be promoted. This may include specific sale of a single before a label releases an **album**, and the album is released either internationally or nationally or distributed through a "major" distribution system. A label may justify the nonrelease of an album, as it may be deemed commercially unviable.

In an effort to force a label to release an album an artist may request a guaranteed release date. This clause establishes that all rights will be returned to the original **author** if a certain level of performance was not achieved by a publisher or record label. In a recording contract, this section may state that all rights would be returned to the author if a commercial recording were not released nationally within a specified period. Record labels may require an **artist** to return all **advance**s before allowing the band to reacquire all rights to their recording. A songwriter may include in a contract a release clause that would return all rights if **royalty** payments were not received within a specified period. In such cases an author would be permitted to seek offers from other organizations. A guaranteed release clause is often only granted to artists with an established recording history.

See also: **catalog**; **copyright**; **public domain**; **royalty**; **termination rights**

RESERVES

A record manufacturer's practice permitting retailers to return unsold merchandise for exchange or credit.

The return percentage allowed varies between manufacturers and ranges from 0 percent to 100 percent. As **artist**s are paid **royalties** based on the number of products sold (not shipped) manufactures withhold or reserve a percentage of the royalty payments as a means of compensation for returned goods. Often reserved royalties are withheld for a period of time before reverting back to the artist. In a recording **contract**, a record label can withhold the payment of royalties to an **artist** until unsold and returned **album**s have been accounted for. Also known as "Reserve for Returns," a recording company will base the withholding amount on their "best business judgment." Artists will often negotiate the removal of this clause or settle for a shorter withholding period from the date a recording has been shipped. Furthermore, artists will insist on a specific ceiling percentage as well as a period of time in which the label can withhold royalties. This practice is standard in most recording contracts, even in the case of electronic distribution.

See also: **distribution**; **independent record label**; **major record label**; **retail**

Further reading: Bhattacharjee (2006); Leeds (2008); Levy and Weitz (1995)

RETAIL

The sale of goods in small quantities for the direct consumption by the general public.

Traditionally, retailing consisted of the sales of goods or merchandise from a fixed location, such as a freestanding store or a department store. However, the advent of the World Wide Web has seen the development of online music retailing and **e-commerce**. The process of retailing, also known as the supply chain management, begins with a retailer buying goods or products in large quantities from a wholesaler, manufacturer, or from an importer. Once the retailer has received the goods, it will sell smaller quantities to the customer or the end-user. Retail classification is based on size, location, and function. At one end of the spectrum are small, "brick-and-mortar" stores run by individuals, often referred as "mom-and-pop" stores. Most mom-and-pop stores purchase recordings from **one-stop** distributors. Due to the limited floor space in these retailers, most have a limited specialized inventory catering to specific needs found in that region. Bricks and Click stores combine a physical presence and an online component. Often found near colleges are alternative stores. Alternative stores are heavily **consumer** oriented and often deal in second-hand recordings as well as other merchandise ranging from DVDs, books, action figures, and clothing. As with mom-and-pop stores, most of the new inventory is purchased from a one stop. Chain stores are multiple retail units that often operate under a common owner. These retail outlets rely on a central buying and controlling system to maximize profit margins. Finally, music megastores such as Tower Records (now defunct), Virgin, and HMV have developed a **catalog** selection that provide vast information on works sold, thus also providing the convenience of a one-stop shopping. These music retailers offer on average over 60,000 stock-unit items including recordings, books, and DVDs. However, with the advent of the Internet and legal and illegal downloading, many of these large retailers have closed. This declining trend has been exacerbated by the growth of recorded music sales in big-box retailers such as Wal-Mart, Target, and Best Buy. These retailers stock smaller units of recordings (on average of approximately 5,000 units in comparison to a Megastore carrying over 50,000 units), often using this section as a loss-leader to generate sales in other areas such as electronics. Another form of music retail are **record clubs**. This model allows record labels to sell directly to the retailer. Although deep discounts are offered to consumers due to efficiencies in distribution, today record clubs are declining due to increasing pressure from online music stores. Online retail has developed with the creation of **MP3** players such as Apple's iPod. Originally online retailers sold physical copies of CDs to consumers, but with the creation of the iPod and the corresponding digital media player application, iTunes, consumers can download music, music video, podcasts, and movies.

See also: **album**; **Audio Home Recording Act**; **breakage allowance**; **ERA**; **GERA**; **GATT**; **Harry Fox Agency**; **IFPI**; **Minimum Advertised Price (MAP)**; **NARAS**; **Published Price to Dealers (PPD)**; **rack jobber**; **RIAA**

Further reading: Bhattacharjee (2006); Fox (2005); Leeds (2008); Levy and Weitz (1995)

REVERSION

Within **copyright** law the right of an **author** to end the transfer of ownership in a copyright to a publisher or other organization.

Typically, this may occur during a 5-year period, 35 to 40 years after the transfer of all rights. The statutory rights or **termination rights** in publishing can be exercised during a 5-year period, 40 years after the date of transfer or 35 years after the date of first publication. In most situations, the reversion of all rights is negotiated through a contractual agreement. Publisher will often release a nonexclusive **license** if there are no unrecouped **advance**s outstanding.

See also: **catalog**; **copyright**; **public domain**; **royalty**; **termination rights**

Further reading: Halloran (2007); Passman (2006); Schulenberg (2005)

RIDER

A contractual amendment or attachment that lists additional provisions beyond the requirements found in an initial contract.

Typically found in live performance and **tour**ing contracts, riders cover specific technical requirements and issues dealing with the comfort of an **artist** on the day of a performance. Technical riders are provided to parties concerned well in advance of a performance. Riders dealing with hospitality issues are provided to venues or promoters closer to the date to the performance. Common hospitality rider requests include requests for specific foods and beverages, transportation, accommodation, complementary **ticket**s, and security. Technical riders cover issues such as sound reinforcement (PA systems, sound desks, microphones); monitor requirements, lighting, and backline (**venue** provides the equipment including sound, lighting and musical instruments); and risers, staging and crew. Merchandise rider provisions deal with the sale of merchandise at the venue, the method the merchandise is sold, and payment methods (venues usually chare 15% to 40% of gross sales from merchandise). **Ticket** rider provisions address issues such as complementary tickets, box office accounting, and use of tickets not sold.

See also: **agent**; **IATSE**; **manager**; **promoter**; **road manager**

Further reading: Brabec and Brabec (2006); Halloran (2007); Holden (1991)

RINGTONE

An audible sound made by a telephone to indicate an incoming call.

The term is used most often in regard to mobile or cell phones but may be applied to other personal digital assistants (PDA), pagers, and any other communication devices operating on wireless communication networks. The ringtone market has become an important income source for the music industry, especially with reduced CD physical sales. As cell phone usage grew, it became obvious that ringtone differentiation would become important. Modern cell phones support a wide frequency range that allows for several seconds of music to be played, both monophonically (single tones) and polyphonically (multiple simultaneous tones). This has led to the development of prerecorded ringtones (often known as trutones, song-tones, mastertones, or master ringtones) that consist of short samples of sound recordings.

Today cell phones come with a selection of built-in ringtones or accept new ones from one or more ringtone services that are down-loaded for a fee. The popularity of ringtones have been the driving force in the creation of m-commerce (mobile commerce) services via social media features such as composing, sharing, and rating ringtones. This further highlights vertical telecommunication convergence (crossing of multiple industries) as music companies are now integrating with tele-communication firms. Ringtone royalties are processed as a **mechanical license** through the **Harry Fox Agency** (**HFA**) for **distribution** between ringtone manufacturers and publishers. As with **phonorecord**s, standard **compulsory license** and statutory mechanical rates apply to ringtone sales, as they are considered to be digital phonorecord deliveries (PDPs). On October 3, 2008, the Copyright Royalty Board established a mechanical royalty rate of 24 cents per mastertone ring-tones from a full recording. Mono and polyphonic ringtones are not included. HFA **license**s also require the licensee to implement **Digital Rights Management** (**DRM**) systems to protect the copying of the ringtone.

Information for **royalty** payments from ringtones is collected by Nielsen and presented on the company's RingScan chart. RingScan, a division of Nielsen Entertainment, collects weekly sales data from mobile carriers and general retailer stores. Utilizing a product's UPC code at point-of-sale registers, **PRO**s use the information for estimating royalty payments. This information also forms the basis of *Billboard Magazine*'s weekly ringtone **chart**s.

See also: **ASCAP**; **BMI**; **circumvention**; **MP3**; **RIAA**

Further reading: Alderman (2001); Bhattacharjee (2006); Blockstedt (2006); Diese (2000); Fellenstein (2000); Hill (2003); McCourt (2005); McLeod (2005); Ouellet (2007); Rifkin 2001; Terranova (2000)

ROAD MANAGER

A person who organizes and coordinates the day-to-day business activities of a touring artist or band.

Responsibilities for a road manager vary from act to act depending on the scope and size of the tour in question. Nonetheless, road managers in general coordinate certain aspects of all tours. Often a road manager will be in charge of the advancing of show dates before a performer arrives at the designated **venue**. Duties required of a road manager, therefore, include making travel and hotel arrangements for the tour members, arranging the transportation of equipment and instruments, and overseeing the smooth transition from venue to venue. Other duties include hiring technical specialists for concerts including road crew or stage members; the coordination of an **artist**'s media obligations; and fulfilling contractual requirements set by performers, unions, and **promoters**. A road manager is also required to ensure that contractual **rider**s are adhered to and that tour members fulfill their contractual commitments. The road manager may also be in charge of collecting payments due to the artist at the show and distributing funds in line with union regulations. Managers who work with larger tours are often granted a greater degree of authority in tour operations. Compensation for a tour manager is often based on a weekly salary. In addition, a road manager may be given a per diem while on tour.

See also: **agent**; **IATSE**; **manager**; **venue**

Further reading: Ashton (2007); Kirchner (1994); Leeds (2007); Waddell, Barnet, and Berry (2007)

ROME CONVENTION

A 1961 international intellectual property agreement that set a minimum standard for the protection of performing rights.

Known officially as the Rome Convention for the Protection of Performers, Producers of Phonograms and Broadcasting Organizations, this convention is designed to protect physical manifestations of intellectual property such as LPs and audiocassettes. The convention was developed in response to the creation of tape recorders, which made the reproduction of sounds easier and cheaper than before, and to extend the legal protection offered to **artist**s beyond the **Berne Convention**.

The Rome Convention offers performers protected against certain acts not consented to such as **fixation** of their live performance and the reproduction of that performance. This protection includes secondary uses such as **broadcasting** of **phonorecord**s for commercial purposes. The convention also gave broadcasters protection from the reproduction of broadcasts without the permission of the owner (in such cases as the public performance where an entrance fee is charged). Although international in scope, the convention allowed for certain exceptions in national law. This included the use of excerpts for news purposes, the use of material for education purposes or scientific research, and the private use of protected materials. Protection under the Rome Convention lasts at least for 20 years from when fixation was made or when a performance or broadcast took place. Although the United States is not a signatory to the Rome Convention, recordings can receive "limited" protection in other member nations if they are **released** "within thirty days of its publication in a contracting State" (www.WIPO.int). The Rome Convention is monitored by **WIPO** jointly with the International Labour Organization (ILO) and the United Nations Educational, Scientific and Cultural Organization (UNESCO).

See also: **Buenos Aires Convention; copyright; DMCA; performing rights organization (PRO)**

Further reading: Biederman (1992); Wallis (1992)

ROYALTY

The payment or compensation for the use of a tangible or intangible asset.

In the music industry, this transaction occurs between a user (licensee) and an owner (licensor) for the sale or performance of the use of intellectual property. An **artist**'s royalty rate is determined through negotiation. Because music royalties are strongly linked to individuals, rates vary according to an artist's experience and past record in the music industry. Other variables in calculating a royalty rate include the market and demand structure of the market, territorial extent of the agreement, the inherent risk involved with a particular artist, and cost considerations. This last variable is an estimate of what it costs to recover the expense involved in creating a work. Royalties are determined as a percentage of gross or net sales derived from the use of an asset or a fixed price per unit sold. Other metrics used include royalty interest and the income stream of future royalty payments based on future production or revenues from a given **license**. Licenses are based on the term or length of time that the product can be used, the territory, type of product, and so on. Each term may be subject to separate license and royalty arrangements.

There are four forms of royalties used in the music industry. Each royalty is associated with a specific function within the music industry. **Mechanical royalties** are obtained from the sale of recorded music. Although originally reserved for the sale of physical recordings, such as CDs and Cassettes, today they cover an array of new media such as **ringtone**s, **music video**s, computer games, and musical toys. Royalties for **mechanical rights** are established by the Library of Congress for a **statutory rate**. Royalty rates are reduced to 75 percent under a **controlled composition** clause in a recording **contract**. Furthermore, royalty rates are further reduced after deductions for "packaging," "breakage," "promotion sales," and holdback for "returns." In the United States artists earn royalties amounting to 10 percent to 25 percent of the suggested **retail** price of the recording. Payments are managed by the **Harry Fox Agency** (**HFA**) in the United States. Mechanical royalty payments in the United States varies considerably from practices followed in other countries. HFA is the predominant licensor, collector, and distributor for mechanical royalties. HFA is a state-approved quasi-monopoly and acts in the interest of the composers/songwriters. HFA charges a 6 percent **commission** for the services provided. In the United Kingdom, the Mechanical-Copyright Protection Society (MCPS) collects royalties for the sale of CDs. The rate is 6.5 percent of retail price (8.5 percent of the published wholesale price). Other European **mechanical rights** organizations include SACEM in France, GEMA in Germany, and SFA in Italy. Performance royalties paid to music publishers and songwriters for the public performance of music. Royalties for **performance rights** are established by the Library of Congress' Copyright Royalty Board. Performance royalties include the performance of a song either live or broadcast both on traditional forms or through digital transmission (such as ringtones, downloads, and live Internet streaming), the performance through a physical media, and the playing of recorded music. Copyright Act of 1976 entitles owners of musical works royalties for the sale of recordings. Under this act, record labels and recording artists are not entitled to royalties from **radio** and TV broadcasts (unlike international standards where performers obtain royalties from over-the-air and digital **broadcasting**). The Digital Performing Right in Sound Recording Act granted copyright owners the exclusive license to perform by means of digital audio transmissions but exempted nonsubscription services. Compulsory royalty rate was to be shared at the following rates: 50 percent to the recording companies, 45 percent to featured artists, 2.5 percent to nonfeatured musicians through AFM (nonfeatured vocalists through **AFTRA**). The **DMCA** redefined the DPRA by expanding the statutory license to include three categories of licensees: preexisting satellite digital radio services, new subscription services, and nonsubscription transmission services. A fourth license was created permitting webcasters to make "ephemeral recordings" of a sound recording to facilitate streaming with a royalty to be paid (nonsubscription services qualify if they are non-interactive, do not exceed the sound recording performance complement, provide information on the song title and recording artist, and do not allow any request for songs). Interactive services allow a listener to receive a specially created Internet stream in which the listener dictates the songs to be played. Such services take the Web site out of the **compulsory license** requirement and require instead negotiations with the **copyright** owners. The United Kingdom adopted the **European Union Copyright Directive (EUCD)** in 2003. This includes **distribution** through the Internet as well as traditional media. Synchronized royalties are obtained from the use or adaptation of a musical score on movies, radio, and television commercials. Synchronized royalties are formally collected by Mechanical Rights Agencies and are negotiated between an owner and a licensee. Print royalties are obtained from the sale of sheet music, **folios**, and other printed editions of musical compositions. Royalty rates range between 10 percent and 25 percent of the retail price for each copy sold. Licensing, administration, and collection of royalties is handled through specialized publishing companies. Other royalties in the music industry include **producer** royalties, master recording license royalties, and **foreign royalties**. Producer royalties are given to producers of recordings who have entered into a contractual relationship with either the recording label or artists to assist in the production of **phonorecord**s. Typically a producer will receive a royalty of 2 percent to 4 percent of the retail price. Master recording license royalties are obtained from the sale of phonorecords through **record club**s. Foreign royalties are collected from the sale of music products in other countries. Mechanical royalties produced outside of the United States are negotiable (no compulsory licensing). The rate is based on the wholesale, retail, or suggested retail value of the CDs. Royalty rates are negotiated between companies and range from 7 percent to

20 percent of the suggested retail price for recordings (minus various deductions) and 50 percent to 75 percent for the sale of music compositions through **subpublishing** agreements.

Royalties are paid on a quarterly or semiannual basis. An artist will receive a royalty statement made by a licensee to a licensor or publishing company, including information on the source of income, costs, total sales, royalty rates, and amounts owed.

See also: **ASCAP**; **BMI**; **contract**; **independent record label**; **major record label**; **statutory rate**

Further reading: Hardy (1999); Harrower (2005); Keesan (2008); McCourt (2005); Michel (2006); Towse (1999)

SAMPLING

The process of taking a portion of a sound recording and using it as a new element in another composition.

Samples often consist of a small portion of a song, such as a melody (with or without lyrics) or rhythm that is integrated into a new composition. Sampling is typically achieved with a piece of hardware such as a computer or analog tape loops that consist of short phrases of instrumental, vocal, or even the spoken word in a repeated ostinato. Although sampling has been primarily associated with hip-hop, the technique has seen numerous applications in various genres, including classical music where it is the foundation of musique concrète.

Sampling has been a contentious issue from a legal perspective. Early sampling **artist**s used portions of other artists' recordings without permission. Even today, many musicians argue that digital sampling does not constitute copyright infringement because the final product differs from the original sample. Furthermore, this issue becomes more confusing when sampling is compared to remixing, which U.S. Copyright Law recognizes as a new derivative work. Today artists obtain prior authorization to use a sample. In an effort to legally use sampled music, artists and record labels will use a technique known as "clearing" to gain permission from copyright owners. Obtaining clearance requires paying either an up-front fee or a percentage of the **royalties** to the appropriate owner. However, there still exists the question of how much can be sampled, especially within the boundaries of the **fair-use** doctrine. The U.K.'s national copyright statue under the Copyright Designs and Patents Act (CDPA) does not explicitly define or address the issue of sampling. It does, however, provide the language that recognizes the storing of "the work in any mediums by electronic means" (www.opsi.gov.uk). Works under a Creative Commons license have tried to mitigate this problem by allowing sampling of a work, provided the resulting work is licensed under the same terms.

See also: **circumvention**; **creative commons**; **e-commerce**; **fair use**; **Intentional Inducement of Copyright Infringement Act**; **IFPI**; **peer-to-peer network**; **piracy**; **RIAA**; **TRIPS**

Further reading: Castillo (2006); Hesmondhalgh (2006); Sirois and Martin (2006)

SCALE

A specific hourly rate negotiated by a union for a specific task.

For most music unions, scale rates differ based on national and local unions. National scale is applied to various activities such as master recordings, low-budget master recordings, TV shows, and TV and **radio** commercials (jingles). Local scale often occurs for demo tapes used for publishing or **artist** development and are not for commercial **release**. Both the **American Federation of Musicians** (**AFM**) and the **American Federation of Television and Radio Artists** (**AFTRA**) have established scale rates with major labels for non**royalty** performers. The standard scale for a recording is measured as a period of time. If the recording exceeds this time limit, overtime must be paid to the artist. Additional to the standard scale are payments made that cover health, welfare, and a pension contribution. Cartage for certain instruments such as double base require higher-scale rates. There is also a specific payment for doubling when a musician performs on multiple instruments during the recording. Typically, this raises the scale by an additional 20 percent. Finally, special scale rates apply to musicians for dubbing (also known as overdubbing). AFTRA requires that a musician be paid "for a session as if each overtracking were an additional side" (www.AFTRA.org).

When evaluating scale payments individuals are categorized according to their responsibilities and status. AFTRA classifies members according to employment: soloists or groups, cast **album**s, choral performances of classical music, and so on. Side musicians receive a specific standard rate for recordings and live performance. In comparison leaders receive higher rates than side musicians. AFTRA rates for television and radio vary according to employment category (soloists, groups, narrators, etc.). AFTRA TV commercial scale depends on the advertisement duration, on- or off-camera appearance, **distribution** (national or regional), and the time of day in which the advertisement is aired.

Apart from designating basic rates for recordings and **broadcasting**, employers contribute to special funds set aside for union members. Employers who engage AFM members for a recording will also contribute to several funds including the AFM Phonograph Record Special Payments Fund, the Motion Pictures Special Payments Fund, and the Phonograph Record Trust Fund.

See also: **Associated Actors and Artists of America**; **major record label**; **phonorecord**; **producer**; **venue**

Further reading: Holland (2004)

SCALPING

The act of reselling **tickets** for live entertainment events at often higher prices than the established value.

Scalping, or touting as it is known in the United Kingdom, arises when the amount demanded for a ticket exceed the amount supplied, especially at sold-out events. Scalpers will often purchase tickets at face value and sell them inflated by several thousand percent when the supply of available tickets cannot meet demand. The purchasing of unauthorized tickets also may lead to the customer acquiring counterfeit tickets, which have no monetary value and are not accepted by a **venue**. In the United States scalping occurs on or near a venue (including adjacent parking lots that are officially part of the facility), at hotels, and through online entities such as eBay and may be prohibited by state law. Although these laws vary from state to state, the majority of U.S. states do not have laws in place to limit the value placed on the resale amount of event tickets or where and how these tickets should be sold. To circumvent prosecution of these laws, ticket brokers will sell tickets from out of state. Often conducted through the Internet, ticket brokering has fulfilled a reselling market due to lax state laws (in many states scalping is misdemeanor punishable with a minimal fine) limiting resale of tickets. Brokers often obtain tickets from **promoter**s, performers, and representatives of venues (including box office treasurers and ticket sellers). Legitimate ticket selling companies such as

Ticketmaster have created their own forums for the **distribution** of unwanted tickets. For example, TicketExchange is a fan-to-fan auction site that allows individuals to sell legitimately purchased tickets at set prices.

See also: **agent**; **piracy**

Further reading: Ashton (2007)

SESAC

Originally the Society of European Stage Authors & Composers, SESAC is a U.S. performing rights organization.

Founded in 1930, SESAC originally strove to support underrepresented European **artists** in the United States. Unlike the other two PROs in the United States, SESAC is a for-profit company and unlike its competitors doesn't offer open membership. SESAC **license**s performing rights to all types of genres for a period of five years. Annual fees paid by **radio** and television broadcasters are scaled according to two factors. The market classification (the population of a city where a broadcaster performs and for which receives FCC license and the advertising rate that the broadcaster charges. License fees for nonbroadcast users are based on criteria such as annual entertainment expenditures for hotels and nightclubs, and for auditoriums, fees are calculated on the seating **capacity** of the **venue**.

SESAC distributes **royalties** to members using an allocation system. Credit is based on the total number of **copyright**s, the growth of a **catalog**, promotional activity, and performances.

After deducting administration costs, SESAC grants points for members that equates into a monetary value. Royalties for television and film are calculated using a complex formula that includes a station count (networks receive higher credits than local broadcasters), use type (features, jingles, background, etc.), duration of a work, and the time of day the music was played. In calculating live-performance royalties, SESAC will take into account a venue's size and seating capacity as well as the relative "weight" of a performer. Those performers who are headlining a concert will receive 85 percent of the applicable concert credit, while supporting acts receive 15 percent of the available live concert credit value. For online radio SESAC makes use of **BDS** for some online radio stations, while the company relies on logs and **playlist**s for tracking and payment. In the case of **ringtone**s, SESAC relies on Nielsen's RingScan **chart**s. Because RingScan does not collect information on ringbacks and several other types of ring-tones, SESAC collects information directly from tracking ringtone performance and consumption data from major carriers. Satellite radio stations provide SESAC with information through electronic performance logs. Payments are made on a quarterly basis.

See also: **ASCAP**; **BIEM**; **BMI**; **copyright**; **GERA**; **publishing**

Further reading: Fujitani (1984)

SOUNDEXCHANGE

A nonprofit organization that collects, distributes, and negotiates digital performance royalties.

The **Recording Industry Association of America (RIAA)** originally established SoundExchange as an unincorporated division but it became an independent incorporated in 2003. The organization functions as a **performing rights organization (PRO)** for digital media. Sound recording **copyright** owners (SRCOs) and feature **artist**s are paid **royalties** for digital transmissions including satellite and internet **radio**.

The Digital Performance in Sound Recordings Act of 1995 and the Digital Millennium Copyright Act of 1998, changed the practice of collecting online royalties by granting SoundExchange sole rights to collect and distribute performance royalties accruing from statutory licenses awarded to online performances. A small administrative fee is deducted from an artist's royalties before they are distributed, with remainder being divided between the performing artists and the copyright owner. As the principal administrator of statutory licenses SoundExchange participates in establishing license rate increases. On May 1, 2007, SoundExchange and certain large webcasters agreed to pay minimum fees set by the Copyright Royalty Board. The Copyright Royalty Board (CRB) imposed a minimum fee of $500 per station or channel for all webcasters. The **Digital Media Association (DiMA)** negotiated and settled for a $50,000 fee "cap" for its members. SoundExchange also recently offered alternative rates and terms to certain eligible small webcasters, which allows them to calculate their royalties as a percentage of their revenue or expenses, instead of at a per-performance rate.

Royalties awarded from other countries are on the basis of the awarder entities' reciprocal agreements with SoundExchange for eligible international performances. Furthermore, SoundExchange makes **distribution** of the nonfeatured artist's share to **AFTRA** and **AFM**'s Intellectual Property Rights Distribution Fund. The SoundExchange Board of Directors oversees all operations of SoundExchange and is composed of 18 members.

See also: **airplay**; **ASCAP**; **BMI**; **broadcasting**; **FCC**; **marketing**; **playlist**; **performance rights**; **SESAC**

Further reading: Beville (1988); McBride (2007); Scholl (2008)

SOUNDSCAN

An information system that tracks the sale of music products from over 14,000 **retail** outlets in the United States and Canada.

SoundScan is owned by A.C. Neilson and collects weekly data from traditional retail stores, online-stores, and **venue**s. SoundScan tracks information via barcodes or universal product codes (UPCs) that cash registers use to register sales. This requires stores, both physical and Internet based, have a point-of-sale (POS) inventory system.

Though this includes all major brick-and-mortar retailers, it is not a 100 percent sample of record sales; it excludes music clubs as well as some independent retailers and online outlets. In comparison, the **Recording Industry Association of America**'s **(RIAA)** system is a 100 percent sample of shipments. In order for a retailer to become eligible for reporting, SoundScan requires that the retailer be in business for at least two years and that an annual fee be paid to have data recorded.

See also: **ASCAP**; **BMI**; **broadcasting**; **FCC**; **marketing**; **performance rights**; **playlist**; **SESAC**

Further reading: Beville (1988); Harrison (2007); McBride (2007)

STATUTORY RATE

A **mechanical license** rate established by the U.S. Copyright Office for the sale of recordings.

Established by the Copyright Act of 1909, the rate was set at 2 cents per copy, which prevailed until 1978. The Copyright Act of 1976 changed this and set the price at 2.5 cents per copy or 0.5 cents per minute. Rate increases for mechanical licenses are based on either mechanical rate adjustment proceedings or by the consumer price index (CPI). Since 2004 mechanical rate increases in the United States have been established by the **Copyright Royalty Board** (**CRB**) and have been linked to the CPI. The CPI measures the average price of consumer goods and services. Percentage changes in the CPI are used as a measure of inflation. The CPI is prepared monthly by the Bureau of Labor Statistics and the U.S. Department of Labor in the United States and the Office of National Statistics in the United Kingdom, and prior to CRB, it was the **Copyright Arbitration Royalty Panel** (**CARP**) that established statutory royalty rates.

See also: **artist**; **contract**; **first-sale doctrine**; **Harry Fox Agency**; **MP3**; **piracy**; **RIAA**

Further reading: Bunker (2002); Butler (2005); Kempema (2008); Khon and Khon (2002); Kretschmer (2000)

SUBPUBLISHING

A contractual relationship between a publisher and a foreign publisher for the exploitation, licensing, and collection of **royalties** in the foreign publisher's territory.

The growth of music markets internationally and the success of **artist**s on a global level have become an important source of income for recording and publishing companies. Apart from the **major record label**s or large publishing companies, most publishing companies do not have subsidiaries in a foreign country. Therefore, when a publisher wishes to have **copyright**s from its **catalog** exploited in other markets, it may enter into a subpublishing agreement. Subpublishing agreements may be for specific territories or worldwide. Foreign **agent**s are responsible for the **marketing** and promotion of the work in a specified country as well as the administration of mechanical, performance, and synchronized licenses.

Subpublishing **contract**s range between 1 and 5 years, with extensions depending on the success of the subpublisher exploiting the copyrights in their market. A subpublisher will pay an **advance** to the licensor for the right to represent the catalog in their territory. The amount of the advance depends on the territory and the potential of that market in terms of revenue. Advances in a subpublishing agreement are **recoupable** against future earnings. As with publishing, income in a subpublishing agreement is earned from performance and from mechanical and print royalties. A subpublisher's percentage is usually 20 percent but can range as high as 25 percent for royalties generated from the sale of music. Rates vary based on the type of **royalty** collected. If a publisher is a multinational company, payments are often based on **copublishing** agreement, with the local publisher keeping 50 percent of the earnings and remits the other half to the original publisher. If the publishing company owns foreign affiliates it can cross-collateralize royalties from country to country against advances paid in the original territory. If a publisher doesn't own its foreign affiliates, payment will be on the basis of wholesale or **retail** price.

In certain cases, a publisher may only use a foreign publisher as a collection agent. In this case a foreign publisher will collect monies earned in a specific territory after deducting administrative costs. Contracts are for 2 to 5 years with **commission**s ranging from 15 percent to 25 percent of gross collections.

See also: **ASCAP**; **author**; **best edition**; **BMI**; **copublishing**; **GERA**; **license**; **performance rights**; **performing rights organization (PRO)**; **SESAC**

Further reading: Flack (1989); Garofalo (1999); Morton and Koufteros (2008)

SYNCHRONIZATION LICENSE

The right under **copyright** law to synchronize music with motion pictures for the purpose of **distribution**.

In most cases, synchronization takes the form of a sound track of a movie or background music for television shows or commercials. Music publishers will **license** the synchronization rights in individual numbers and will sometimes license synchronization rights for complete works, subject to the approval of the creators and any preexisting grant from motion picture rights. As with dramatic (grand) rights, there are no set tariffs, compulsory rates, or industry standard rates. Each license is individually negotiated either on a multiterritorial basis or internationally. A publisher usually splits income with a writer 50/50 after deducting administrative costs. In negotiations, rates are often calculated on several factors, including the number of people who will see a work. Major studios will distribute a movie on an international basis, whereas independent studios may enter into a distribution deal with a major studio. Similarly, television operates on a national basis with networks and national cable stations or on a regional **broadcasting** basis.

Budget is another critical factor in determining synchronization rates. Feature films with multimillion dollar budgets usually offer a higher synchronization license than smaller budgets.

See also: **first-sale doctrine**; **Harry Fox Agency**; **MP3**; **nondramatic performance rights**

Further reading: DuBoff (2007); Jacobson (2007); Speiss (1997)

TERMINATION RIGHTS

A term used in **copyright** law that gives an **author** and his or her heirs the right to recapture copyrights after a specific period.

These rights include the termination and transfer of a copyright. In most cases an author will request that all rights in a work be transferred to themselves, as termination rights are inalienable (cannot be transferred). Most termination clauses are for publishing agreements, administration of publishing agreements, and **copublishing** agreements. The act of termination within these agreements has two steps: First, a notice of termination must be given to the previous publisher at least two years (but not more than 10 years) prior to the termination date. Second, a copy of the notice must be filed with the Copyright Office before the termination date. Failure to comply with these requirements can make the termination request null and void, with all rights reverted to the previous publisher.

In the United States, termination of a copyright depends on the date in which the work was filed with the Copyright Office. For works registered on or before December 31, 1977, there are four separate periods of protection: The first term, also known as "the initial term" or "original term," lasts for 28 years from the date of registration. The second term, known as the "renewal term," lasts for an additional 28 years. The third term of protection, namely, the "bonus term," lasts 19 years. The fourth term, known as the "extended term" or "bonus extended term," lasts 20 years. If a work is not renewed it automatically falls into **public domain**. This was altered to allow any copyright work registered between January 1, 1964 and December 31, 1977, to be automatically renewed. Under the Copyright Act of 1976, copyrights registered on or after January 1, 1978, have one period of protection, that is, life of the author plus 70 years. Unlike the previous system, there are no renewal periods of protection.

See also: **agent**; **artist**; **development deal**; **independent record label**; **license**; **major record label**; **royalty**

Further reading: Biederman (1992); Frith (1993); Halloran (2007); Holland (1994); Jones (1992); Negus (1992); Passman (2006); Schulenberg (2005); Wallman (1989)

TERRITORIAL RIGHTS

A contractual agreement that defines market rights in terms of territories.

As a standard clause, territorial rights appear in most recording, management, manufacturing, and publishing **contracts**. Territorial rights cover the **exclusive rights** to sell music in a particular country or region and collect monies from that process. Furthermore, territorial rights limit the extent an individual or company can operate. For example, lawyers in the United States are qualified to practice in a specific jurisdiction. An important factor in assigning territories in a contractual relationships are the various rules associated with that region.

With global markets expanding in the music industry, several international organizations deal with issues associated with fair trading on an international basis. The **World Intellectual Property Organization** (**WIPO**) is an international organization sponsored by signatories to the United Nations. WIPO seeks to promote the development and protection of intellectual property on a global basis. Organizations such as the **World Trade Organization** (**WTO**) negotiate trade rules, both globally and bilaterally (between countries), in an effort to reduce trade barriers between countries that inhibit global trade. Similarly, trade zones, such as the European Union (EU), and trade agreements, such as the North America Free Trade Agreement (NAFTA), endeavor to promote trade by reducing restrictions due to territorial boundaries between countries.

See also: **agent**; **artist**; **development deal**; **independent record label**; **GERA**; **license**; **major record label**; **royalty**; **subpublishing**

Further reading: Blunt (1999); McCalman (2006); Rietjens (2006)

TICKETING

The act of issuing tickets for admission to an event or live performance.

Tickets are sold either through a ticket agent or at the event. Ticket agents are individuals or organizations who resell tickets for live performances, usually on behalf of a **promoter** and **venue**. Large corporations, such as Ticketmaster, provide an array of ticketing options to audience members and venues.

Tickets are divided into several categories based on how a **consumer** can purchase them. Hard tickets are physical tickets sold at a venue's box office or by means of a secondary selling agent. Selling agents will print, distribute, and in some cases run the box office for a **commission**. Hard tickets require a customer to be physically present to obtain the tickets. Hard tickets are often lower priced, especially when the **artist** needs to **paper the house** or widen their fan base. A disadvantage of hard tickets has been the issue of **scalping**. Traditionally, scalping or touting involves the resale of tickets outside or near a **venue**. In an effort to curtail the sale of counterfeit or scalped tickets, many companies have begun to incorporate measures that make the reproduction of tickets difficult. These measures include barcodes or magnetic stripes that range from keeping simple information stored on them to higher-end preventative measures such as imbedded chips and holograms. Recently, in an effort to curtail physical ticket scalping and online ticket brokers, legitimate ticket companies such as Ticketmaster have created forums for the sale of unwanted tickets. These fan-to-fan auction sites allow individuals to sell legitimately purchased tickets at set prices, thereby bypassing inflated prices of scalpers.

Soft tickets are those sold online and away from the event's venue. This is done by a ticketing agencies such as Ticketmaster or by the venue itself through a dedicated Web page. This type of digital ticketing has several advantages over the traditional hard tickets. First, they are secure. It is very difficult for scalpers to alter or counterfeit a digital ticket. Second, they are portable. Their online capability allows for a greater ability to tap into any potential market of consumers. Finally, digital tickets provide the agent or event the ability to obtain funds and an increase in ticket sale almost instantly. This gives a real-time, actual accounting of all tickets sold. This has advantages for accounting and promotion of a performance, especially for music genres dependent on live performances, such as classical music.

Tickets may also have a payment status, paid or unpaid, or reservation status, waitlisted, reserved, or canceled. The status may be changed dynamically. In addition, the ticket ownership can be rewritten when the ticket is transferred. However, it is difficult to allow these changes while still guaranteeing security.

See also: **agent; AFM; FTC; festival; four walling; IATSE; papering the house; road manager**

Further reading: Ashton (2007); Leeds (2007)

TOUR

A series of concerts by a musician, musical group, or both, in different cities or locations.

As an important source of income, tours can last several months and be global in scope. For many **artist**s a tour can be an important source of income or a means to establishing national recognition. Many tours are used as a platform by record labels and artists for the promotion of a new **album**. Often international tours generate millions of dollars in **ticket** revenues as well as income derived from merchandise and ancillary sources such as films, and recordings.

The length of a tour and the number of engagements performed is determined by several factors, including the popularity of the bands performing, the finances, and the public demand. Therefore, an international tour by a major artist may last from few weeks to several months. Balancing the potential profit from a tour, a concert **promoter** must control expenses. Expenses may come from a variety of sources. Salaries are mostly paid for road crew members, security, and concessionaires. Salaries and other wages are often dictated by unions such as the **American Federation of Musicians (AFM)**. Other expenses, such as equipment, transportation, and boarding, are rented from various sources.

Concert tours are often administered on the local level by concert promoters. It is a promoter's job to organize the number and types of performances, the quality and location of performance **venue**s, and all travel and accommodation arrangements. Tour promoters also require a thorough knowledge of various aspects of venues, including acoustics, size of staging area, need for warm-ups, rehearsals, and changing rooms.

See also: **agent; AFM; FTC; festival; four walling; IATSE; papering the house; road manager**

Further reading: Ashton (2007); Kirchner (1994); Leeds (2007); Waddell, Barnet and Berry (2007)

TRADE ASSOCIATION

An organization that promotes a particular trade or profession within a specific industry.

Trade organizations are usually established by corporations that operate in a specific sector and they promote a specific industry though information dissemination, lobbying, and **public relations** campaigns. Often trade associations act as **guild**s by establishing standardization within a particular trade. This not only establishes minimum requirements for a particular field but also acts as a barrier restricting external companies from entering into a particular market. Public relations activities of trade associations range from advertising and educational programs to political donations and lobbying. Lobbying activities of trade associations often take the form of contributions to selected candidates through Political Action Committees (PACs) in return for support on legislation that influences the trade association. The support of public policy has sparked controversy on the purpose and function of trade associations. Non-public-relation activities of trade associations include collaborative activities between members of a similar trade both on a national and international level. Associations may offer other services, such as producing conferences, networking, or charitable events, or offering classes or educational materials.

As most trade associations in the United States are nonprofit organizations they are governed by bylaws and a board of directors elected by the general membership. Membership is usually open to individuals and corporations that operate within a particular area. Fees collected from these organizations are used to run and administer the trade associations programs and activities.

Most noticeable music trade associations in the United States include the **Recording Industry Association of America (RIAA)**, the **National Association of Recording Merchandisers (NARM)**, the **National Academy of Recording Arts and Sciences (NARAS)**, and the **Digital Media Association (DiMA)**.

See also: **AGMA**; **ERA**; **GERA**; **IATSE**; **IFPI**

Further reading: Armbrust (2004); De Veuax (1988); Passman (2006), Seltzer (1989)

TRADEMARK

A distinctive word, logo, design, or symbol used by a business organization or other legal entity that uniquely identifies a product and or service to **consumer**s.

Qualification for trademark protection may be applied to any sign that is capable of performing the essential trademark function. This includes a range of nonconventional signs such as shapes (three-dimensional trademarks), smells, tastes, and perhaps even texture. In order to obtain full protection, a trademark must be registered often with a governmental agency. In the United States trademarks are registered with the Patent and Trademark Office, whereas in the United Kingdom trademarks are established through the U.K. Intellectual Property Office.

As with a **copyright**, a registered trademark confers a bundle of **exclusive rights** upon the registered owner. These rights include the exclusive use of the mark in relation to specific products or services. Trademarks, like copyrights, are protected from any unauthorized use of the mark in relation to products or services, which are identical or similar to the "registered" products or services. This not only protects the company from unauthorized use, but, more importantly, protects the consumer who may get confused about the identity of the source or origin.

The ™ symbol is used when trademark rights are claimed in relation to a mark. However, this symbol does not indicate whether a mark has been registered with a government trademark office of a particular country or jurisdiction. When a mark has been registered a company may use the ® symbol as an indication.

The owner of a registered trademark may commence legal proceedings for trademark infringement to prevent unauthorized use of that trademark. However, registration is not required. The owner of a common law trademark may also file suit, but an unregistered mark may be protected only within the geographical area within which it has been used or in geographical areas into which it may be reasonably expected to expand. Trademarks rights must be maintained through actual lawful use of the trademark. These rights will cease if a mark is not actively used for a period of time, normally 5 years in most jurisdictions. In the case of trademark registration, failure to actively use the mark in the lawful course of trade or to enforce the registration in the event of infringement may also expose the registration itself to become liable for the removal from the register after a certain period on the grounds of "nonuse."

In the United States, failure to use a trademark for this period, aside from the corresponding impact on product quality, will result in abandonment of the mark, and consequently, any party may use the mark. An abandoned mark is not irrevocably lost in the **public domain**; instead, it may be reregistered by any party that has reestablished exclusive and active use or is associated or linked with the original mark owner. If a court rules that a trademark has become "generic" through common use (such that the mark no longer performs the essential trademark function and the average consumer no longer considers the exclusive rights attach to it), the corresponding registration may also be ruled invalid. When a trademark is used in relation to services rather than products, it may sometimes be called a service mark.

Trademarks are inherently limited by territorial application, often on a national basis. With the advent of globalization, a range of international trademark laws and systems has come into force to facilitate the protection of trademarks. The **World Trade Organization (WTO)** agreement on **Trade-Related Aspects of Intellectual Property Rights** (TRIPS) establishes legal compatibility between member jurisdictions by requiring the harmonization of applicable laws. Article 15(1) of TRIPS provides a definition for a "sign" that is used as or forms part of the definition of "trademark" in the trademark legislation of many jurisdictions around the world.

See also: **audiovisual work; best edition; collective work; compulsory license; contract; Copyright Royalty Arbitration Panel (CARP); Copyright Royalty Board (CRB); Copyright Term Extension Act; creative commons; dramatic rights; first-sale doctrine; IFPI; RIAA**

Further reading: Burshtein (2005); Myers (1996)

TRADE-RELATED ASPECTS OF INTELLECTUAL PROPERTY RIGHTS (TRIPS)

A comprehensive international agreement that established minimum standards for international intellectual property regulation.

Administered by the **World Trade Organization (WTO)**, TRIPS was negotiated at the conclusion of the Uruguay Round of the **General Agreement on Tariffs and Trade** (GATT) in 1994 and introduced intellectual property law into the international trading system. As TRIPS is a compulsory requirement for WTO membership, any country seeking to obtain access to international markets established by the WTO must enact the strict intellectual property laws mandated by TRIPS.

The treaty contains laws that cover a variety of areas such as **copyright** protection for performers, producers of sound recordings, and **broadcasting** organizations. The agreement also sets standards for **trademark**, patent, geographical indication, and industrial design protection. An important principle of the TRIPS agreement is that intellectual property should "contribute to technical innovation and the transfer of technology, both for producers and users" (www.wto.org).

TRIPS in general includes topics on enforcement procedures, remedies, and arbitration measures among member nations. Under TRIPS copyright terms must extend to 50 years after the death of the **author**. As with the **Berne** Convention, copyright protection is granted automatically for fixed works, however, not on formalities such as registration or renewal. Producers of phonograms have the right to authorize or prohibit direct or indirect reproduction of their phonograms. Within the TRIPS agreement a producer may prohibit the reproduction of a recording on the basis that the work distorts, mutilates, or modifies the original, thus violating the producer's **moral rights**. Equitable remuneration of right holders in respect of the rental of phonograms may be maintained if the rental of phonograms does not impair the **exclusive rights** of reproduction of right holders. The **fair-use** doctrine used in TRIPS is dependent on the Berne Convention three-step test. Finally, TRIPS provided performers the protection from unauthorized recording of live performances.

Unlike other treaties on intellectual property, TRIPS has a powerful enforcement mechanism. States can be disciplined through the WTO's dispute settlement mechanism. All parties have a right issue a written notice that includes sufficient information on the claims. This procedure also requires all parties to substantiate their claims and to present relevant evidence. Remedies for violating intellectual property law include injunctions, such as ordering a party to desist from an infringement, compensation for the damage or loss the right holder has suffered as a result of the infringement, the recovery of profits lost, and expenses incurred during the trial. The TRIPS agreement also provides the right to order that pirated or counterfeited material be disposed or destroyed. Under the convention willful copyright **piracy** on a commercial scale can be considered a criminal offence.

Although TRIPS has a broad overarching framework, new developments and use of technology have surpassed this legal instrument's original scope. This includes areas such as sampling, which has not been clearly addressed in this document and goes against TRIPS's primary intent of harmonizing international intellectual property law. Furthermore, this situation results in the implementation of a weaker national legislation on copyright enforcement, thus preventing uniform application of copyright protection among member states.

See also: **circumvention**; **creative commons**; **e-commerce**; **fair use doctrine**; **Intentional Inducement of Copyright Infringement Act**; **IFPI**; **peer-to-peer network**; **piracy**; **RIAA**; **sampling**

Further reading: Adeloye (1993); Castillo (2006); Dutfield (2005); Kretschmer (2000); Maskus (2000); Rietjens (2006); Shadlen (2007); Ullrich (2003)

UNIVERSAL COPYRIGHT CONVENTION (UCC)

An international convention established by the United Nations Educational, Scientific and Cultural Organization (UNESCO) for the protection of **copyright**.

Adopted in 1952, the UCC functioned as an alternative to the **Berne Convention** in an attempt to enable several countries such as the Union of Soviet Socialist Republics (USSR) and the United States to adhere to a multilateral treaty on copyright protection. Consequently, the United States was able to retain much of its copyright protection without major modification to its copyright law. Although the UCC expanded international copyright law, many Berne Convention states were concerned that members may renounce the Berne Convention in favor of the UCC. To mitigate a migration to the UCC a clause was included in the treaty that penalized states for such action. As with the Berne Convention, the UCC provided protection to **author**s and other copyright owners of literary, scientific, and artistic works, including musical, dramatic, and cinematic works. The UCC requires as a condition of copyright protection the compliance that states must abide by formalities such as deposit, registration, notice, notaries certificates, and payment of fees as would apply in a specific contracting state. For a work to obtain copyright protection under the UCC it must contain a copyright notice and be registered at the copyright office of the signatory nation. In contrast, the Berne Convention provides copyright protection for a single term based on the life of the author and does not require registration or the inclusion of a copyright notice.

In 1989, the United States became a willing partner to the Berne Convention under the Berne Convention Implementation Act and changed its copyright laws as required. With most states being members of the **World Trade Organization (WTO)** and the ratification of the Agreement on **Trade-Related Aspects of Intellectual Property Rights (TRIPS)**, the UCC no longer has significance as an international convention.

See also: **Buenos Aires Convention**; **copyright**; **DMCA**; **performing rights organization (PRO)**

Further reading: Adeloye (1993); Dubin (1954); Koelman (2006); Wallman (1989)

VENUE

A fixed physical entity where an organized gathering, such as a concert or other musical performance, takes place.

Venues are categorized by several factors, including capacity, music genre, location, and permanent status. Size plays an important role in the function and musical style performed at a venue. Smaller venues often have a duel function. Typical to this category are nightclubs, clubs, bars, coffee houses, and restaurants that not only offer food and beverages but may also have live music performed on a regular basis. These venues also tend to cater to a single genre of music, for example, jazz clubs or folk music in coffeehouses. Medium-sized venues tend to exhibit a wider array of genres. Some of the larger concert halls cater to only one genre, for example, opera houses, which traditionally were designed only for opera performances. In an effort to keep a venue profitable, many opera houses today are part of larger performing arts centers that offer a range of performing arts including theater and opera. Another variable for categorizing venues is permanence. The majority of venues are permanent structures; however, temporary venues exist, often in conjunction with specific purposes or genres. An example of a temporary venue are those associated with **festivals**. They often have a dual function, such as a sports stadium or a farm as in Woodstock festival. Temporary venues are those that cater to seasonal requirements, especially in regard to summer performances such as Tanglewood in Massachusetts. Music venues may be the result of private or public enterprises. A recent trend within folk music are house concerts. These are performances at an individual's house, usually a living room or outdoors. They are sponsored by a community, neighborhood, or state folk alliance.

Venues generate revenue through attendance. Apart from the venue generating income directly from attendance and any other ancillary items, such as food and liquor at clubs, venue owners have various formulas for leasing their space. Most common is a flat fee charged to a promoter or performer. In this arrangement, the venue will charge a fee for use of the space, security, box office staff, clean up, stage hands, and so on. A simplified version of a flat fee is **four walling** or the four-walls deal, in which the venue will charge the promoter only for the space and not include any ancillary services. In an effort to increase possible future profits and reduce risks, a venue owner may enter into an agreement with a promoter. Methods of this type of agreement run from a simple split of the tickets sold to flat fee against a percentage of the door (the venue obtains whichever is greater) or payment after the promoter has broken even. Associated with attendance is the sale of tickets. Ticket sales are not only important in securing a venue by only allowing those who have a genuine ticket to enter the venue and generating income but they can also be used as a means of measuring actual attendance, thus guaranteeing fair payment to all parties concerned. Tickets may be bought in advance of a performance, both for individual use and for group use. The advantage of advance tickets is that organizations, especially those in the performing arts and seasonal venues, can improve their cash flow during the off season. An incentive for subscription or advance ticket purchases are deep discounts that range from 10 percent to 50 percent. In contrast to the sale of advance tickets, walk-up tickets are sold only on the day of the performance. Although certain venues rely on walk-ups, it is not a reliable method as numerous external variables, including weather, can impact the sale of tickets. Tickets are also classified according to physical characteristics. Hard tickets are physical tickets sold at a venue's box office or by means of a secondary selling agent. Selling agents will print, distribute, and, in some cases, run the box office for a commission. Unlike soft tickets, hard tickets require a customer to be physically present to obtain the tickets. Hard tickets are often lower priced, especially when the artist needs to **paper the house** or widen their fan base. Electronic tickets or e-ticket are e-mailed to the purchaser, who is then able to print it or e-mail it to a friend who may use it. The printed e-ticket contains a unique barcode that is scanned upon entry to the event. Once it is scanned, the ticket is no longer useable. Buyers benefit from the assurance of obtaining an authentic ticket for an event.

See also: **AFM**; **FTC**; **festival**; **four walling**; **IATSE**; **papering the house**; **promoter**; **road manager**

Further reading: Ashton (2007); Kirchner (1994); Leeds (2007); Waddell, Barnet, and Berry (2007)

WEIGHTING FORMULA

A method used by **performing rights organization**s (**PROs**), such as **ASCAP, BMI,** and **SESAC** to distribute **royalties** to members.

Designed as an efficient survey and **distribution** system, a PRO's weighting rules and formulas enable them to track music used on **radio**, television, the Internet, live performances, and other media. The goal of collecting this data is the distribution of appropriate royalty payments to **copyright** owners. These payments are meant to fairly reflect the value of performances on various media. Royalty distribution, therefore, reflects the **license** fees paid by or attributable to users in that medium. According to ASCAP, different types of performances have different values, even within the same medium. ASCAP conducts periodic sample surveys of performances of its members to determine each member's share of a royalty. An ASCAP Classification Committee takes into consideration several factors in determining a royalty payment. These include factors related to the work itself, such as the nature of the work (any work that is hummed or whistled on camera in a television program is not considered a feature performance and has a lower ranking in the evaluation process; www.ASCAP.com), its length, and its **originality**. A member's **catalog** influences a weighting formula such as the nature, character, and prestige of the works within the catalog. External influences include the popularity of a work in the current market, the time of day a work is performed, the type of media used, and the use of the music such as feature performances, cues, jingles, advertising, and so on. For example, a work performed on a public television program between 6:00 a.m. and 12:59 a.m. will receive 100 percent of the applicable credit. If the same work was performed on other television programs, it would only receive 100 percent of the applicable credit if it was performed between the hours of 7:00 p.m. and 12:59 a.m. (www.ASCAP .com). All distributions are fully and clearly disclosed to all members by their respective PRO. A review board using an arbitration mechanism is established to resolve members' complaints in regard to distribution of revenues.

Weighting formulas came into existence after an amended final judgment in 1950 when the U.S. Court of Appeals for the Second District ordered that ASCAP's distribution to members be made "on a basis which gives primary consideration to the performance of the compositions of the members as indicated by objective surveys of performances periodically made by or for ASCAP" (United States v. ASCAP, ¶62,595, S.D.N.Y. 1950). A 1960 order required that performance surveys be conducted and revenue distribution be made to ASCAP members on the basis of an objective scientific survey, replacing a somewhat arbitrary survey that gave undue emphasis to network **broadcasting** performances. The survey put into effect an initial "Weighting Formula" to be used by ASCAP when determining the amount of distribution to be made to each member.

See also: **publishing**; **royalty**; **subpublishing**

Further reading: Fujitani (1984)

WORK-MADE-FOR-HIRE

A work prepared by an employee or a commissioned work to an individual, corporation, or organization where the parties agree that composition is for hire.

Under the U.S. Copyright Act of 1976, a work-made-for-hire (work for hire or corporate authorship) is an exception to the general rule that the person who actually creates a work is the legally recognized **author** of that work. This principal allows for corporations, employers, and individuals other than the creator to purchase a work and obtain the rights and privileges associated with copyright ownership. As such, the creator may or may not be publicly credited for the work. Generally, a work-made-for-hire is specially ordered or commissioned for use as a contribution to a **collective work**, such as part of a motion picture or other **audiovisual work**. Terms of the use and ownership of the work are expressed in an advanced written agreement between the parties. In complex works, which contain multiple copyrighted works, for example, a film, it is in the company's best interest to control the copyright of all elements—film, music, choreography, and so on—so that the entity cannot be limited by individual sections. Furthermore, if there is no work-made-for-hire a company may be forced to rely on an implied license, thereby reducing the hiring party's rights to alter, update, or transform the work for which it paid. Certain circumstances allow the creator of a composition the ability to retain some rights to the material following this **assignment**, either through provisions of a **contract** surrounding the assignment or through statute. For example, the Copyright Act of 1976 and the "Sonny Bono" **Copyright Term Extension Act of 1998** increased U.S. copyright terms and allowed creators of preexisting works to reclaim the copyright when the previous shorter term would have expired.

In the United States a "work-made-for-hire" (published after 1978) attracts a special copyright duration, of either the shorter period of 95 years from publication or 120 years from creation. This extends the life of a work from the standard copyright duration of life of the author plus 70 years. In the European Union the duration of protection is in general the same as the copyright term for a personal copyright, 70 years from the death of the author, or in the case of works of joint authorship, 70 years from the death of the last surviving author. The **Berne Convention** for the Protection of Literary and Artistic Works recognized "**moral rights**" as including the right of the actual creators to publicly identify themselves as such and the ability to maintain the integrity of the work.

See also: **Berne Convention**; **copyright**; **moral rights**

Further reading: Blume (2000); Brabec and Brabec (2006); Frith (1988); Holland (2000)

WORLD INTELLECTUAL PROPERTY ORGANIZATION (WIPO)

A United Nations (UN)–operated specialized agency created in 1967 "to encourage creative activity, to promote the protection of intellectual property throughout the world" (www.WIPO.int).

Located in Geneva, Switzerland, WIPO has over 180 member states and administers over 20 international treaties. As the organization is not an elected body, it attempts to reach decisions by consensus. Unlike other UN organizations, WIPO allows one vote to each member, regardless of population or contribution to the organization. WIPO works with a wide spectrum of stakeholders, including other intergovernmental organizations, nongovernmental organizations, and representatives of civil society and industry groups.

WIPO's purpose is to promote the development of intellectual property legislation, standards, and procedures among its member states. This includes further development of international laws and treaties regarding patents, **trademarks**, **copyright,** and related rights. The organization administers important intellectual property treaties including the **Berne Convention**, the Phonogram Convention, the Paris and **Rome Conventions**, and the **WIPO Copyright Treaty and Performances and Phonograms Treaty**.

WIPO meetings regularly bring together stakeholders from governments, rights holders' groups and civil society in order to facilitate constructive debate on current challenges. The organization has several important committees in which issues related to international intellectual property are resolved. The Standing Committee on Copyright and Related Rights (SCCR) deals with all copyright issues, and the Advisory Committee on Enforcement (ACE) coordinates with certain organizations and the private sector to combat counterfeiting and **piracy** activities, public education, and exchange of information on enforcement issues through the establishment of an electronic forum. WIPO is largely self-financing. About 90 percent of the organization's budgeted expenditure comes from earnings from the services that WIPO provides to users of the international registration systems. The remaining 10 percent is made up of revenue from WIPO's arbitration and mediation services, sales of publications, and contributions from member states.

See also: **Buenos Aires Convention**; **copyright**; **DMCA**; **performing rights organization (PRO)**

Further reading: Blunt (1999); Castillo (2006); Maskus (2000); Masson (2002); McCalman (2006); Rietjens (2006)

WIPO COPYRIGHT TREATY

An international **copyright** treaty adopted by member states of the **World Intellectual Property Organization (WIPO)** in 1996.

The WIPO Copyright Treaty provides protection for copyright due to advances in information technology. The treaty requires that member states provide adequate protection for software by prohibiting devices used for circumventing protective measures such as digital management. This includes the prohibition of **circumvention** of technical protection measures, even where such circumvention is used in the pursuit of legal and **fair-use** rights. Furthermore, the treaty ensures that computer programs are protected as literary works and that arrangement and selection of material in databases are protected. The treaty also provides **author**s control over the rental and distribution of their works, measures not protected under the **Berne Convention**. In this treaty there is no reference to copyright term extension beyond the existing terms of the Berne Convention. The WIPO Copyright Treaty was implemented in the United States through the **Digital Millennium Copyright Act (DMCA)** of 1998. During the same week, the United States passed both the Digital Millennium Copyright Act (DMCA) and **Copyright Term Extension Act**, extending the copyright term beyond the Berne Convention. The European Union had adopted the Directive Harmonizing the Term of Copyright Protection in 1995. In 2000, the European Council approved the treaty on behalf of the European Union.

See also: **Buenos Aires Convention**; **copyright**; **DMCA**; **performing rights organization (PRO)**

Further reading: Blunt (1999); Flint (2004); McCalman (2006); Rietjens (2006)

WIPO PERFORMANCE AND PHONOGRAMS TREATY

An international treaty signed by the members of the **World Intellectual Property Organization (WIPO)** in 1996.

The treaty was created to address numerous issues in regard to economic, cultural, and technological developments affecting the rights of performers and producers of **phonorecord**s. This treaty endeavors to maintain a balance between the creators of phonorecords and the interests of the public, especially in regards to education, research, and access to information, in regards to the **fair-use** doctrine.

The WIPO Performance and Phonogram treaty granted performers four kinds of economic rights in their performances fixed on a phonorecord. First, the treaty provides performers with the right to authorize direct or indirect reproduction of phonogram in any manner or form. Second, this treaty provides a performer the right to distribute the original phonogram and copies through the sale or other transfer of ownership. Third, the treaty provides a performer the right to commercially rent the original and copies of a phonogram to the public, as determined in the national law of signatory nations. Finally, the WIPO treaty provides a performer the right to make available a performance fixed on a phonogram via wire or wireless means. Specifically, this right covers on-demand and interactive performances available through the Internet. To protect the right of performance over the Internet, the Performance and Phonogram Treaty obliges contracting parties to provide legal remedies against the **circumvention** of technological measures. This includes the removal or altering of information (rights management information) indicating the identity of a performer, producer, or phonogram used for licensing or the collection and distribution of **royalties**. The treaty also established that the term of the protection should be for a period of 50 years from **fixation** of the phonorecord. Finally, regardless of a performer's economic rights, the treaty upheld the **moral rights** of an **author** against any distortion, mutilation, or modification of their work that would be "prejudicial" to their reputation.

In 1998, the United States implemented sections of the WIPO Performances and Phonograms Treaty into the **Digital Millennium Copyright Act (DMCA)** via the WIPO Copyright and Performance and Phonograms Treaties Implementation Act. Apart from the rights set forth in the WIPO treaty, the DMCA provided additional protection against the circumvention of copy prevention systems and prohibited the removal of **copyright** management information.

See also: **Berne Convention**; **Buenos Aires Convention**; **copyright**; **DMCA**; **performing rights organization (PRO)**

Further reading: Blunt (1999); McCalman (2006); Masson (2002); Rietjens (2006); Zohar (2005)

WORLD TRADE ORGANIZATION (WTO)

An international organization designed to promote and enforce trade agreements between member nations.

Established as a successor to the **General Agreement on Tariffs and Trade** (**GATT**), the WTO was founded in 1995. Most of the WTO's rulings are based on polices negotiated during the Uruguay Round and earlier negotiations under GATT.

The stated goal of the WTO is the improved welfare of people within its membership. The WTO achieves this goal by ensuring "that trade flows as smoothly, predictably and freely as possible" (www.WTO.org). This mission is framed within five principles that form the core functions of the organization. The first principle is nondiscrimination between countries in regards to intellectual property. This principle is divided into two categories, the most-favored-nation rule that requires a nation to apply the same conditions on all trades to other WTO members, and the national treatment policy, which means that both imported and locally produced goods should be treated equally. The second principle is reciprocity between members for access to foreign markets. The third principle states that all commitments are binding and enforceable. The fourth principle is transparency between members. Finally, the fifth principle is the establishment of safety values that provide members the opportunity to restrict trade for economic reasons. The WTO does not offer member nations a forum for the negotiation and implementation of trade agreements; nevertheless, it acts as an arbitrator for disputes between member nations. Apart from negotiating and implementing trade agreements, the WTO requires members to apply **Berne Convention** standards in their **copyright** laws.

Other important WTO treaties that affect the music industry include the General Agreement on Trade in Services (GATS), which provides a system for merchandise trade, especially for services. Prior to the WTO's Uruguay Round, services were not included in international trade agreements. This agreement has opened world markets to the development of information technologies and the Internet. Another important agreement that has implications for the music industry is the **Trade–Related Aspects of Intellectual Property Rights (TRIPS)** agreement. TRIPS contains requirements that member nations must meet for copyright rights, geographical indications, **trademark**s, and patents. Finally, the Technical Barriers to Trade (TBT) agreement ensures that technical negotiations and standards, as well as testing and certification procedures, do not create unnecessary obstacles to trade between member nations.

See also: **Buenos Aires Convention**; **copyright**; **DMCA**; **performing rights organization (PRO)**

Further reading: Blunt (1999); Castillo (2006); Kirkham (2002); McCalman (2006); Maskus (2000); Rietjens (2006)

Bibliography

Aaker, D.A., Kumar, V., and Day, G.S. (1998) *Marketing Research*, 8th edn, Chichester: John Wiley.

Adeloye, A. (1993) 'The Uruguay Round: A Discussion of the Trade Related Aspects of Intellectual Property Rights,' *Journal of Information Science*, 19(5): 395–400.

Adorno, T.W. (1941) 'On Popular Music,' *Studies in Philosophy and Social Sciences*, 9: 17–48.

Alderman, J. and Schwartz, F.E. (2001) *Sonic Boom: Napster, MP3, and the New Pioneers of Music*, New York: Perseus.

Allen, R. (1987) *Challenges of Discourse: Television and Contemporary Criticism*, London: Methuen.

Alliance of Artists and Recording Companies (2007) Available at: www.aarcroyalties.com (accessed August 30, 2008).

American Federation of Musicians (2007) Available at: www.afm.org (accessed August 30, 2008).

American Federation of Television and Recording Artists (2007) Available at: www.Aftra.com (accessed August 30, 2008).

American Guild of Musical Artists (2007) Available at: www.agma.org (accessed August 30, 2008).

American Society of Composers, Authors and Publishers (2007) Available at: www.ascap.com (accessed August 30, 2008)

Andersen, B., Hesbacher, P., Etzkorn, K.P., and Dennisoff, R.S. (1980) 'Hit Record Trends, 1940–1997,' *Journal of Communication*, 30(2, Spring): 31–43.

Andersen, C. (2006) *The Long Tail: Why the Future of Business is Selling Less of More*, New York: Hyperion.

Angwin, J. (2006) 'Record Labels Turn Piracy Into a Marketing Opportunity,' *Wall Street Journal*, 248(92): B1.

Appadurai, A. (ed.) (1986) *The Social Life of Things: Commodities in Cultural Perspective*, Cambridge: Cambridge University Press.

———. (1990) 'Disjuncture and Difference in the Global Cultural Economy,' *Theory, Culture and Society*, 7: 295–310.

162

Arbitron (2008) Available at: www.arbitron.com (accessed August 30, 2008).

Armbrust, R. (2004) 'AFTRA, AFM Push FCC,' *Back Stage*, 45(51): 7.

Ashton, R. (2007) 'Promoters Will Tout Own Tickets, Says Concert Chief,' *Music Week*, 24 February: 5.

———. (2007a) 'Ofcom Under New Pressure to Reform Music Creators' Rights on Television,' *Music Week*, 21 February: 4.

Attali, J. (1985) *Noise: The Political Economy of Music*, Minneapolis, MN: University of Minnesota Press.

The Australian Music Industry: Economic Evaluation (1987) Music Board of the Australian Council, Sydney: The Board.

Bagdikian, B. (1990) *The Media Monopoly*, Boston: Beacon Press.

Banks, J. (1996) *Monopoly Television: MTV's Quest to Control the Music*, Boulder, CO: Westview Press.

Barnes, K. (1988) 'Top 40 Radio: A Fragment of the Imagination,' in S. Frith (ed.) *Facing the Music*, New York: Pantheon.

Barnett, R.J. and Cavanagh, J. (1994) *Global Dreams: Imperial Corporations and the New World Order*, New York: Simon & Schuster.

Barrett, C. (2001) 'Industry Looking for New Ways to Cure Old Problems,' *Music Business International*, 11(6): 23–24.

Barrow, T. and Newby, J. (1996) *Inside the Music Business*, London: Routledge.

Baumol, W.J. and Baumol, H. (1968) *Performing Arts: The Economic Dilemma*, Cambridge, MA: MIT Press.

Bayler, M. (2006) 'The Music Industry Must Tread Carefully With Advertisers,' *New Media*, 14.

Beard, C. and Gloag, K. (2005) *Musicology: The Key Concepts*, London: Routledge.

Bennett, A. (2000) *Popular Music and Youth Culture: Music, Identity and Place*, London: Macmillan.

Bennett, T., Frith, S., Grossberg, L., Shepherd, J., and Turner, G. (1993) *Rock and Popular Music: Politics, Policies, and Institutions*, London: Routledge.

Beville, H.M. (1988) *Audience Ratings: Radio, Television, Cable*, Hillsdale, NJ: Lawrence Erlbaum Associates.

Bhattacharjee, S., Gopal, R.D., Lertwachara, K., and Marsden, J.R. (2006) 'Consumer Search and Retailer Strategies in the Presence of Online Music Sharing,' *Journal of Management Information Systems*, Summer: 129–159.

Biederman, D.E., Pierson, E.P., Silfen, M.E., Glasser, J.A., and Berry, R.C. (1992) *Law and Business of the Entertainment Industry*, New York: Praeger.

Bishop, J. (2005) 'Building International Empires of Sound: Concentrations of Power and Property in the "Global" Music Market,' *Popular Music and Society*, 28(4): 443–471.

Blake, A. (1992) *The Music Business*, London: Batsford.

Blazek, J. (2008) *Nonprofit Financial Planning Made Easy*, Hoboken, NJ: John Wiley.

Block, M. (2007) 'Critics Fault FCC for Stopping Payola Inquiry,' *All Things Considered*, N.P.R., 22 January.

Bloom, J. (2008) 'Book and Record Clubs Sold by Bertelsmann,' *New York Times Online*, http://www.nytimes.com/2008/07/14/books/14arts-BOO ANDRECOR_BRF.html?scp=1&sq=record%20clubs&st=cse (accessed May 12, 2009).

Blume, J. (2006) *The Business of Songwriting: A Practical Guide for Doing Business as a Songwriter*, New York: Billboard Books.

Blunt, R. (1999) 'Bootlegs and Imports: Seeking Effective International Enforcement of Copyright Protection for Unauthorized Musical Recordings,' *Houston Journal of International Law*, 22: 169–208.

Bockstedt, J.C., Kauffman, R.J., and Riggins, F.J. (2006) 'The Move to Artist-Led On-Line Music Distribution: A Theory-Based Assessment and Prospects for Structural Changes in the Digital Music Market,' *International Journal of Electronic Commerce*, Spring, 10(3): 7–38.

Bordowitz, H. (2007) *Dirty Little Secrets of the Record Business: Why So Much Music You Hear Sucks*, Chicago: Chicago Review Press.

Boyd-Barrett, O. and Newbold, C. (1995) *Approaches to Media: A Reader*, New York: St. Martin's Press.

Brabec, J. and Brabec, T. (2006) *Music, Money and Success: The Insider's Guide to Making Money in the Music Industry*, 5th edn, New York: Schirmer Books.

Brackett, D. (1995) *Interpreting Popular Music*, Cambridge: Cambridge University Press.

Brake, M. (1980) *The Sociology of Youth and Youth Subcultures*, New York: Routledge.

Breen, M. (1994) 'Editor's Introduction,' *Popular Music*, 13(3): 239–242.

Breen, M. and Forde, E. (2004) 'The Music Industry, Technology, and Utopia – An Exchange Between Marcus Breen and Eamonn Forde,' *Popular Music*, 23(1): 79–89.

Brierly, S. (2002) *The Advertising Handbook*, London: Routledge

Bringham, D. (1998) 'Webnoize Warns: Music Industry Must Evolve,' *US Press Release*, 4, March.

Broersma, M. (1998) 'Cyber Music: Fad or Future?,' *Excite*, 17 July (http://www.excite.com).

Brooks, T. (2004) *Lost Sounds: Blacks and the Birth of the Recording Industry 1890–1919*, Urbana, IL: University of Illinois Press.

Brophy-Warren, J. (2007, 2 June) 'Gold Bust: When the Hit Parade Slows,' *Wall Street Journal – Eastern Edition*, 249(128): P1–P3.

Brown, Ian. (2006) 'The Evolution of Anti-Circumvention Law,' *International Review of Law, Computers and Technology*, 20(11): 239–260.

Bruno, A. (2005, 3 December). 'The Future of Music: Industry Transformation is Just Getting Started.' *Billboard*, p. 49.

Bunker, M. (1992) 'The Implications of Ownership Changes on Concentration and Diversity in the Phonogram Industry,' *Communication Research*, 19: 749–769.

———. (1993) 'The Popular Music in Transition,' *Popular Music and Society*, 17(1): 87–114.

———. (2002) 'Eroding Fair Use: The "Transformative" Use Doctrine After Campbell,' *Communication Law and Policy*, 7(1): 1–24.

Burkart, P. and McCourt, T. (2006) *Digital Music Wars: Ownership and Control of the Celestial Jukebox*, Lanham, MD: Rowan & Littlefield.

Burnett, R. (1996) *The Global Jukebox*, London: Routledge.

Burshtein, L.M. (2005) 'Would a Brand by Any Other Name Sound Just as Sweet?,' *Canadian Musician*, May/June, 24(3): 62.

Butler, S. (2004) 'Streamling the License Clearance Process', *Billboard*, 116(46): 14.

———. (2005) 'Can Labels Control DPD Statutory Rates?,' *Billboard*, 117(17): 38.

———. (2007) 'Harry Fox Agency Synching Up?,' *Billboard*, 119(33): 20.

Buzzard, K. (2002) 'The Peoplemeter Wars: A Case Study of Technological Innovation and Diffusion in the Ratings Industry,' *Journal of Media Economics*, 15(4): 273–291.

Cable, M. (1977) *The Music Industry Inside Out*, London: W. H. Allen.

Carlin, D. (2007) 'Europe vs. Apple: Facing the Music', *Business Week Online*, http://www.businessweek.com/globalization/content/jan2007/gb20070131_49265.html.

Carlisle, G. and Chandak, N. (2006) 'Issues and Challenges in Securing Interoperability of DRM Systems in the Digital Music Market,' *International Review of Law, Computers and Technology*, 20(3): 271–281.

Castillo, T. (2006) 'Conflicting Beats: Proposing the Adoption of an Additional Obligation Within the WTO TRIPS Agreement Under Article 14 to Recognize Digital Sampling and Digital Sampling Infringement,' *Texas Review of Entertainment & Sports Law*, 7(1): 32.

Caves, R.E. (2002) *Creative Industries: Contracts Between Art and Commerce*, Cambridge, MA: Harvard University Press.

Chaffee, S. (1985) 'Popular Music and Communication Research,' *Communication Research*, 12: 413–424.

Chambers, I. (1995) *Urban Rhythms, Pop Music and Popular Culture*, London: Macmillan.

Channon, D.F. (ed.) (1997) *The Blackwell Encyclopedic Dictionary of Strategic Management*, Oxford: Blackwell.

Chapple, S. and Garafolo, R. (1977) *Rock 'n' Roll Is Here to Pay: The History and Politics of the Music Industry*, Chicago: Nelson Hall.

Christianen, M. (1995) 'Cycles of Symbolic Production? A New Model to Explain Concentration, Diversity and Innovation in the Music Industry,' *Popular Music*, 14(1): 55–95.

Clarke, D. (ed.) (1995) *The Penguin Encyclopedia of Popular Music*, New York: Penguin.

Cohen, R. (2004) *Machers and Rockers: Chess Records and the Business of Rock & Roll*, New York: Norton.

Cohen, S. (1991) *Rock Culture in Liverpool: Popular Music in the Making*, Oxford: Clarendon Press.

Compaine, B.M. and Read, W.H. (eds) (1999) *The Information Resources Policy Handbook: Research for the Information Age*, Cambridge MA: MIT Press.

Cooper, C.L. and Argyris, C. (eds) (1998) *The Concise Blackwell Encyclopedia of Management*, Oxford: Blackwell.

Cooper, L. (2007) 'American Disc Jockeys, 1945–1975: A Bibliographic and Discographic Survey,' *Popular Music and Society*, 30(3): 401–423.

Cornyn, S. and Scanblon, P. (2001) *Exploding: The Highs, Hits, Hype, Heroes and Hustlers of the Warner Music Group*, New York: Harper Entertainment.

Cort, D. (1958) 'All Alone in the Supermarket,' *Nation*, 187(17): 380–383.

Cortada, J.W. (2001) *21st Century Business: Managing and Working in the New Digital Economy*, London: Prentice Hall.

Craig-Lees, M., Joy, S., and Browene, B. (1995) *Consumer Behavior*, Chichester: John Wiley.

Crane, D. (1992) *The Production of Culture: Media and the Urban Arts*, Newbury Park, CA: Sage.

Crawford, T. and Mankin, L. (1999) 'The Sony Bono Copyright Term Extension Act,' *Communication Arts*, 41(2): 48–50.

Crisell, A. (1994) *Understanding Radio*, 2nd edn, London: Routledge.

Cronje, G.J. de, Toit, G.S. du, and Motlatla, M.D.C. (2004) *Introduction to Business Management*, 6th edn, Cape Town: Oxford University Press.

Cross, B. (1993) *It's Not About a Salary: Rap, Race and Resistance in Los Angeles*, New York: Verso.

Cunningham, M. (1996) *Good Vibrations: A History of Record Production*, Chessington: Castle Communications.

Cuppitt, M., Ramsay, G., and Shelton, L. (1996) *Music, New Music and All That: Teenage Radio in the 90s*, Sydney: Australian Broadcasting Authority.

Curtis, J. (1987) *Rock Eras: Interpretations of Music and Society 1954–1984*, Bowling Green, OH: Bowling Green State University Press.

Cusic, D. (1995) 'Country Green: The Money in Country Music' in C. Tichi (ed.) *Readin' Country Music: Steel Guitars, Opry Stars and Honky Tonk Bars: The South Atlantic Quarterly*, 94(1, Winter): 231–241.

———. (1996) *Music in the Market*, Bowling Green, OH: Bowling Green State University Press.

Dannen, F. (1991) *Hit Men: Power Brokers and Fast Money Inside the Music Business*, New York: Vintage Books.

Das, S (2000) 'The Availability of the Fair Use Defense in Music Piracy and Internet Technology,' *Federal Communications Law Journal*, 52(3): 727–748.

Davis, G.B. (ed.) (1997) *The Blackwell Encyclopedic Dictionary of Management Information Systems*, Oxford: Blackwell.

Dawson, T. (1998) *Principles and Practice of Modern Management*, 2nd edn, London: Tudor.

Deise, M.V., Nowikow, C., King, P., and Wright, A. (2000) *Executive's Guide to E-Business: From Tactics to Strategy*, Chichester: John Wiley.

Delchin, R.J. (2004) 'Music Copyright Law's Past, Present and the Future Online Music Distribution,' *Cardoza Arts and Entertainment Law Journal*, 235(94): 1–44.

Dennisoff, R.S. (1975) *Solid Gold: The Popular Record Industry*, New Brunswick, NJ: Transaction.

———. (1986) *Tarnished Gold: The Recording Industry Revisited*, New Brunswick, NJ: Transaction.

———. (1988) *Inside MTV*, New Brunswick, NJ: Transaction.

Dennisoff, R. and Romanowski, W. (1991) *Risky Business: Rock in Film*, New Brunswick, NJ: Transaction.

Denton, J. (1998) *Organizational Learning and Effectiveness*, New York: Routledge.

De Veuax, D. (1988) 'Bebop and the Recording Industry: The 1942 AFM Recording Ban Reconsidered,' *Journal of American Musicological Society*, 51(1): 126–165.

Dorat, G. (1997) 'Finding Fixation: A copyright With Teeth for Improvisational Performers,' *Columbia Law Review*, 97: 1363–1405.

Dubin, B. (1954) 'The Universal Copyright Convention,' *California Law Review*, 42(1): 89–120.

Duboff, L. (2004) 'Navigating the Maze of Music Rights,' *TechTrends*, 51(3): 10–24.

Duffy, M. (2000) 'Lines of Drift: Festival Participation and Performance a Sense of Place,' *Popular Music*, 19(1): 51–65.

Du Gay, P. and Negus, K. (1994) 'The Changing Sites of Sound: Music Retailing and the Composition of Consumers,' *Media, Culture and Society*, 16(3): 395–413.

Dunbar, D.S. (1990) 'Music and Advertising,' *International Journal of Advertising*, 9(3): 97–203.

Dutfield, G. and Suthersanen, U. (2005) 'DNA Music: Intellectual Property and the Law of Unintended Consequences,' *Science Studies*, 18(1): 5–29.

The Economist. 'Music's Brighter Future, Special Report on the Music Industry, The Effect of Multimedia Technologies and E-commerce'.

Edgar, A. and Sedwick, P. (eds) (1999) *Key Concepts in Cultural Theory*, London: Routledge.

Ehrlich, C. (1989) *Harmonious Alliance: A History of the Performing Rights Society*, New York: Oxford University Press.

Eisenberg, E. (1988) *The Recording Angel: Music, Records and Culture from Aristotle to Zappa*, London: Pan Books.

Eisenschitz, T. (2006) 'Moral Rights and Information Content in Published Works,' *ASLIB Proceedings*, 58(4): 316–329.

Ekelund, R.B. and Herbert, R.H. (1996) *A History of Economic Theory and Method*, 4th edn, New York: McGraw-Hill.

Eliot, T.G. (1993) *Rockonomics: The Money Behind the Music*, New York: Franklin Watts.

Elliot, D. (1982) '*The Rock Music Industry*,' Science, Technology and Popular Culture (1) Milton Keynes: Open University Press.

Ellis, S. and Dick, P. (2000) *Introduction to Organizational Behavior*, New York: McGraw-Hill.

Ennis, P.H. (1992) *The Seventh Stream: The Emergence of Rock 'n Roll in American Popular Music*, Hanover: Wesleyan University Press.

Erickson, M.K. (2005) 'Emphasizing the Copy in Copyright: Why Noncopying Alterations Do Not Prepare Infringement Derivative Works,' *Bingham Young University Law Review*, 5(3): 1261–1330.

Erlewine, M. Bogdanov, V., and Woodstra, C. (eds) (1995) *All Music Guide to Rock*, [AMG], San Francisco: Miller Freeman.

Evans, M. (2003) 'Where Next for Peer-to-Peer Music Distribution?,' *Managing Intellectual Property*, 131: 4.

Fabrikant, G. and Weinraub, B. (1996) 4 February, 'Having Gotten the Part, Bonfman Plays the Mogul,' *New York Times, Money and Business*, Section 3, p. 1/13.

Far, J. (1994) *Moguls and Madmen: The Pursuit of Power in Popular Music*, London: Pocket Books.

Feihl, J. (1981) *Music Trends: Characteristics of the Billboard Charts, 1955–1977*, Ottawa: Canadian Radio-television and Telecommunications Commission.

Fellenstein, C. and Wood, R. (2000) *Exploring E-Commerce, Global E-business and E-societies*, Upper Saddle River, NJ: Prentice Hall.

Felton, M. (1980) 'Policy Implications of a Composer Labor Supply,' in W.S. Hendon, J.L. Shanahan, and A.J. MacDonald (eds), *Economic Policy for the Arts*, pp. 186–198, Cambridge, MA: Abt Books.

Ferguson, T. (2002) 'GERA Endorses Reducing Music Tax,' *Billboard*, 114: 40, 61.

Fink, M. (1989) *Inside the Music Business: Music in Contemporary Life*, New York: Schirmer/Macmillan.

Fiske, J. (1989) *Understanding Popular Culture*, Boston: Unwin Hyman.

Flack, S. (1989) 'The Real Music in Music Publishing,' *Corporate Finance*, March.

Flanagan, E. (1994) 'Inside the Bootleg Industry,' *Musician Magazine*, 191: 36–95.

Flandez, R. (2006) 'DJs Left Spinning by Couples Who Program IPods for Wedding Music,' *Wall Street Journal – Eastern Edition*, 248(46): B1–B2.

Flint, D. (2004) 'Countdown to Meltdown,' *Business Law Review*, 25(4): 96–98.

Florida, R. (2002) *The Rise of the Creative Class*, New York: Basic Books.

Foot, M. and Hook, C. (1999) *Introducing Human Resource Management*, 2nd edn, Harlow: Addison Wesley Longman.

Fornas, J., Lindberg, U., and Sernhede, O. (1995) *In Garageland: Rock, Youth and Modernity*, London: Routledge.

Fox, B. (1993) 'Danger in Downloading the Perfect Digital Copy,' *Music Business International*, 3(5): 501–519.

Fox, M. (2005) 'Market Power in Music Retailing: The case of Wal-Mart,' *Popular Music and Society*, 28(4): 501–519.

Fox, T. (1986) *In the Groove*, New York: St. Martin's Press.

Frascogna, X. and Hetherington, H. (2004) *The Business of Artist Management*, 4th edn, New York: Billboard Books.

Frey, B.S. (2000) *Arts and Economics*, Berlin: Springer.

Friedlander, P. (1996) *Rock and Roll: A Social History*, Boulder, CO: Westview Press.

Friedman, Jack P. (2007) *Dictionary of Business Terms*, 4th edn, New York: Barron's Educational Series.

Frith, S. (ed.) (1981) *Sound Effects*, New York: Pantheon.

————. (1986) 'Art Versus Technology,' *Media, Culture and Society*, 8: 263–279.

————. (1988) 'Copyright and the Music Business,' *Popular Music*, 7: 57–75.

————. (1993) *Music and Copyright*, Edinburgh: Edinburgh University Press.

————. (1996) *Performing Rites: On the Value of Popular Music*, Cambridge, MA: Harvard University Press.

Fujitani, J. (1984) 'Controlling the Market Power of Performing Rights Societies: An Administrative Substitute for Antitrust Regulation,' *California Law Review*, 72(1): 103–137.

Gammond, P. (ed.) (1991) *The Oxford Companion to Popular Music*, Oxford: Oxford University Press.

Garnham, N. (1987) 'Concepts of Culture: Public Policy and the Cultural Industries,' *Cultural Studies*, 1(1): 23–27.

Garofalo, R. (ed.) (1992) *Rockin' the Boat: Mass Music and Mass Movements*, Boston: South End Press.

————. (1993) 'Whose World, What Beat: The Transnational Music Industry, Identity, and Cultural Imperialism,' *The World of Music*, 35(2): 16–32.

————. (1999) 'From Music Publishing to MP3: Music and the Industry in the Twentieth Century,' *American Music*, 17(3): 318–353.

Gasser, U., and Silke, E. (2006) 'EUCD Best Practice Guide: Implementing the Su Copyright Directive in the Digital Age,' *Berkman Center for Internet and Society*, Harvard University, http://www.cyber.law.harvard.edu/2006/EUCD-best_practice_guide.

Gillen, M. and Sutter, G. (2006) 'DRMs and Anti-Circumvention: Tipping the Scales of the Copyright Bargain?', *International Review of Law, Computers and Technology*, 287–294.

Gillespie, T. (2007) *Wired Shut: Copyright and the Shape of the Digital Culture*, Cambridge, MA: MIT Press.

Gillet, O., Essid, S., and Gael, R. (2007) 'On the Correlation of Automatic Audio and Visual Segmentations of Music Videos,' *IEEE Transactions on Circuits and Systems for Video*, 17(3): 347–355.

Glanvill, R. (1989) 'World Music Mining: the International Trade in New Music,' in F. Hanly and T. May (eds), *Rhythms of the World*, London: BBC.

Gomes, L (2000) 'Napster Stakes Out "Fair Use" Defense of Music Sharing,' *Wall Street Journal*, 236(2): B2.

Goodman, F. (1993) 'Future Shock: How the New Technologies Will Change the Music Business Forever,' *Musician*, December, 9: 32–49.

Gottlieb, A. (1991) December, 'Almost Grown: A Survey of the Music Business,' *Economist*, 21:1–18.

Gow, J. (1992) 'Music Video as Communication: Popular Formulas and Emerging Genres,' *Journal of Popular Culture*, 26(2): 41–70.

Greco, A.N. (ed.) (2000) *The Media and Entertainment Industries: Readings in Mass Communications*, Boston, MA: Allyn & Bacon.

Gronow, P. (1983) 'The Record Industry: The Growth of a Mass Medium,' *Popular Music*, 3: 53–77.

Gronow, P. and Saunio, I. (1997) *International History of the Recording Industry*, London: Cassell.

Gross, M.J. Jr, Larkin, R.F., and McCarthy, J.H. (2000) *Financial and Accounting Guide for Not-for-Profit Organizations*, Hoboken, NJ: John Wiley.

Gurbernick, L. (1989) 'We Are a Society of Collectors,' *Forbes*, 144(2): 80.

Halloran, M. (ed.), (2007) *The Musician's Business and Legal Guide*, 4th edn, Englewood Cliffs, NJ: Prentice-Hall.

Halsey, J. (2000) *How to Make It in the Music Business*, New York: Hawk Publishing.

Hansmann, H. (1981) 'Nonprofit Enterprise in the Performing Arts,' *Bell Journal of Economics*, 12(2, Autumn): 341–361.

Hardy, D. and Laing, D. (1990) *The Faber Companion to 20th Century Popular Music*, London: Faber & Faber.

Hardy, P. (1985) *The British Record Industry*, IASPM-UK Working Paper.

———. (1999) 'The European Music Business: A Market Undergoing the Process of Restructuring,' *Cultural Trends*, 9(34): 57–61.

Haring, B. (1996) *Off the Charts: Ruthless Days and Reckless Nights Inside the Music Industry*, New York: OTC.

———. (2000) *Beyond the Charts: MP3 and the Digital Music Revolution*, New York: OTC.

Harker, D. (1980) *One for the Money: Politics and Popular Song*, London: Hutchinson.

———. (1997) 'The Wonderful World of IFPI: Music Industry Rhetoric, the Critics and Classical Marxist ...,' *Popular Music*, 16(1): 45–80.

Harrison, T. (2007) 'Empire: Chart Performance of Hard Rock and Heavy Metal Groups, 1990–1992,' *Popular Music and Society*, 30(2): 197–225.

Harrower, A. (2005) 'Copyright Issues in Internet Music,' *Music Review*, 24(6): 483–488.

Harvard Law Review (2003) 'California Labor Code Section 2855 and Recording Artists Contracts,' 116(8): 2632–2653.

————. (2005) 'Copyright Law – Sound Recording Act – Sixth Circuit Rejects De Minimis Defense to the Infringement of a Sound Recording Copyright. – Bridgeport Music, Inc. v. Dimension Films, 383 F.3d 390 (6th Cir. 2004),' 118(4): 1355–1362.

Harwood, E.D. (2004) 'Staying Afloat in the Internet Stream: How to Keep Web Radio from Drowning in Digital Copyright Royalties,' *Federal Communications Law journal*, 56(3): 673–696.

Hebdige, D. (1979) *Subculture: The Meaning of Style*, London: Methuen.

————. (1987) *Cut 'N' Mix*, London: Comedia.

Heilbrun, J. and C.M. Gray (2001) *The Economics of Art and Culture*, Cambridge: Cambridge University Press.

Heinauer, L. (2001) 25 April, 'Music Industry Continues to Sell Violent Fare to Children, FTC Says,' *Wall Street Journal – Eastern Edition*, 237(81).

Hellman, H. (1983) 'The New State of Competition in the Record Industry,' *Sociologia*, 20: 355–367.

Helms, M.M. (1999) *Encyclopedia of Management*, 4th edn, London: Gale.

Hemphill, T.S. (2002) 'Self-Regulation, Public Issue Management and Marketing Practices in the U.S. Entertainment Industry,' *Journal of Public Affairs*, 3(4): 220–296.

Hendon, W.S., Shanahan, J.L., and MacDonald, A.J. (eds) (1980) *Economic Policy for the Arts*, Cambridge, MA: Abt Books.

Hennion, A. (1989) 'An Intermediary Between Production and Consumption: The Producer of Popular Music,' *Science, Technology and Human Values*, 14(4): 400–424.

Hesmondhalgh, D. (1996) 'Flexibility, Post-Fordism and the Music Industries,' *Media, Culture and Society*, 18(3): 469–488.

Heylin, C. (1996) *Bootleg: The Secret History of the Other Music Business*, New York: St. Martin's Press.

Hill, B. (2003) *Digital Songstream*, New York: Routledge.

Hindle, T. (2000) *Pocket MBA*, London: Economist Book.

Hirsch, P. (1970) *The Structure of the Popular Music Industry: The Filtering Process by Which Records are Preselected for Public Consumption*, Ann Arbor: Institute for Social Research, University of Michigan.

————. (1970a) *The Structure of the Popular Music Industry*, Survey Research Center, Ann Arbor: University of Michigan.

————. (1972) 'Processing Fads and Fashions: An Organizational Set Analysis of Cultural Industry Systems,' *American Journal of Sociology*, 77(4): 639–659.

————. (1985) 'US Cultural Productions: The Impact of Ownership,' *Journal of Communication*, 35, Summer.

Hitchock, H.W. and Saide, S. (1986) *New Grove Dictionary of American Music*, London: MacMillan.

Holden, S. (1991) 24 March, 'Pop View: Big Stars, Big Bucks and Big Gamble,' *New York Times*, 24.

———. (1994) 'Home Recording Act Royalties Coming Soon to Labels, Artists,' *Billboard*, 106(44): 5–7.

———. (2000) 'New Analysis, Arts Rights in Focus,' *Billboard*, 112(44): 5.

Holland, B. (2004) 'Funds Seek Sidemen,' *Billboard*, 116(50): 1.

Hollis, T. (2006) *Mouse Tracks: The Story of Walt Disney Records*, Jackson: University Press of Mississippi.

Howard-Spink, S. (2000) 'Digital Revolution Has Little Impact on A&R Function,' *Music Business International*, 7(6): XIII.

Hull, G. (2002) 'The Audio Home Recording Act of 1992: A Digital Dead Duck, or Finally Coming Home to Roost,' *Journal of the Music & Entertainment Industry Educators Association*, 2(1): 76–112.

———. (2004) *The Recording Industry*, 2nd edn, London: Routledge.

International Federation of Phonographic Industries (2007) Available at: www.ifpi.org (accessed August 30, 2008).

Jablin, F.M., Putman, L.L., Roberts, K.H., and Porter, L.W. (2001) *The Handbook of Organizational Communication*, Newbury Park, CA: Sage.

Jackson, J. (1994) *Big Beat: Alan Freed and the Early Years of Rock and Roll*, New York: Schirmer.

———. (1998) *American Bandstand: Dick Clark and the Making of a Rock 'n Roll Empire*, New York: Oxford University Press.

Jacobson, M. (2007) 'Advertising Dollars Should Be an Important Revenue Stream,' *Billboard*, 119(45): 1c.

Jefkins, M. and Yadin, D. (1998) *Public Relations*, 5th edn, London: Pitman.

Jhally, S. (1990) *The Codes of Advertising: Fetishism and the Political Economy of Meaning in the Consumer Society*, New York: Routledge.

Joffrain, T. (2001) 'Deriving a (Moral) Right for Creators,' *Texas International Law Journal*, 36(4): 735–794.

Jones, R. and Cameron, E. (2005) 'Full Fat, Semi Skimmed or No Milk Today – Creative Commons Licenses and English Folk Music,' *International Review of Law, Computers and Technology*, 19(4): 259–275.

Jones, S. (1993) 'Who Fought the Law? The American Music Industry and the Global Popular Music Market,' in T. Bennett, S. Frith, L. Grossberg, J. Shepherd and B. Turner (eds), *Rock and Popular Music: Politics, Policies and Institutions*, London: Routledge.

Jones, S. and Schumacher, T. (1992) 'Muzak: On Functional Music and Power,' *Critical Studies in Mass Communications*, 9: 156–169.

Kalma, V. (2002) *Label Launch: A Guide to Independent Recording, Promotion, and Distribution*, New York: St. Martin's Press.

Kao, A. (2004) 'RIAA V. Verizon: Applying the Subpoena Provision of the DMCA,' *Berkeley Technological Law Review*, 19(1): 405–426.

Kaplan, E. A. (1987) *Rocking Around the Clock: Music, Television, Postmodernism, and Consumer Culture*, New York: Methuen.

Kashif and Greenberg, G. (1996) *Everything You Better Know About the Record Industry*, New York: Brooklyn Boys Books.

Kealy, E. (1982) 'Conventions and the Production of the Popular Music Aesthetic,' *Journal of Popular Culture*, 16: 100–115.

Keesan, J. (2008) 'Let it Be?: The Challenges of Using Old definitions for Online Music Practices,' *Berkeley Law Journal*, 23(1): 353–372.

Kempema, J. (2008) 'Imitation is the Sincerest Form of … Infringement?: Guitar Tabs, Fair Use and the Internet,' *William & Mary Law Review*, 49: 2265–22307.

Kennedy, R. and McNutt, R. (1999) *Little Labels – Big Sound: Small Recording Companies and the Rise of American Music*, Bloomington, IN: Indiana University Press.

Khon, A. and Kohn, B. (1992) *Art of Music Licensing*, Upper Saddle River, NJ: Prentice Hall.

———. (2002) *Kohn on Music Licensing*, 3rd edn, New York: Aspen Law & Business.

Killmeier, M. (2001) 'Voices Between Tracks: Disc Jockeys, Radio and Popular Music,' *Journal of Communication Inquiry*, 25(4): 353–375.

Kimpel, D. (2006) *How They Made It: True Stories of How Music's Biggest Stars Went From Start to Stardom*, New York: Hal Leonard.

Kinkle, R.d. (1974) *The Complete Encyclopedia of Popular Music and Jazz, 1900–1950*, New Rochelle, NY: Arlington House.

Kirchner, T. (1994) 'The Lalapalooziation of American Youth,' *Popular Music and Society*, 18(1): 69–89.

Kirkham, Richard. (2002) 'Indies Lobby EU on Trade Issues,' *Billboard*, 114(20): 4.

Klinefetter, A. (2001) 'Will the First Sale Doctrine Disappear?,' *Information Outlook*, 5(5): 45–47.

Knab, C. and Bartley, F.D. (2007) *Music Is Your Business: The Musicians Forefront Strategy for Success*, Seattle, WA: Fourfront Media and Music.

Knoedelseder, W. (1993) *Stiffed: A True Story About MCA, the Music Business and the Mafia*, New York: HarperCollins.

Koelman, K.J. (2006) 'Fixing the Three-Step Test,' *European Intellectual Property Review*, August 15.

Koller, F. (2001) *How to Pitch and Promote Your Songs*, New York: Allworth.

Kotler, P. (1994) *Marketing Management: Marketing, Planning, Implementation and Control*, 8th edn, Upper Saddle River, NJ: Prentice Hall.

Kotler, P. and Armstrong, G. (1999) *Principles of Marketing*, 9th edn, Upper Saddle River, NJ: Prentice Hall.

Krasilovsky, W., Shemel, S., Gross, J., and Feinstein, J. (2007) *This Business of Music*, 10th edn, New York: Billboard Publications.

Kretschmer, M. (2000) 'Intellectual Property in Music: A Historical Analysis of Rhetoric and Institutional Practices,' *Studies in Cultures, Organizations and Societies*, 6(2): 197–223.

Kretschmer, M., Klimis, G. M., and Wallis, R. (1999) 'The Changing Location of Intellectual Property Rights in Music: A Study of Music Publishers, Collecting Societies and Media Conglomerates,' *Prometheus*, 17(2): 163–187.

Kronemyer, D. (1987) 'The New Payola and the American Record Industry,' *Harvard Law Review*, summer: 521.

Kuhn, I. (ed.) (1988) *Handbook for Creative and Innovative Management*, New York: McGraw-Hill.

Kwok, S.H. and Lui, S.M. (2002) 'A License Management Model for Peer-to-Peer Music Sharing,' *International Journal of Information Technology and Decision Making*, 1(3): 541–558.

Laing, D. (1985) 'Music Video: Industrial Product, Cultural Form,' *Screen*, 26(2).

———. (1986) 'The Music Industry and "Cultural Imperialism" Thesis,' *Media, Culture and Society*, 8: 331–341.

Landau, M. (2005) 'Copyrights, Moral Rights and the End of the Right of Attribution Under U.S. Trademark Law,' *International Review of Law, Computers and Technology*, 19(1): 37–64.

Lanza, J. (1995) *Elevator Music: A Surreal History of Muzak Easy-Listening and Other Moodsong*, New York: Picador.

Lathrop, T. (2007) *This Business of: Global Music Marketing – Global Strategies for Maximizing Your Music's Popularity and Profits*, New York: Billboard Books.

Lea, G. (1999), "Moral Rights and the Internet – Common Law Perspectives," in D.F. Pollaud (eds), *The Internet and Author's Rights*, London: Sweet and Maxwell.

Leeds, J. (2007) 21 December, 'Top Concert Promoter Sets Up a Challenge to Ticketmaster,' *New York Times*, Section A, p. 3.

Lessig, L. (2004) *Free Culture: How Big Media Uses Technology and the Law to Lock Down Culture and Control Creativity*, New York: Penguin.

———. (2005) *Free Culture: The Nature and Future of Creativity*, New York: Penguin.

Levin, A., Dato-on, M., and Ree K. (2004) 'Money for Nothing and the Hits for Free: The Ethics of Downloading Music from Peer to Peer Web Sites,' *Journal of Marketing Theory & Practice*, 12(1): 48–60.

———. (2008) 10 January, 'Radiohead Finds Sales, Even After Downloads,' *New York Times*, Section A, p. 1.

Levy, M. and Weitz, B.A. (1995) *Retailing Management*, Chicago: Irwin McGraw-Hill.

Lewis, G. (1978) 'The Sociology of Popular Culture,' *Current Sociology*, 122–261.

Lewis, L.A. (ed.) (1992) *The Adoring Audience: Fan Culture and the Popular Media*, London: Routledge.

Lichtman, I. (2000) 'Harry Fox Agency Forges MP3.com Royalty Plan,' *Billboard*, 112(44): 12.

Lim, M., Hellard, M., Hucking, J., Aitken, P., and Campbell, K. (2008) 'A Cross-Sectional Survey of Young People Attending a Music Festival: Association Between Drug Use and Musical Preference,' *Drug and Alcohol Review*, 27(4): 439–441.

Lopes, P. (1992) 'Innovation and Diversity in the Popular Music Industry, 1969–1990,' *American Sociological Review*, 57: 56–71.

———. (1992a) 'Aspects of Production and Consumption in the Music Industry, 1967–1990,' *American Sociological Review*, 57(1): 46–71.

Lovering, J. (1998) 'The Global Music Industry: Contradictions in the Commodification of the Sublime,' in A. Leyshon, D. Matless, and G. Revill (eds), *The Place of Music*, New York: The Guilford Press.

Lull, J (ed.) (1987) *Popular Music and Communication*, London: Sage.

McAuliffe, R. (ed.) (1997) *The Blackwell Encyclopedic Dictionary of Managerial Economics*, Oxford: Blackwell.

McBride, S. (2007) 'New Way to Count Listeners Shakes Up Radio,' *Wall Street Journal*, 250(56): B1–B2.

McCalman, P. (2006) 'Parallel Imports and the Lot of a Starving Artist,' *Journal of International Trade and Economic Development*, 15(1): 49–62.

McCourt, T (2005) 'Collecting Music in the Digital Realm,' *Popular Music & Society*, 28: 249–225.

McLeod, L (2005) 'MP3s Are Killing Home Taping: The Rise of Internet Distribution and Its Challenge to the Major Label Music Monopoly,' *Popular Music & Society*, 28: 521–531.

Magil, F.N. (ed.) (1997) *International Encyclopedia of Economics*, London: Fitzroy Dearborn.

Maitland, I. (1998) *The Small Business Marketing Handbook*, London: Cassell.

Mann, B. (2000) *I Want My MP3! How to Download, Rip & Play Digital Music*, New York: McGraw-Hill.

Marshall, A. (1999) *Principles of Economics*, 8th edn, London: Macmillan.

Marshall, L. (2003) 'For and Against the Record Industry: An Introduction to Bootleg Collectors and Tape Traders,' *Popular Music*, 22(1): 57–72.

Masiyakurima, P. (2005) 'The Trouble With Moral Rights,' *Modern Law Review*, 68(3): 411–434.

Maskus, K. (2000) *Intellectual Property Rights in a Global Economy*, Washington, DC: Institute for International Economics.

Maslow, A.H. (1970) *Motivation and Personality*, New York: Harper and Row.

Masson, G. and Lofthus, K.R. (2002) *Billboard*, 3/9/2002.

Mattelart, A. (1984) *International Image Markets: In Search of an Alternative Perspective*, London: Comedia.

May, T. (2007) *Promoting Your Music*, New York: Routledge.

Michel, N. (2006) 'Digital File Sharing and Contracts in the Music Industry: A Theoretical Analysis,' *Review of Economic Research on Copyright Issues*, 3: 29–42.

Millard, A.J. (1995) *America on Record: A History of Recorded Sound*, Cambridge: Cambridge University Press.

Miller, D. (1998) *A Theory of Shopping*, Cambridge: Polity Press.

Mitchell, D. (2007) 29 December, 'Piracy and Privacy,' *New York Times*, Section A, p. 5.

Monthly Labor Review (1992) 'Television and Movie Agreement,' *U.S. Department of Labor*, 115(8): 61.

Moorefield, V. (2005) *The Producer as Composer: Shaping the Sounds of Popular Music*, Cambridge, MA: MIT Press.

Morden, T. (1999) *An Introduction to Business Strategy: A Strategic Management Approach, Text and Cases*, 2nd edn, New York: McGraw-Hill.

Morse, S. (1998) *Successful Product Management: A Guide to Strategy, Planning and Development*, London: Kogan Page.

Morton, N. and Koufteros, X. (2008) 'Intention to Commit Online Music Piracy and Its Antecedents: An Empirical Investigation,' *Structural Equation Modeling*, 15(3): 491–512.

Mulholland, P. (1989) *The Music Recording Industry in Australia*, Fitzroy, Victoria, Australia: Victorian Commercial Teachers Association and Victoria Education Department.

Muller, P. (1994) *The Music Business – A Legal Perspective*, New York: Quorum Books.

Myers, G. (1996) 'Trademark Parody: Lessons From the Copyright Decision in Campbell v. Acuff-Rose Music, Inc.,' *Law and Contemporary Problems*, 59(2): 181–212.

Napoli, P. (2003) *Audience Economics: Media Institutions and the Audience Marketplace*, New York: Columbia University Press.

Negroponte, N. (1995) *Being Digital*, New York: Alfred Knopf.

Negus, K. (1992) *Producing Pop: Culture and Conflict in the Popular Music Industry*, London: Edward Arnold.

———. (1993) 'Global Harmonies & Local Discords: Transitional Policies and Practices in the European Recording Industry,' *European Journal of Communications*, 8(3): 293–316.

———. (1995) 'Where the Mystical Meets the Market: Commerce and Creativity in the Production of Popular Music,' *Sociological Review*, 43(2): 316–41.

———. (1996) 'Globalization and the Music of the Public Sphere,' in S. Braman and A. Sreberny-Mohammadi (eds), *Globalization, Communication and the Transnational Public Sphere*, Derby: Hampden Press.

Newman, D. (1981) *Subscribe Now: Building Arts Audiences Through Dynamic Subscription Promotion*, New York: Consortium Book Sales.

Nexica, I.J., (1997) 'Music Marketing: Tropes of Hybrids, Crossovers and Cultural Dialogue Through Music,' *Popular Music and Society*, 21(3): 22–87.

Niva, E. (2007) 'Making Room for Consumers Under the DMCA' *Berkeley Technology Law Journal*, 22(3): 270–281.

Nye, W. (2000) 'Some Economic Issues in Licensing of Music Performance Rights: Controversies in Recent ASCAP–BMI Litigation,' *Journal of Media Economics*, 13(1): 15–25.

O'Connell, J. (ed.) (1997) *The Blackwell Encyclopedic Dictionary of International Management*, Oxford: Blackwell.

Office of Communications (2008) Available at: www.ofcom.org.uk (accessed August 30, 2008)

Oppenheim, C. (1996) 'Moral rights and the electronic library,' available at: www.ariadne.ac.uk/issue4/copyright/ (accessed 14 October 2005).

Ouellet, J. (2007) 'The Purchase Versus Illegal Download of Music by Consumers: The Influence of Consumer Response Towards the Artist and Music,' *Canadian Journal of Administrative Sciences*, 24(2): 107–119.

Owens, J. (1992) *Welcome to the Jungle: A Practical Guide to Today's Music Business*, New York: HarperCollins.

Pallister, J. and Daintith, J. (2006) *A Dictionary of Business and Management*, New York: Oxford University Press.

Palmer, A. and Hartley, B. (1999) *The Business and Marketing Environment*, 3rd edn, New York: McGraw-Hill.

Park, D.J. (2007) *Conglomerate Rock: The Music Industry's Quest to Divide Music and Conquer Wallets*, Boston: Lexington Books.

Passman, D. (2006) *All You Need to Know About the Music Business*, 6th edn, New York: Simon & Schuster.

Patchen, R. and Kolessar, R. (1999) 'Out of the Lab and Into the Field: A Pilot Test of the Personal Portable Meter,' *Journal of Advertising Research*, 39(4): 55–68.

Patchet, F. (2003) 'Content Management for Electronic Music Distribution,' *Communication of the ACM*, 46(4): 71–75.

Pease, E. and Dennis, E. (eds) (1995) *Radio – The Forgotten Medium*, New Brunswick, NJ: Transaction.

Peers, M. and Ramstad, E. (2000) 'Prices of CDs Likely to Drop, Thanks to FTC,' *Wall Street Journal*, 235(94): B1.

Peters, L.H., Greer, C.R., and Youngblood, S.A. (eds) (1998) *The Blackwell Encyclopedic Dictionary of Human Resource*, Oxford: Blackwell.

Peterson, R. (ed.) (1976) *The Production of Culture*, London: Sage.

———. (1982) 'Five Constraints on the Production of Culture: Law, Technology, Market, Organizational Structure and Occupational Careers,' *Journal of Popular Culture*, 16: 158–173.

Perterson, R. and Berger, D. (1975) 'Cycles in Symbol Production: The Case of Popular Music,' *American Sociological Review*, 40: 158–173.

Pike, G. H. (2007) 'First Sale Doctrine Put to the Test,' *Information Today*, 24(9): 17–19.

Pindyck, R.S. and Rubinfeld, D.L. (1995) *Microeconomics*, 3rd edn, Englewood Cliffs, NJ: Prentice Hall.

Png, I. (1998) *Managerial Economics*, Oxford: Blackwell.

Qualen, J. (1985) *The Music Industry: The End of Vinyl?*, London: Comedia.

Radcliffe, Mark F. (2006) 'Grokster: The New Law of Third Party Liability for Copyright Infringement Under United States Law.' *Computer Law and Security Report*, 22: 137–149.

Rajan, M. (2002) 'Moral Rights in the Digital Age: New Possibilities for Democratization of Culture,' *International Review of Law, Computers and Technology*, 16(2): 187–197.

Randel, D.M. (ed.) (1986) *The New Harvard Dictionary of Music*, Cambridge, MA: Harvard University Press.

Rashad, Abdel-Khalik, A. (ed.) (1998) *Encyclopedic Dictionary of Accounting*, Oxford: Blackwell.

Reder, M. (1940) 'The Doctrine of Moral Rights: A Study in the Law of Artists, Authors and Creators,' *Harvard Law Review*, 53(4): 28–52.

Reyes Matta, F. (1982) 'Popular Song, the Recording Industry, and Their Alternative Facets,' *Media Development*, 1: 12–20.

RIAA (2007) Inside the Recording Industry: A Statistical Overview, New York: Recording Industry Association of America.

RIAA. Recording Industry Association of America, Annual Reports.

Rietjens, B. (2006) 'Copyright and the Three Step Test: Are Broadband Levies too Good to Be True?,' *International Review of Law Computers*, 20(3): 323–336.

Rifkin, J. (2001) 21 March, 'Where Napster Has Gone, Others Will Follow,' *Los Angeles Times*. Available at: http://www.latimes.com/news/comment/2000821/t000078663.htm.

Riodan, J. (1991) *Making It in the New Music Business*, Cincinnati, OH: Writer's Digest Book.

Rothenbuhler, E. and Dimmick, J. (1982) 'Popular Music: Concentration and Diversity in the Industry, 1974–1980,' *Journal of Communication*, 32: 143–149.

Ruling, K. (1993) 'IATSE Turns 100,' *Theatre Crafts International*, 27(8): 20–22.

Runci, M.A. and Albert, R.S. (eds) (1990) *Theories of Creativity*, London: Sage.

Russell (2005) 'Sony's Payola,' *Multinational Monitor*, 26: 70.

Rutten, P. (1991) October, 'Local Popular Music on the National and International Markets,' *Cultural Studies*, 294–305.

Ryan, J. (1985) *The Production of Culture in the Music Industry: The ASCAP-BMI Controversy*, Lanham, MA: University Press of America.

Sanjek, R. (1988) *American Popular Music and Its Business. The First Four Hundred Years, Volume III: From 1900 to 1984*, New York: Oxford University Press.

Sanjek, R. and Sanjek, D. (1991) *American Popular Music Business in the 20th Century*, New York: Replica Books.

Schneider, M. and Henten, A. (2004) 'DRMs, ISP and the EUCD: Technology and Law,' *Telematics and Informatics*, 22: 25–39.

Scholl, G. (2008) 'A Sound Exchange?,' *Billboard*, 120(36): 3–8.

Schowater, D. F. (2000) 'Remembering the Dangers of Rock and Roll: Toward a Historical Narrative of the Rock Festival,' *Critical Studies in Media Communication*, 17: 86–103.

Schulenberg, R. (2005) *Legal Aspects of the Music Industry*, 2nd Rev. edn, New York: Billboard Books.

Schuler, R.S. and Van de Ven, A.H. (eds) (1997) *The Blackwell Encyclopedic Dictionary of Organizational Behavior*, Oxford: Blackwell.

Schwartz, D. (1995) 'Strange Fixation: Bootleg Sound Recordings Enjoy the Benefits of Improving Technology,' *Federal Communications Law Journal*, 47(3). (http://www.law.indiana.edu/fclj/pubs/v47/no3/schwartz.html (last visited February 7, 2001).

Schwartz, D.D. (2005) *I Don't Need a Record Deal! Your Survival Guide for the Indie Music Revolution*, New York: Billboard Books.

Schwartz, L.M. (2007) *Making Music Videos: Everything You Need to Know from the Best in the Business*, New York: Billboard Books.

Scott, A. and D. Power (eds) (2004) *Cultural Industries and the Production of Culture*, London: Routledge.

Segrave, K. (1994) *Payola in the Music Business: A History 1880–1991*, Jefferson, NC: McFarland.

Seifert, M. and Hadida, A. (2006) 'Facilitating Talent Selection Decisions in the Music Industry,' *Management Decision*, 44: 790–808.

Seigel, A.H. (1991) *Breaking Into the Music Business*, London: Pocket Books.

Seltzer, G. (1989) *Music Matters: The Performer and the American Federation of Musicians*, Landham, MD: Scarecrow Press.

Senge, P.M. (1990) *The Fifth Discipline: The Art and Practice of the Learning Organization*, New York: Currency/Doubleday.

Shadlen, K. (2007) 'Intellectual Property and Development: Can Foes Be Friends?,' *Global Governance*, 13(2): 171–177.

Shepard, W.G. (1996) *The Economics of Industrial Organization*, Upper Saddle River, NJ: Prentice Hall.

Shepherd, J., Horn, D., Laing, D., Oliver, P., and Wicke P. (eds) (2003) *Continuum Encyclopedia of Popular Music of the World,* Volume I: Media, Industry and Society, London: Continuum.

Sheth, J.N. and Parvatiyar, A. (2000) *Handbook of Relationship Marketing*, London: Sage.

Shim, J.K., Siegel, J.G., and Simon, A.J. (1997) *The Vest-pocket MBA*, Upper Sadddle River, NJ: Prentice Hall.

Shirky, C. (2001) February, 'Where Is Napster Taking the Publishing World,' *Harvard Business Review*, 143–148.

Shuker, R. (1998) *Key Concepts in Popular Music*, London: Routledge.

———. (2001) *Understanding Popular Music*, 2nd edn, London: Routledge.

Shur, R. (2006) 'Steal This Music: How Intellectual Property Law Affects Musical Creativity,' *American Studies*, 47(2): 139–140.

Sireois, A. and Martin, S. (2006) 'U.S. Copyright Law and Digital Sampling: Adding Color to a Grey Area,' *Information and Communications Technology Law Review*, 15(1): 1–32.

Sklair, L. (1984) *Rocking America: How All-Hit Radio Stations Took Over*, New York: St. Martins Press.

Slack, N. (ed.) (1997) *The Blackwell Encyclopedic Dictionary of Operations Management*, Oxford: Blackwell.

Smith, E. (2004) 'EMI, Sony BMG Set License Accord for Music Catalogs,' *Wall Street Journal – Eastern Edition*, 244: B5.

Smith , P. (2006) 'The Politics of UK Television Policy: The Making of Ofcom,' *Media, Culture and Society*, 28(6): 929–940.

Soocher, S. (1999) *Financial Management for Musicians*, New York: Schirmer.

Spahr, W. and Lesrand, E. (2004) 'Rights Row Flares,' *Billboard*, 116(7): 8–56.

Speiss, T.J., (1997) ' "Heigh Ho, Heigh, Ho": A Synchronization License Granted to Use Musical Composition in Film and on Television Does Not Include Videocassette,' *Journal of Arts Management, Law and Society*, 27(2): 101–118.

Stallabrass, J. (1996) *Gargantua: Manufactured Mass Culture*, New York: Verso.

Stambler, I. (1989) *Encyclopedia of Rock and Soul*, 2nd edn, New York: St. Martins Press.

Statt, D.A. (1999) *Concise Dictionary of Business Management*, 2nd edn, London: Routledge.

Stern, Richard (2000) 'Napster: A Walking Copyright Infringement,' *IEEE Micro*, 20(6): 4–6.

Sternberg, R.J. (ed.) (1988) *The Nature of Creativity*, Cambridge: Cambridge University Press.

Stewart, C. (1998) *Gower Handbook of Management Skills*, Aldershot: Gower.

Stokes, G. (1977) *Star Making Machinery*, New York: Vantage.

Stover, S. (1990) 'The "Fair Use" of Sound Recordings: A Summary of Existing Practices and Concerns,' *Association for Recorded Sound Collections Journal*, 21(2): 232–240.

Strasser, R. and Shirley, J. (2005) *The Savvy Studio Owner*, New York: Hal Leonard Corporation.

Stratchan, R. (2007) 'Micro-Independent Record Labels in the UK,' *European Journal of Cultural Studies*, 10(2): 139–140.

Stratton, J. (1982) 'Between Two Worlds: Art and Commercialism in the Record Industry,' *Sociological Review*, 39: 267–285.

———. (1983) 'Capitalism and the Romantic Ideology in the Record Business,' *Popular Music*, 3: 143–156.

Strauss, N. (1999) 18 July, 'The MP3 Revolution: Getting With It,' *The New York Times*, Section 2: 29.

Sullivan, P.H. (1998) *Profiting from Intellectual Capital: Extracting Value from Innovation*, Chicester: John Wiley.

————. (2000) *Value-driven Intellectual Capital: How to Convert Intangible Corporate Assets into Market Value*, Chichester: John Wiley.

Sundbo, J. (1998) *The Theory of Innovation: Entrepreneurs, Technology and Strategy*, Cheltenham: Edward Elgar.

Sutton, C. (1998) *Strategic Concepts*, London: Macmillan Business.

Swingwood, A. (1977) *The Myth of Mass Culture*, London: Macmillan.

Tagg, P. (1982) 'Analyzing Popular Music: Theory, Method and Practice,' *Popular Music*, 2: 37–69.

Tapscott, D., Lowy, A., and Ticoll, D. (eds) (1998) *Blueprint for the Digital Economy: Creating Wealth in the Era of E-Business*, London: McGraw-Hill.

Tavani, H. (2005) 'Threat to Democratic Ideals in Cyberspace: Lessons Learned from Verizon v. RIAA Case,' *IEEE Technology and Society Magazine*, 24(3): 40–44.

Terranova, T. (2000) 'Free Labor: Producing Culture for the Digital Economy,' *Social Text*, 18: 33–58.

Thall, P.H. (2006) *What They Never Tell You About the Music Business: The Myths, the Secrets, the Lies (and a Few Truths)* rev. updated edn, New York: Billboard Books.

Therien, J. (2001) 'Exercising the Specter of a "Pay-Per-Use" Society: Toward Preserving Fair Use and the Public Domain in the Digital Age,' *Berkeley Technology Law Journal*, 16: 979–1144.

Thorp, J. (1998) *The Information Paradox: Realizing the Business Benefits of Information Technology*, London: McGraw-Hill.

Towse, R. (1999) 'Copyright and Economic Incentives: An Application to Performers' Rights in Music Industry,' *Kylos*, 52(3): 369–390.

Toynbee, J. (2000) *Making Popular Music: Musicians, Creativity and Institutions*, London: Arnold.

Tremlett, G. (1990) *Rock Gold: The Music Millionaires*, London: Unwin Hyman.

Truzzi, M. (1977) 'Towards a General Sociology of the Folk, Popular and Elite Arts,' in R. Jones (ed.), *Research in Sociology of Knowledge, Sciences and Art*, Greenwich, CN: JAI Press.

Turow, J. (1991) 'A Mass Communication Perspective on Entertainment Industries,' in J. Curran and M. Gurevitch (eds), *Mass Media and Society*, New York: Routledge.

Ullrich, H. (2003) 'IP-Antitrust in Context: Approaches to International Rules on Restructure Uses of Intellectual Property Rights,' *The Antitrust Bulletin*, 48(4): 837–883.

United States v. ASCAP, 1950–1951 Trade Cas. ¶62,595 (S.D.N.Y.1950).

Van Camp, J. (1994) 'Creating Works of Arts from Works of Art: The Problem of Derivative Works', *Journal of Arts Management, Law and Society*, 24(5): 209–225.

Vandermerwe, S. (1999) *Customer Capitalism: The New Business Model of Increasing Returns in New Market Spaces*, London: Nicholas Brealey.

Velluci, S. (1998) 'Bibliographic Relationships and the Future of Music Catalogs,' *Fontes Artis Musicae*, 45: 213–227.

Vernallis, C. (2006) *Experiencing Music Video: Aesthetics and Cultural Context*, New York: Columbia University Press.

Vink, P. Koningsveld, E.A.P. and Dhondt, S. (eds) (1998) *Human Factors in Organizational Design and Management* – VI, Amsterdam: Elsevier.

Vogel, H. L. (2007) *Entertainment Industry Economics: A Guide to Financial Analysis*, 7th edn, New York: Cambridge University Press.

Wacholtz, L.E. (1997) *Star Tracks: Principles for Success in Music and Entertainment Business*, Nashville, TN: Thumbs up Publishing.

Waddell, R.D., Barnet, R., and Berry, J. (2007) *This Business of Concert Promotion and Touring: A Practical Guide to Selling, Organizing and Staging Concerts*, New York: Billboard Press.

Wadhams, W. (1990) *Sound Advice: The Musician's Guide to the Record Industry*, New York: Schirmer.

Walker, J.L. (2008) *This Business of Urban Music: A Practical Guide to Achieving Success In the Industry, From Gospel to Funk to R&B to Hip-Hop*, New York: Billboard Books.

Wallis, R. and Malm, K. (1992) *Media Policy and Music Activity*, London: Routledge.

Wallis, R., Baden-Fuller, C., Kretschmer, M., and Klimis, G. M. (1999) 'Contested Collective Administration of Intellectual Property Rights in Music: Challenge to the Principles of Reciprocity and Solidarity,' *European Journal of Communications*, 14(1): 5–34.

Wallman, J. (1989) 'The Berne Convention and Recent Changes in U.S. Copyright Law,' *Cum notis variorum*, 132: 8–10.

Warner, J. (2006) *How to Have Your Hit Song Published*, New York: Hal Leonard Books.

Waters, H.J. (1960) 'The Hit of the Week: A History and Discography,' *Record Research*, 26(3): 2–18.

Watson, M. (2006) 'Award Ceremony as an Arbiter of Commerce and Canon in the Popular Music Industry,' *Popular Music*, 25: 41–56.

Weissman, D. (2006) *Making a Living in Your Local Music Market*, New York: Hal Leonard Books.

Werhane, P.H. and Freeman, R.E. (eds) (1997) The *Blackwell Encyclopedic Dictionary of Business Ethics*, Oxford: Blackwell.

Westmacott, P. (2006) 'Moral Rights of Paternity and Integrity,' *Managing Intellectual Property*, 158: 62.

Whitburn, J. (1988) *Top 40 Hits*, New York: Guinness.

Wicke, P. (1990) *Rock Music: Culture, Aesthetics and Sociology*, Cambridge: Cambridge University Press.

Wiley, L. (1998) 'Bootleggers Turning to Burning: RIAA Says CD-R Piracy Is on the Rise,' *EMedia Professional*, 11(6): 11–14.

Williamson, J. and C. Martin (2007) 'Rethinking the Music Industry,' *Popular Music*, 26(2): 305–322.

Wilmshurst, J. and Mackay, A. (1999) *The Fundamentals of Advertising*, 2nd edn, Oxford: Butterworth-Heinemann.

Wolfe, A. (2004) 'Over to You: Can Europe Restrain Microsoft's Threat to Freedom of Musical Expression in Computer-Mediated Communication?,' *Popular Music*, 23(1): 63–78.

Wolff, J. (1981) *The Social Production of Art*, New York: St. Martin's Press.

World Trade Organization (2007) Available at: www.wto.org (accessed August 30, 2008).

York, N. (ed.) (1991) *The Rock File: Making It In the Music Business*, Oxford: Oxford University Press.

Zager, L. (2007) *Music Production: A Manual for Producers, Composers, Arrangers, and Students*, Lanham, MD: Scarecrow Press.

Zhang, Micheal X. 'A Review of Economic Properties of Music Distribution,' in *Music Industry – Emerging Paradigms*, 2006, ICFAI Press.

Zohar, E. (2005) 'Complex But Reasonable Relationship: The Chamberlain Lesson on Access Control and Copyrights,' *Journal of Internet Law*, 9(2): 3–12.

INDEX

Note: page numbers in **bold** indicate entry for a subject.